THE PLAYWORLD OF SANSKRIT DRAMA

THE PLAYWORLD OF SANSKRIT DRAMA

ROBERT E. GOODWIN

MOTILAL BANARSIDASS PUBLISHERS
PRIVATE LIMITED • DELHI

First Edition: Delhi 1998

ISBN: 81-208-1589-0

Also available at:

MOTILAL BANARSIDASS

41 U.A. Bungalow Road, Jawahar Nagar, Delhi 110 007
8, Mahalaxmi Chamber, Warden Road, Mumbai 400 026
120 Royapettah High Road, Mylapore, Chennai 600 004
Sanas Plaza, 1302, Baji Rao Road, Pune 411 002
16 St. Mark's Road, Bangalore 560 001
8 Camac Street, Calcutta 700 017
Ashok Rajpath, Patna 800 004
Chowk, Varanasi 221 001

PRINTED IN INDIA

BY JAINENDRA PRAKASH JAIN AT SHRI JAINENDRA PRESS,
A-45 NARAINA, PHASE I, NEW DELHI 110 028
AND PUBLISHED BY NARENDRA PRAKASH JAIN FOR
MOTILAL BANARSIDASS PUBLISHERS PRIVATE LIMITED,
BUNGALOW ROAD, DELHI 110 007

Contents

Preface

This book is fundamentally a collection of essays and articles published during a six-years period in various places. All have gone through some revision, several through major restructuring or rewriting. I have decided to make a book of them for two reasons. First, they represent a thematic and methodological unity and should be read with reference to each other. Second, the lack of regular bibliographical publications in Indology almost assures their obscurity as journal or anthology articles. Only a book can bring these ideas to the attention of the broader Indological community and interested general readers.

The Introduction is original here, with some material borrowed from my AO article 'Aesthetic and Erotic Entrancement in the *Śakuntalā*.' Chapter 1 is a revision of the first part of an anthology essay titled 'The Playworld of Sanskrit Poetry: Model *Śakuntalā*'—the anthology is *God's Play: Līlā in South Asia,* edd. William S. Sax and John Carman. Chapter 2 combines portions of the article and essay just mentioned, while adding a new section on the Dharmic Father. Chapter 3 is a revision of a JRAS article with the same title. Chapter 4 is a complete rewriting of an article of the same title which appeared in JSAL. Chapter 5, also revised, originally appeared in a Festschrift for a distinguished professor of comparative literature. Titled *The Scope of Words: In Honor of Albert S. Cook.* Chapter 6 is a revision of another JRAS article with almost the same title. Chapter 7, also revised, is has appeared as the Introduction to an abridged translation of *Mṛcchakaṭika* by the late A. L. Basham, edited by Arvind Sharma. See the Bibliography for publication details.

I would like to thank Prof. David Pingree of Brown University, my former guru and colleague, who always supported and encouraged my work, even though it was very different from his own. I also thank Prof. Charles Segal of the Classics Department at Harvard University, another former teacher, and Prof. Terence Diggory of the Department of English at Skidmore college, both of whom have generously read my work (outside their own fields) and given much helpful advice and encouragement. I thank my wife Sarah Webster Goodwin, herself a Professor of English at Skidmore College, who has helped me not only with careful reading and comments but by her own professional example—and this says nothing about the emotional encouragement that only a true friend can give. Special thanks to Prof. Edith Croft of San Francisco State University's Classics Department who introduced me to Sanskrit, which I initially envisioned as merely a linguistic adjunct to Latin and Greek. Special thanks too to Prof. Steven Hoffmann of Skidmore College who hand-delivered the proofs from Delhi. Nor can I forget my parents, Burnley J. and Eleanor M. Goodwin, who made it possible for me to return to school 22 years ago when I was foundering and prospects were dim. *Sine his omnibus nihil sum.*

Introduction

This book, an interpretive study of seven representative Sanskrit dramas, fills a gap in the critical literature, which is of two kinds: the impressionistic 'appreciation' and the formal presentation of generic conventions and aesthetic canons. There are several problems with the 'appreciative' criticism—its subjectivism, its tendency to hyperbole, its defensiveness or condescension—but the main one is its failure to situate its universalist claims of 'greatness' (or the lack of it) in the context of Indian aesthetic culture. Perhaps the most influential case is Rabindranath Tagore's interpretive essay 'Sakuntala: Its Inner Meaning' (1920). Tagore treats Kālidāsa's play as the drama of the moral bankruptcy of sensual love and its redemption by suffering, and never once refers to *śṛṅgāra* or *karuṇa rasa* (the aesthetic 'savors,' respectively, of 'erotic' and 'pathetic' situations). Thus he and the many critics who follow him implicitly condemn the hedonism of the courtly ethos depicted in the play, as if that ethos had nothing to do with the production of *kāvya*,[1] its subject matter and treatment, and indeed the whole system of aesthetics which it assumes. Even those who argue against his thesis do so on general humanistic grounds, plausible only if we make assumptions of authorial intent more proper to nineteenth-century European literature. On the other hand, the purely formal criticism does not go far enough. If it refers to the dramatic or poetic literature at all it is only to illustrate the rules of the game. Its inability or refusal to imagine that the tastes enshrined in classical Indian aesthetics might be reflected in the emotional responses of characters in a play, or, in general, that aesthetic emotion can have anything to do with real-life concerns, is a prime example of critical myopia. The point of view of this book is, by contrast, that aesthetical values are in fact *values*, with emotional and ethical implications, and as such are dramatized in the plays against the backdrop of a broader cultural ideology of self-restraint. According to this ideology, which reflects the influence of asceticism on *dharma* (duty, law), emotion with its fulcrum in desire (*kāma*) is but the affective side of ignorance, a troublesome irritant at best and at worst the source of pain, illusion, and the loss of wholistic identity.[2]

The plays' advancement of affective values associated with *rasa* and the problems that result from this may indeed constitute their only authentically dramatic character. For otherwise it would be as Daniel H. H. Ingalls has written:[3]

> The Sanskrit play is not a drama, for the word *drama* means action and can only refer to a piece where action and the conflict (*agonia*) of character and principle are essential factors of the piece. The Sanskrit play has been described by those who best knew it, as a *dṛśyakāvya,* a spectacle-poem. Its text is lyric rather than dramatic and this text functions as an accompaniment to pantomime, dance, and music. The object of this combination of arts is the unfolding of mood [*rasa*]. Always it is mood rather than plot which determines the content and selection of a Sanskrit play. The mood of love [*śṛṅgāra*], for example, must be furnished in both major varieties, as love-in-enjoyment [*saṃbhoga*] and love-in-separation [*vipralambha, viraha*].

This point of view depends on our regarding curses and other conflictive incidents as mere literary devices which provide plausible narrative cover for the progression from one mood to another. This is adequate for formal analysis, but it does not allow for the operation of contentual suggestion in the minds of members of the audience. In the *Śakuntalā,* for example, it is significant that the curse which protracts the separation of the lovers comes from an irascible ascetic. Likewise in Bhāsa's *Svapnavāsavadattā* it matters that separation is brought about by considerations of political necessity. In the former play *kāma* (desire) is in conflict with *dharma* (duty) backed by ascetical anger (*tapas, krodha*), in the latter with a combination of *dharma* and *artha* ('profit,' particularly in the political sphere). Ingalls is right enough to see no 'conflict of character' in Sanskrit drama, since all characters are stereotypes, but these stereotypes do, I argue, align themselves with conflicting 'principles.'

In each of the plays we study, the protagonist—mostly a king, but in one case a sentimental minister and in another a bourgeois citizen (*nāgarika*)—is a 'man of heart' (*sahṛdaya*) or of 'feeling' (*rasika*). These are synonymous terms which are usually understood to apply only in the context of literary or aesthetical appreciation. The *rasika-sahṛdaya* is the 'connoisseur' of poetry, who can distinguish the genuine article from poetistic artifice.[4] Thus the poetician Abhinavagupta (fl. 1000 AD) defines the *sahṛdaya* as:

> One who shares in a concordance of heart (*hṛdayasaṃvāda*), i.e., who has the capacity to become one with (*tanmayībhavana*) what the poem depicts in a mirror-like mind made clear by the constant cultivation of and practice with poetry.[5]

But when we examine the notion of 'concordance of heart,' we find it impossible to restrict it to a purely aesthetical context. For one thing, it is not clear how we can establish the limits of an aesthetic experience. The term 'concordance of heart' (*hṛdayasaṃvāda*) probably derives from a much earlier passage in *Nāṭyaśāstra* 7:

> The emotional state (*bhāva*) associated with a subject that agrees with the heart (*hṛdayasaṃvādin*) gives rise to aesthetic emotion (*rasa*). By this the body is permeated, as dry wood by fire.[6]

This suggests that the 'concordance of heart' precedes aesthetic emotion as such, i.e., that it derives from real-life emotional proclivities. It also suggest the resultant emotion is something vital and gripping.

Other passages from the NŚ reinforce this impression. First the characterization of the ideal 'spectator' (*prekṣaka*), which constitutes the earliest portrait of the *rasika* or *sahṛdaya* we have, though neither term is used:

> Familar with words and meters, learned in the various *śāstras* [law, government, erotics, etc.]: such are the spectators of drama. Possessing refined organs of sense, skilled in logical thought, capable of recognizing (aesthetic) defects, having an emotional [or 'passionate,' *anurāgin*] temperament: such is the spectator of drama. One who feels happiness at the portrayal of happiness, grief at the portrayal of grief, misery at the portrayal or misery: such is the spectator of drama.[7]

We see, therefore, that the emotional temperament (*anurāgitā*) is a prerequisite of proper literary or dramatic response. The latter part of this ideal definition recalls an earlier passage from the same chapter, where the distinction is made between the two types of 'success' (*siddhi*) a play may have. One is human (*mānuṣī*): this is when spectators become so caught up in the drama that they laugh aloud, boo the villain, clap, stand up from their seats, tear their clothes, etc. The other is called 'divine' (*daivikī*), indicating a more sophisticated response. It is characterized by 'purity' (*sattva*), 'feeling' (*bhāva*), and a hushed silence.[8] The latter alone is what concerns the writers on aesthetics. It apparently alludes to the state of entrancement known as *rasāvāda* (the 'savoring' of aesthetic mood), which Masson and Patwardhan have aptly rendered as 'aesthetic rapture.'[9] It will be one of the chief concerns of this book to bring out the implications of *rasāvāda* or *daivikī siddhi,* but this can be done only if one keeps in mind the connection between aesthetic entrancement and the emotional concerns of the audience of Sanskrit drama. The identification (*tanmayībhavana*) with poetic subjects of which Abhinavagupta speaks has, we insist, both a sophisticated and a naively sentimental aspect.[10] The *rasika-sahṛdaya* does not suddenly come into being in the heightened aesthetic experience, but is a person with tastes, assumptions, ideas, and values who is capable of the sophisticated response.

The hero (*nāyaka*) of drama is an idealized projection of the *sahṛdaya* in both naive and sophisticated senses.[11] I do not refer to instances of his response to properly aesthetic situations, though the texts do portray him as ideally sensitive to the arts—an example is Cārudatta in Act Three of the *Mṛcchakaṭika.*[12] First of all, he is a feeler rather than a thinker or doer, a sensibility rather than a mind, a sentimentalist easily fatigued by demands that promise no emotional reward. He is quick to sympathize (Udayana with the imagined sorrow of bees in *Svapnavāsavadattā* 4, Duḥṣanta with the family of a shipwrecked merchant in *Śakuntalā* 6) or otherwise betray a passionate temperament (Udayana's heroic anger confronting ambush in *Pratijñāyaugandharāyaṇa* 1, Rākṣasa's impetuous trust of all who seem his friend in the *Mudrārākṣasa*). He is even quicker to fall in love, and his love has a distinctly asthetic cast to it. He does not simply feel desire for the heroine (*nāyikā*), the beautiful object *par excellence* in *kāvya,* but savors her, acutely conscious of the nuances of his own feeling, which he capably renders into elaborate poetic figures (*alaṃkāra*). Aestheticians like Abhinavagupta, drawing on NŚ 6, make the distinction between *bhāva* as personal feeling and *rasa* as its aesthetic distillation, but in the hero it is impossible to make such a distinction: for him *bhāva* is already *rasa.* Even as he feels emotion he savors it.

This, of course, is entirely consistent with the sociological matrix of *kāvya,* the court and urbane bourgeois circles with their cultivation of refined manners and tastes. The 'townsman' (*nāgarika*), whose amusements are catalogued (or prescribed) in *Kāmasūtra*

1.4, is an exaggerated portrait of the *sahṛdaya* as a social type: dedicated to the arts, personal grooming, stylish living arrangements, polite entertainments, and—the crowning glory—love. He is a member, like Cārudatta again, of a literary *goṣṭhī* or club, where the arts (including drama) are discussed, dabbled in, and patronized. It is entirely indicative of the idealistic bent of the secondary literature that the *nāgarika* and the *sahṛdaya* are treated as distinct types.[13] Yet we have clear testimony from poetic sources that the *sahṛdaya* by name was something more or less than a high-minded aesthete. A passage from the *Kuṭṭanīmata* (*A Bawd's Advice*) by Dāmodaragupta (fl. 800 AD) portrays him as a young, amorous, and impecunious sentimentalist somewhat in the style of Cārudatta:

> The worry that comes from the acquisition of wealth
> does not touch the man of heart's heart,
> bursting with deep passion
> and watered with the nectarous juice of youth.[14]

Here is *sahṛdaya* in the same breath with *rasa*, used in *double* or rather *triple entendre:* 'juice, liquid,' 'love, desire,' and 'aesthetic sentiment.'[15] Another example of worldly usage is in this lyric (*muktaka*) from the anthology of love-poetry *Amaruśataka*, where one woman counsels another:

> Women are deceiving innocents who lure a lover away despite attempts to stop them.
> So why languish and lament? You only do them a favor.
> Desirous, fond of sport, young, a man of heart: such is a lover, timid girl.
> What use are blubbering reproaches? Assail him with endearments and so win him over.[16]

It is also no doubt significant that the *Kāmasūtra* calls the model lover and beloved of a love affair 'hero' and 'heroine' (*nāyaka* and *nāyikā*), the implication being that life imitates art, which had more than a purely aesthetic effect on the *sahṛdaya*. If we want to get at the heart of *kāvya* we can not persist in treating the *sahṛdaya* solely as an aesthetic formalist of a philosophical bent. We have many indications in the poems and plays, as well as outside sources, of his emotional concerns.[17] There is a mean between Vātsyāyana's quasi-parodic portrait of the urbane hedonist and the noble-minded aesthete of S.K. De and others. What we need to do now is probe beneath *kāvya's* placid surface for the trouble spots, the conflicts, the area where sentiment implies principle.

There have been three other attempts to use the principles of aesthetics and dramaturgy as interpretive tools, but they differ markedly from the method of this book. M. Christopher Byrski makes his most concerted effort in *Methodology of the Analysis of Sanskrit Drama,* where he applies the minutiae of plot-structure (the *sandhi-sandhyaṅga* scheme[18]) to the analysis of Bhāsa's two Yaugandharāyaṇa plays (pp. 115 ff.). As in his other work, his aim is to uncover an implicit dharmic world-view which has its basis in the Brāhmaṇas' idealization of sacrifice as cosmic process. For all its painstaking detail, however, Byrski's work is too reverently idealistic: he makes nothing of court culture, the prominence of eros, the *rasika's* cult of feeling, and the sentimental tenor of the plays. Barbara Stoler Miller's introductory essay to a translation of Kālidāsa's plays is more interesting.[19] Above all, she makes the connection between 'aesthetic rapture' (*rasāsvāda*) and the hero's fascination with the heroine. But she does not develop her insights into a coherent picture, and in fact ends—illogically, in my opinion—by implicitly endorsing Tagore's reading of the *Śakuntalā.*

The most significant attempt to integrate form and content, however, is Edwin Gerow's article 'Plot Structure and the Development of *Rasa* in the Śakuntalā,' which has in common with Byrski's *Methodology* the detailed employment of the *sandhi-sandhyaṅga* scheme in conjunction with other dramaturgical structures.[20] But where Byrski virtually ignores *rasa,* Gerow, in Part 1, makes it his main interpretive concern. Gerow's strategy is to translate the *Śakuntalā's* principal *rasas* into thematic equivalents—*vīra* (the heroic) into duty and *śṛṅgāra* (the erotic) into love—so that they can be treated within the traditional *puruṣārtha* scheme. He then plots thematic development according to *sandhi-sandhyaṅga* analysis. It is a virtuoso feat, if not entirely persuasive. We trace a kind of musical dialectic of love and duty themes from an initial association that is morally inauthentic, through opposition and hostility, to separation, suffering, and finally reunion in moral authenticity. But, as we can see from this sketch, which does no justice to Gerow's ingenuity, the tenor of the argument is essentially ethical, a recasting of Tagore's thesis that avoids sentimental character judgments. Gerow's view of the aesthetic experience is highly abstract and intellectual; *rasa* is purely thematic, not really a feeling at all. The emotional dialectic thus becomes a ritualistic ratification of a moral vision. Gerow's emphasis on formal complexity has much to do with his interest in aquitting Sanskrit drama of the charge of melodramatic naiveté.[21] But, as with Byrski, no importance is attached to the fact that Sanskrit drama developed and throve in the context of courtly and urbane culture with its affects and manneristic codes.

My approach, by contrast, emphasizes emotional appeal, the audience's involvement in the *nāyaka's* desire, and the problems it poses. It assumes, as I have stated, an identification of the audience with its hero on the basis of both the *sahṛdaya* sensibility and behavioral code on the sophisticated, 'divine' level as well as a more naively 'human' fantasy involvement in his loves and sorrows. Where Gerow minimizes sentiment, I stress it as the key to understanding the *rasika* psychology. The dialectic between *kāma* and *dharma* (as well as *artha* and *mokṣa-tapas*[22]), therefore, must be seen as enacted within the *rasika* sensibility with the ideal representative of that sensibility in the starring role. We must bear in mind that *kāvya,* as regarded in the *rasa* poetic, is a medium naturally aligned with *kāma.* Thus questions of duty, etc., become questions of feeling about duty, feeling whose end is pleasure. The hero's plight thus seems to me to carry mythic weight, telling the paradigmatic story of the 'man of heart' within the broader Indian (mainly Hindu) culture. It is, in other words, the *sahṛdaya's* self-portrayal as both hero and victim, privileged sensibility and bewildered Everyman. My guiding principle is Wallace Stevens' characterization of poetry as the rhetoric of the imagination, which I take to mean that poetry is a form of persuasion even—and even especially—when it is most artfully beautiful. With every successful artistic creation we enter into a world of the imagination that strikes us as a compellingly plausible configuration of the emotional life.

The central element of the *rasika-sahṛdaya* myth is eros, for it is through his highly cultivated erotic sensibility that the *sahṛdaya* hero enters into an idyllic playworld that suggests the transcendent realm certain poeticians celebrate as the 'poetic universe' (*kāvyasaṃsāra*). But that heady elation succumbs at length to other powerful forces, deriving from both the outside world (social role, practical necessity, ascetical disdain) and the internal paradoxes of aestheticized love. A break occurs and the emotional tone shifts from eros to pathos. Suddenly we are looking at the hero from the outside, knowing more than he does about his situation. We find ourselves linked in point of view with a principle of intelligence, embodied in a guru-figure, that seems foreign to the *rasika* sensibility because of its pragmatic and ascetical associations, and yet pointedly suggests the authorial intelligence of the plays. Against the initial aesthetic-erotic model of the poetic playworld appears a second model which ironizes and implicitly criticizes the first, without, however, offering a true synthesis. We are at the limits of what a conventional poetry allows itself to understand about itself.

What then is the *rasika* myth? It is, in a nutshell, the portrait of the sentimental hero in his struggle with cultural norms that attach a low value to emotion and individual autonomy. The *rasika* by definition idealizes emotion, cultivates it as an inner truth, finds its apotheosis in a dreamy eroticism, formalizes it in an aesthetic pleasure that is never far removed from erotic feeling, and creates an alternate world of the imagination in which it is the primary value. In this 'poetic universe' the impersonal ideal of dharmic ritualism is converted into a nexus of affective bonds: men are linked in friendship and loyal devotion (*bhakti, sneha*), while women love them faithfully and provide them with inspiration. Naturally the hero himself is the focus of all this affection. The question of power is resolved symbolically: the hero is its visible, charismatic representative, while real authority remains hidden, aligned with the sage's esoteric wisdom and ascetical energy (*tapas*). Against the undermining force of the ascetical intelligence, which is never fully defused by the hero's passive, sentimental triumphs, the myth posits the ideal of *līlā* (play) which exerts a magnetic force in the opposite direction. The transcendent implications of ascetic renunciation (source of the sage's power), with its concomitant disdain or at best condescending regard for the fool's paradise of sentiment, are thereby met by the transcendent implications of serenely ecstatic play. Here the artwork, which houses and embodies the floral paradise and its feminine principle (Śrī), posits itself as the solution, and sentiment is redeemed on the higher level of contemplative, but still eroticized, *rasa*. The ascetical death-drive is sublimated into aesthetic detachment, a refusal of complete psychological identification with the hero, but not an angry refusal:

the subtle, bemused irony of tone that we recognize as peculiarly *kāvya's* replaces a more aggressive critical stance toward sentimental values. We call this a myth because it functions as a narrative paradigm of a world-view, depicting essential areas of conflict and smoothing them over with symbolic mediations.[23] It is the *rasika* myth because of the central place of self-consciously aesthetic sentiment and because it constantly thematizes the role(s) of art or poetry itself.

This book has taken shape over a seven-year period, and portions of it have been published in Indological journals and elsewhere. It follows no single methodology but has been influenced by various notions and practices of modern criticism, structuralism, including psychoanalytic criticism, structuralism, receptivity theory, and deconstruction. Its basic method is the heuristic combination of close reading typically associated with the by now old New Criticism and constant reflection on meaning in context. I have tried to make my argument accessible to students and the general reader without sacrificing attention to philological detail and the important technicalities. It is not possible to be accurate or incisive without using Sanskrit terminology, which has necessitated the inclusion of a glossary.[24] There is also for the general reader an appendix outlining the *rasa* system. As a teacher of Sanskrit literature in translation in addition to normal Sanskrit courses, I have been struck by the lack of good secondary literature beyond the introductory level. With the growing requirement in the U.S. at least for the teaching of non-Western literatures to undergraduates there needs to appear a critical literature which addresses the would-be expositor (most likely a member of an English department) as well as the student in an intelligent and informed manner without hiding behind technicalities and well-meaning but usually insipid idealizations. I believe that Sanskrit drama has a more than museum-piece claim to a place in world literature, and that, if presented as a complex literature engaged in basic human concerns, it cannot fail to draw the comparatist's attention.[25] It should have a special interest for those who work with other court poetries, and I hope my interpretation of its under-the-surface dynamics may resonate for them. I make, however, no objective claim to having unlocked the secrets of Sanskrit drama. My conclusions are heuristic, meant to stimulate interest and further discussion, not seal it off.

A final word on the seven plays and the chapters that deal with them. The two by Bhāsa (probably 4th century AD) and the three by Kālidāsa (probably 5th) are among the earliest in the extant corpus.[26] The other two, by Śūdraka and Viśākhadatta, are harder to date and may go anywhere in the 5th-9th century range. The representativeness of the seven is beyond dispute: they are the most discussed plays in Sanskrit literature, and effectively define the genre.[27] The great majority of the other plays in the corpus, while not without interest, are clearly derivative. Only the three plays of Bhavabhūti (8th C.), which are not considered here, have an equal status. After the opening theoretical chapter on the implications of the aesthetic-erotic playworld, comes a chapter on Kālidāsa's *Śakuntalā,* which best illustrates the dilemma of the playworld. Then a chapter each on the same poet's *Mālavikāgnimitra,* which brings out its metadramatic character in the areas of *rasāsvāda* and strategic 'success' (*siddhi*), and his *Vikramorvaśīya,* where the issue, critical to the understanding of Sanskrit poetry, is the tension between mannered form (*alaṃkāra*) and sentimental content (*rasa*). Chapter 5 focuses on the unresolved split between intelligence and emotion in Sanskrit drama and the precariousness of the conventional world-view that supports *rasa*-aesthetics: the subject is Viśākhadatta's great 'problem-play' *Mudrārākṣasa.* It is based on an essay that was intended wholly for non-specialists and may provide the easiest access to the non-Sanskritic or non-Indological reader. Chapter 6 is on Bhāsa's *Pratijñāyaugandharāyaṇa* and *Svapnavāsavadattā,* both minister plays, though not to the same degree as the *Mudrārākṣasa.* Again the focus is on the division between emotion and intelligence, but this time with the accent on conflicting valuations of the playworld: paradise or prison cell? The final chapter takes us away from the court into the urban center of Ujjayinī with its 'bourgeois' (*nāgarika*) hero. Here we see something we saw more tentatively in the *Svapnavāsavadattā,* that is, a certain ethical emphasis on love. For the unassuming hero of the *Mṛcchakaṭika* love is not so much the entrance into an aesthetic-erotic play-world as it is the crowning symbol of affective solidarity among 'persons of heart' and therefore the key to a utopian society transformed by 'sympathetic generosity' (*hṛdayasaṃvāda*) or *rasa* redefined as virtue (*guṇa*).

namo gaṇeśāya

Notes

1. The general term for Sanskrit poetry. Drama (*nāṭya, nāṭaka*) is one of *kāvya's* principal forms, rivaled only by *mahākāvya* (typically translated as 'court epic') in importance.
2. This is the place to introduce the scheme of the four 'human goals' (*puruṣārtha*) without which no discussion of classical Indian culture can proceed. Three pertain to life in the world and are, in order of importance, *dharma* ('law, duty'), *artha* ('material success, profit'), and *kāma* (desire, pleasure'). The last is *mokṣa* ('liberation' from the cycle of rebirth). *Dharma* can be conceived objectively as the socio-religious order which extends throughout the cosmos. One's duty is determined by one's place in the social hierarchy and by one's stage of life (student, householder, forest dweller, renouncer). *Artha* has special significance for a ruler, since his success theoretically maintains the dharmic order for all others. *Kama* is of value—according to the scheme, which inherently reflects the dharmic perspective—only in the householder stage, when it accounts for offspring. In other stages it is the distraction which keeps us from *mokṣa,* the supreme good. Without desire and its concomitant ignorance there could be no world to have to escape.
3. Ingalls, 'General Introduction,' p. 38.
4. Ānandavardhana, *DhĀ* 1.1-4, 3.41-42.
5. *DhĀL* 1.1 (towards the end): *yeṣāṃ kāvyānuśīlanābhyāsavaśād viśadībhūte manomukure varṇanīyatanmayībhavanayogyatā te svahṛdayasaṃvādabhājaḥ sahṛdayāḥ/*
6. *NŚ* 7.7:

   yo'rtho hṛdayasaṃvādī tasya bhāvo rasodbhavaḥ/
   śarīraṃ vyāpyate tena śuṣkaṃ kāṣṭham ivāgninā//

   Translation mine, as is the case with all Sanskrit texts throughout this book except where otherwise noted. All citations from the NŚ are from the KSS ed. I have checked all readings against the GOS text and found no variations which would affect assertions made in this book. The *Nāṭyaśāstra* (*The Teaching on Drama*) is the principal, and earliest, extant manual on the art of drama. Parts of it probably go back to the 5th century BC, when the grammarian Pāṇini referred to texts called *naṭasūtras* ('actors' manuals'): *Aṣṭādhyāyi* 4.3.110-11, 129. It is attributed to the sage Bharata (regarded as the ancestor of all actors—their caste debasement is explained in the last chapter of the NŚ), but is actually a compilation which probably took something like its present shape in the 3rd or 4th century AD. For a discussion of the textual problems see Ch. 1 of P. V. Kane, *History of Sanskrit Poetics.*
7. *NŚ* 27.53-55:

   śabdacchandovidhānajñā nānāśāstravicakṣaṇāḥ/
   evaṃvidhās tu karttavyāḥ prekṣakā nāṭyadarśane//
   avyagrair indriyaiḥ śuddha uhāpohaviśāradaḥ/
   vyaktadoṣo'nurāgi ca so nāṭye prekṣakaḥ smṛtaḥ//
   yas tuṣṭau tuṣṭim āyāti śoke śokam upaiti ca/
   dainye dīnatvam abhyeti sa nāṭye prekṣakaḥ smṛtaḥ//

   Compare the key term *anurāgin* here with *śṛṅgārin* and *vītarāga* in Ānandavardhana's praise of the poet as world-creator, cited in section 2 of the title chapter.
8. *NŚ* 27.16-17:

   sā sattvātiśayā jñeyā bhāvayuktā tathaiva ca/

nāṭye samprekṣakair jñeyā nityaṃ siddhis tu daivikī//
na śabdo naiva ca kṣobho cotpātananidarśanam/
sampūrṇatā ca raṅgasya sā siddhir daivikī smṛtā//
The description of *mānuṣī siddhi* occupies vv. 3-15.

9. See their book of that title.
10. A helpful discussion of the spectrum of aesthetic identification can be found in Hans Robert Jauss, *Aesthetic Experience and Literary Hermeneutics*, sections A and B.
11. Henceforth I use *rasika* and *sahṛdaya* interchangeably with no distinction of meaning.
12. See ch. 7. I refer to the *rasika* with the masculine pronoun advisedly. Though the *rasika* may indeed be female, the fact is that *kāvya* is written from a male point of view, where women are primarily *objects* of desire. See Ch. 1, section 2.
13. See, for example, S.K. De in Dasgupta and De, *A History of Sanskrit Literature*, pp. 24-25. Paul Thieme is one of very few to keep the *sahṛdaya's* worldliness in mind. See, for example, his remarks on the 'piquant charm' of Śakuntalā as a courtly beauty in the grab of a naive ascetical maiden: 'Das indische Theater,' pp. 95-96.
14. *KM* 548 (Tripathi ed.):
    gāḍhānurāgabhinnaṃ tāruṇyarasāmṛtena saṃsiktam/
    na bhajati sahṛdayahṛdayam vibhavārjanasaṃbhavā cintā//
    I owe my awareness of this passage to David Smith, *Ratnākara's Haravijaya*, p. 46.
15. The fact that *rasa* is a typical word for 'love' or 'desire'—and the same is true of *bhāva*, another key term of aesthetics—is yet another indication of the worldly associations of Indian aesthetics.
16. *AŚ* 9 (Devadhar ed.):
    nāryo mugdhaśaṭhā haranti ramaṇaṃ tiṣṭhanti no vāritās
    tat kiṃ tāmyasi kiṃ ca rodiṣi mudhā tāsāṃ priyaṃ mā kṛthāḥ/
    kāntaḥ kelirucir yuvā sahṛdayas tādṛk priyaḥ kātare
    kiṃ no barbarakarkaśaiḥ priyaśatair ākramya vikrīyate//
    The interpretation of the last line is vexed.
17. There is a whole subgenre of drama called *bhāṇa* or 'monologue play,' which features the *nāgarika-sahṛdaya* as sole actor. It has, however, hardly received any critical attention.
18. The *sandhi-sandhyaṅga* scheme is a complicated method of dividing major plays up into 5 developmental sections containing 64 nodes or 'elements.' See *NŚ* 21, the collected excerpts of G. K. Bhat, or handbooks such as those of Levi, Keith, and S. N. Shastri.
19. 'Kālidāsa's World and His Plays,' particularly pp. 26-38.
20. The 5 'stages' (*avasthās*) of action and the 5 'plot-constituents' (*arthaprakṛtis*). T. G. Mainkar's work *The Theory of the Sandhis and Sandhyaṅgas*, unlike Gerow's and Byrski's studies, is exegetical rather than interpretive, pulling examples from various plays (including Shakespeare) to illustrate the practical meaning of Sanskrit terms.
21. Gerow, I. 564, 570; II. 282.
22. *Mokṣa* or spiritual liberation is not in itself a concern of drama, but asceticism (*tapas*) and a kind of magical intelligence is associated with it in the Indian imagination. The word *tapas* means 'heat,' and describes both asceticism itself

and the energy gained by it. *Tapas* is an important concept as early as the late portions of the *Ṛgveda* (c. 1000 BC), where it is the heat that generates the cosmos from the primordial waters. It was even then, but more systematically in the *Brāhmaṇa* texts (2nd layer of the *Vedas*, c. 1000-800 BC), associated with the fire of sacrifice, which was itself mystically identified with the cosmic process. In both stages it also connotes sexual energy—stored up by deprivation to be used for special purposes. When ritual was internalized in Upaniṣadic thought (late Vedic stage, beginning c. 800 BC), the sacrificial idea was overtly reconciled with ascetical practice, which was probably pre-Aryan in origin. The ascetic is thus a very potent figure, who combines various levels of religious belief in transcendent or 'magical' power and stands behind every imposing Brahmanical figure in Sanskrit and derived literatures. Contrary to idealistic notions that prevail especially in the West, *tapas* and other techniques were not primarily practised in order to gain liberation (*mokṣa, nirvāṇa*), but for supernormal powers. Thus, the sage is always a virtual magician in myth, legend, tale, and more sophisticated poetic compositions.

23. My use of 'myth' corresponds to that of Roland Barthes in the interpretive portion of *Mythologies*, which in my paraphrase is a narrative coding of ideological-cultural values according to the subliminal wishes of a community or subcommunity (in this case, Indian aesthetic culture). The pseudo-scientific, jargonized definition he offers in the final theoretical chapter does not concern me.
24. It is not either advisable or possible to translate key terms in a rigidly consistent manner. There are no exact English equivalents. When the same term gets different translations it is because it shows a different facet in a different context. The reader who feels confused should use the glossary as an anchor and see the particular translation as part of the word's legitimate scope. Sanskrit words are notorious for their wide metaphorical extensions of meaning and many technical usages.
25. I will take this opportunity to insist that Sanskrit literature is not simply an Indian heritage. It belongs to the world, as much as the Greek and Latin classics. In my judgment, too much is made of the differences between East and West. This has led to absurdities like the West claiming critical thought as its own, and certain Indian thinkers agonizing over their compromised Indianness because they employ it. If new methods and ideas remained the possession of the cultures which evolved them there would never be any advance in human knowledge.
26. Sanskrit drama is known to have existed in some form as early as the grammarian Pāṇini, 5th C. BC (see *supra*), though it may have been more dance than drama at that time. From another grammarian, Patañjali possibly 2nd C. BC), we hear of a drama that included several speaking parts, but it is unclear whether or not we are dealing with a poetic form (*kāvya*) or more popular and/or religious entertainment. There are a few fragments of poetic drama, which is what we mean when we speak of Sanskrit drama (*nāṭya, nāṭaka*), from approximately the 2nd century AD—by the Buddhist poet Aśvaghoṣa, two of whose 'literary epics' (*mahākāvya*) survive almost complete. Bhāsa's plays (of the thirteen plays arguably attributed to him, at least two or three and most likely more are sure to be his) are the earliest extant whole plays in the corpus, and Kālidāsa's (whose three plays were apparently his

whole dramatic output) are next. The next plays we can securely date are those of Harṣa, in the early 7th C.

27. The 'genre' I refer to here is that of serious poetic drama, which includes the forms *nāṭaka, prakaraṇa, troṭaka* (or *toṭaka*), and *nāṭikā*. There are also minor forms such as *bhāṇa* and *prahasana*, which are also very interesting, but have a less idealistic character. See the handbooks of Keith, Levi, and others, or go straight to the *Nāṭyaśāstra* or *Daśarūpaka* for descriptions. The differences among the forms of the plays studied here have little essential significance, but see the appropriate notes in the chapters of *Mālavikāgnimitra* and *Mṛcchakaṭika*.

CHAPTER 1

The Playworld of Sanskrit Drama

Most general readers will be at least dimly aware of the importance of the concept of play or sport (*līlā, krīḍā*) in Indian (specifically Hindu) religion and philosophy. It is one of the main attractions of Indian thought in the West. Who can resist the appeal of rising to a level of understanding that would permit us to revel not only in the world-spectacle, but in the vicissitudes of our own experience, our pains, frustrations, fears, rejections, etc.? To take an aesthetic view of our own lives and really hold it, insulated from outside threats, to feel nothing but pleasure and of the most enlightened kind, to be divine in fact, to understand that the world is only ourselves, the dream we dream in our character as cosmic artist. The Homeric gods enjoyed the freedom of the playworld, but they were a privileged aristocracy off on the distant heights of Olympus—and no one ever imagined them as cosmic artists. But Indian thought (or one facet of it) removes the barrier between god and man and makes everything possible to the enlightened: 'The gods are only your Self.' Of course, when we pay close attention to the particular systems of Indian philosophy and religious practice, when we decide to investigate and study the details of this attractive view, we encounter all sorts of difficulties. The textual problems are enormous, for instance. There seem to be no definitive texts, but rather multiple versions needing much editorial emendation. And then there is the matter of format: dogmatic assertion followed by scholastic commentary and subcommentary virtually without end. But even if we have the patience to get to the bottom of this, fitting all the pieces of the puzzle together to discove a representative system, we find that the principal ideas are riddled with paradoxes and even contradictions. At that point the more philosophically minded scholar might experience a revelation: The endlessly baroque argumentation is itself a form of play. It brings a smile to the lips: the pursuit of paradox and complication as liberation. But was such a game ever understood as such by the players themselves? Were scholastics like Abhinavagupta amused by their own erudition? I suspect the answer is No, yet is the insight invalid? Perhaps our less literal perspective is more in the spirit of play, though less 'theologically' authentic, than reams of scholarly polemic.

The argument of this book follows a similar course. Sanskrit drama (indeed *kāvya* as a whole) tacitly enshrines the ideal of play, which we find connected to the idea of a 'poetic universe,' created by the poet for his own and the *rasika–sahṛdaya's* delight. In this new world the laws of karmic causality (*niyati*) become the rules of a game, i.e., the rococo of poetic forms and conventions that support *rasa* (aesthetic mood), the elixir that converts all emotion to relish. The model reminds us of metaphysical *līlāvāda* (play-doctrine) in Vedānta and in Kashmiri Śaivism, the latter being of particular importance because it provided the philosophical background for theoretical aesthetics, which was largely a Kashmiri phenomenon. Yet the closer we look at the aesthetic playworld, the more attention we pay to its central myth, the more problematic it becomes. There are two areas in particular which will concern us. One is structural, inherent in the very idea of play: the trend to solipsism, which brings up the question of the status of the aesthetic object and beyond that the much larger issue of subjectivity and objectivity in the human relations which *kāvya* depicts. We shall see that we cannot speak of aesthetics in the Indian context (perhaps any context) without bringing in the erotic. In a practical sense this means that aesthetic questions take on a more human dimension, in as much as they come to focus on the issue of an ideal relationship between lovers. It is here that the playworld of poetry begins to appear less than an envelopment in a rare atmosphere of delight, for it becomes a ground for the exploration of hopes and fears that remain rooted to real-life concerns despite *sui generis* (*alaukika*) aesthetic claims. The other area of concern is a byproduct of the emphasis on creative freedom and autonomy: the issue of power. Is the *rasika* in fact the creator of his own world of fancy? Or does the poet speak as well for other cultural forces, even those that are at odds with the cultivation of emotional subtlety? How does poetry *qua* playworld—a form of *kāma* (desire) with quasi-mokṣic pretensions (*mokṣa* = transcendence)—mythicize its own status vis-à-vis the ritualism of *dharma*, the drive to ascetical purgation (*tapas*), the cult of emotionlessness (*vairāgya*), the demands of practical reality (*artha*)? In the following chapters we will be examining individual plays in great detail to gain insight into these matters. This chapter, however, will be more programmatic, concerned only with establishing the ideological connection between the metaphysical and aesthetic conceptions of *līlā*. Perhaps, like our imaginary scholar of metaphysics, we will come in the course of the book to the understanding that the process of worrying out the details is as close as we will come to enlightenment.

1. The Metaphysics of Play

I deal here only with the monistic version of the play-idea, leaving alone, for example, the dualistic literature of Vaiṣṇava *bhakti*, where God's sport with the world is typified as Krishna's play with the Gopis (personifying the *jīvas* or human souls). I do this because I am approaching *kāvya* through mainstream Indian aesthetical theory, and it is the monistic tradition of Kashmiri Śaivism and—to a much lesser extent—Vedānta which is pertinent to this. The dualistic model, with its adulation of Krishna as child, master, lover, companion, etc., would also afford insight into kāvyic patterns, since we see almost every *nāyaka* (protagonist, hero) adulated in the same ways in the poems and plays. And, as we shall see, the monistic bias of the aesthetic play-ideal cannot be sustained. But we will postpone the application of devotional (*bhakti*) aesthetics to a later chapter.[1]

I further restrict myself to three monistic models: the Vedāntic conceptions of Śaṅkara and Rāmānuja and Trika Śaivism.[2] The Vedāntic versions come out of *Brahmasūtra* 2.1.33, the *līlāsūtra*,[3] which solves the problem of the Absolute's relation to the world by appeal to sport. Only a play-relation to the world can save God's transcendence, since play simultaneously assumes action and freedom from the need to act: if God creates for a *reason*, he/it is not autonomous. Both Śaṅkara and Rāmāunja point to courtly amusements as the probable referent of the *sūtra's lokavat* ('as in the world'), which is of interest to us in view of the predominantly courtly atmosphere of *kāvya* and its status as a court poetry.[4] Already we have hints of the pleasure-garden and its erotic charms. For Śaṅkara, however, the play-doctrine can only be figurative,[5] part of the 'lower knowledge' (*aparā vidyā*) that helps us make the leap into the unfathomable (see *BSBh* 4.4.8 ff.). He is led to this position, doubtless, because he knows that play represents a genuine paradox. It must be absorbing, in order to bring delight. But whatever absorbs the attention is obviously a threat to the autonomy and transcendence of consciousness. Even an imaginary object succumbs to reification, causing forgetfulness of Self. So Śaṅkara stoutly maintains that *saṃsāra* is the superimposition of a false vision on the absolute ground of being. The result is another paradox, which critics like Rāmānuja delight in pointing out: how error or illusion can arise in the first place, since there is only Ātman, transcendant consciousness without a second, to serve as its subject.[6] Nevertheless, Śaṅkara's negation of *saṃsāra* is instructive. He is probably right to see that the psychological implications of aestheticizing metaphysics are more of a threat to monism than logical paradox. The valorization of *līlā* and its delights introduces the problematics of Eros and the living ghost of the Other.[7]

The genteel asceticism of Śaṅkara's Vedānta, its conversion of renunciation (*saṃnyāsa, tapas*) into objectless knowledge (*jñāna*), made it very prominent among educated Brahmins, with a prestige that is felt strongly even today. For this reason, and also because he is a less sophisticated thinker than Śaṅkara, we tend to discount the Upaniṣadic roots of Rāmānuja's Vedāntic system, with its ontological validation of *saṃsāra*. For Rāmānuja, however, transcendence does not preclude immanence. God (Īśvara) not only creates the world, He is the world—along with the individual *jīvas* or souls it forms his body. When the liberated soul realized its paradoxical identity as Ātman (paradoxical because it remains separate from Ātman in the full sense) the *māyā*-world does not disappear, as it does in Śaṅkara's system, but simply loses its power to bewilder and bind. It accordingly becomes a playground to be entered at will. Rāmānuja even accords the liberated soul the same power as Īśvara to create worlds out of its own power of imagination (*satyasaṃkalpatva*), though all these have to fit somehow into Īśvara's structure.[8] The soul may relish these worlds (*līlārasa, ŚBh* 3.2.12, 4.13-14), whether created by Īśvara or itself, either in a bodiless dream-presence or by taking bodily form (the equivalent of divine *avatāra*). Where Śaṅkara draws his chief inspiration from the *neti neti* tenor of texts like *BĀU* 4.3.21-22, 4.3.32-33, and 4.5.15, Rāmānuja draws his from *ChU* passages that affirm the liberated soul's delight in what is nevertheless continued sense-experience, though now purified and transformed into Self-achievement. Thus *ChU* 7.25.2 and 8.12.1-3:

> The Self (*ātman*) is this All. He who sees thus, thinks thus, understands thus is one whose pleasure is in the Self (*ātmarati*), whose sport is in the Self (*ātmakrīda*), whose intercourse is with the Self (*ātmamithuna*), whose happiness is in the Self (*ātmānanda*). He is autonomous (*svarāṭ*) and in all worlds he has movement according to his desire (*kāmacāra*). But those who know otherwise are ruled by others (*anyrājānaḥ*), their worlds are perishable, and in all worlds they do not have movement according to their desires.[9]

> Verily, there is no freedom from pleasure and pain for one while he is incorporate. Verily, while one is bodiless, pleasure and pain do not touch him. The wind is bodiless. Clouds, lightning, thunder—these are bodiless. Now as these, when they arise from yonder space and reach the highest light, appear each with its own form, even so that serene one [the liberated soul], when he rises up from this body and reaches the highest light, appears with his own form. Such a one is the supreme person (*uttamapuruṣa*). There such a one goes around laughing, sporting (*krīḍan*), having enjoyment with women or chariots or friends, not remembering the appendage of this body. As a draft-animal is yoked in a wagon, even so this spirit (*prāṇa*) is yoked in this body.[10]

Such an idea of liberation—kinglike (*svarāṭ*) movement through the worlds according to one's desire—does not regard the sensuous manifold itself as a delusion, but rather only that bondage to action and desire that keeps the soul confused about its identity and confined within the cycle of rebirth. Note too the evocation of an aristocratic or courtly ethos even at this early stage (8th-6th C. BC, when courts were very rudimentary compared to what they would be in Nanda times), complete with erotic idealizations: *ātmarati* and *ātmamithuna* give suggestive meaning to *kāmacāra* in the first passage, and in the second play with women and chariots is specifically mentioned as a mokṣic treat. *Līlāmokṣa* posits an experience of *saṃsāra* that is simultaneously transcendent and immanent, like a dream in which one is conscious of dreaming and so is omniscient artist and spectator of a world in which one also plays the leading part and indeed all the parts (cf. *BĀU* 4.3.7-38). No one who has experienced the conscious dreaming phenomenon—one of the most powerful aesthetic experiences available to us—can fail to feel an exhilarating sense of revelation.

But perhaps the most extensive development of this idea comes in Kashmiri Śaivism. I quote the *Śivasūtra* with Kṣemarāja's commentary *in extenso* both because it and statements like it are still not very well-known and because, as I said, Śaiva metaphysics formed the intellectual and religious background for India's mainstream aesthetical theory.

> *The self* (*ātman*) *is the actor.* He acts, i.e., in the mere sport of self-vibration (*svaparispandalīlayaiva*)[11] he manifests, in self-differentiation, the manifold world which consists of various rôles in the waking and dreaming states—which world, however, is firmly based in the essential nature concealed within it. . . . Thus Bhaṭṭa Nārāyaṇa says (*Stavacintāmaṇi* 59):
>
> You have introduced the cosmic drama, Hara,
> into which you have released the seeds of all beings.
> Who then but you are the poet
> to bring it to a conclusion? . . .
>
> *The individual self* (*antarātman*) *is the theater.* He (Śiva) delights therein, by means of the self (*ātman*) that is the basis (*āśraya*) for the manifestation of the sport which is the cosmic drama . . . . Thus, having made his abode (in the embodied self), he manifests the cosmic drama through the vibration of his own senses. *The senses are the audience.* The eyes, etc., of the *yogin* witness, when they are turned inward, the absolute essence (or 'identity,' *sva-svarūpa*) that is filled with delight by the manifestation of the drama of *saṃsāra.* As this performance develops (or 'intensifies,' *tatprayogaprarūḍhyā*), the senses produce a plenum of wondrous delight (*camatkāra*) and *rasa,* in which all division drops away.[12]

One could produce many other passages along these lines, but they would not add anything essential. The universe in the absolute perspective is a work of art, a play (in both senses), for it is nothing but transcendental consciousness taking form for its own delight. The sensuous manifold is the self-manifestation (*ābhāsa*) of Śiva, the absolute subject (our metaphysical 'I'), arising spontaneously from him by the power of his *śakti* or *pratibhā* (= Māyā, Parā Vāc, Devī, etc.) and knownfelt,[13] in an orgasmic shudder (*spanda*), as a blissful experience of Self in imaginary Other. This is far from Śaṅkara's notion of *māyā* as the inexplicable ignorance that leaves absolute consciousness—for which it does not exist any more than does the illusory snake for the rope—

completely untouched. For Śaṅkara all self-consciousness is already false.[14] Monistic Śaivism is fundamentally an aesthetical mysticism, as we see in Kṣemarāja's reference to *rasa* and *camatkāra* in the passage cited above. Thus Abhinavagupta's view of the aesthetic experience as a foretaste of the mystical experience, from which it does not differ in kind.[15] The adept's experience of *samsāra* is, therefore, one in which there is no bondage, no pain, no personal limitation, etc.[16] All is, and is savored as, the 'sport of self-vibration' (*svaparispandalīlā*).

What distinguishes monistic Kashmiri Śaivism, Rāmānuja's Qualified Non-dualism (*viśiṣṭādvaita*), and other systems which take the play-doctrine seriously from those that do not is a reluctance to turn one's back completely on the world of experience. Instead we find what seems to be an impulse to recuperate the phenomenal world in the face of a radical ascetical drive to renunciation. Perhaps the guiding sense is the dread of loss. To repudiate the world entirely is to deprive the notion of bliss of any experiential ground. To sacrifice a vibrant sense-awareness for an impersonal 'knowledge' that does not even include self-consciousness, to reject imagination and memory for hope of bliss that rests in complete abstraction (*nirvikalpatva*)—there is something fundamentally impractical about such a Pascalian wager. We sense in the desire to be rid of desire the deep longing for rest that Freud has called the death-drive. The model for such an idea of bliss is dreamless sleep rather than the conscious-dreaming phenomenon that seems to underlie the *līlā*- ideal. The *līlāvādins,* therefore, instead of finding play an aporia that threatens the self-repose of ultimate consciousness see in it the possibility of achieving that repose with eyes open onto a world of iridescent charm which reflects the mystery of self-identity. It is the repose of a mystical sensitivity to emotion, *rasāsvāda* (*rasa*-savoring) on the highest possible level.[17]

On the other hand we should not underestimate the force of submerged asceticism[18] even in what may strike us as an apotheosis of the leisure-class play-ethos. We must remember, for instance, that the end result of Śaiva monism, for all its relish of the sensuous manifold, is a transcendental solipsism. The thrill (*camatkāra*) of cosmic vibration is, in crude but not I think misleading terms, onanistic. Śiva remains alone in his very fullness. Mystical absorption in the orgasmic bliss of union with his feminized *śakti*—as in the *yogin's* self-absorption in the ritual intercourse of the *Kulayāga*—does not disguise a certain reductive impoverishment of affect implicit in any monism. Love loses its meaning when it dissolves into a self-absorbed ecstatic shudder. With the narcissistic appropriation of the Other, love cease to be a site of vital disclosure. We see this also on the level of purely aesthetical doctrine. In the philosophical understanding of aesthetic delight (*rasāsvāda, camatkāra,* etc.) every emotional response, though engendered by an imaginative engagement in a virtual world, becomes nothing but the spectator's own blissful self-savoring. Aesthetic representation then exists only as a vehicle for an inner pleasure: not to arouse curiosity, to provide inspiration, to make us see better or marvel at the world itself. Not only is it completely without the referential function, it is ultimately, and paradoxically, not even a fascinating object in its own right. So we see that in the *līlāvāda* of Kashmiri Śaivism and its associated aesthetics the ascetical impulse that characterized Śaṅkara's uncompromising non-dualism reappears as the rejection of emotional engagement in the world, a reduction of all 'you' to 'It,' and all 'It' to a modality of 'I.'[19]

The metaphysical idealization of poetry has a profound general significance. Above all, it points to a profound sense of transformation in the *rasika's* emotional response to poetry. It seems to me that Bhaṭṭa Nāyaka, Abhinavagupta, and those who followed their lead had a genuine insight into the depth of the *rasika's* longing for transcendence of affective limitation, i.e., for a breakthrough into freedom-in-feeling. As we shall see in the next section, *rasa* afforded the 'man of heart/feeling' (*sahṛdaya, rasika*) an entry—temporary, perhaps, but all-enveloping—into a different universe, in which personal feeling was atmospherically suffused (cf. *dravaṇa, rasa's* melting sensation) and felt as bliss. *Rasāsvāda* is related to *brahmāsvāda* (savoring of Brahman) most importantly on the affective level, because the *rasika* cannot accept a *mokṣa* that excludes sentiment. All the profound longing for deliverance that underlies the spiritual ideal in Indian culture is invested by him with a positive emotional significance. We have seen that *līlāmokṣa* gives us religious models of the convergence of these two domains. We shall see, however, that the *rasika's* playworld retains a human poignancy that we altogether miss in the monistic perpective we have examined.

Thus the real question for us, as we move from metaphysics to aesthetics, regards the status of affect in *kāvya*. Does the solipsizing *rasa*-doctrine of Abhinavagupta accurately describe what really goes on in the *rasika-sahṛdaya's* imaginative experience? It would be easy simply to answer No and go on with a more humanistic analysis. But this would be to ignore something essential in the aestheticizing consciousness. Does not connoisseurship in any tradition involve a certain reduction, whereby things become mere bearers of savor? All the Indian tradition does in this respect—though it is a major alteration—is mysticize the meaning of aesthetic savor. Inevitably, however, there is a tension between art and life, the savor and the vehical, and it centers on the question of love—in aesthetic terms the *śṛṅgāra* theme—not only because it is the dominant theme of *kāvya* but because it is where the status of the 'You' is most problematic. It is easy to abandon a world that is only a disturbance, but how can one abandon what one loves—or wishes to love—without destroying one's ability to savor anything? The *rasika,* however, is as much of an aesthete as he is a lover, and we see his plight dramatized in the *nāyaka's* (protagonist's) erotic response to the *nāyikā* (heroine). That is to say, it is very difficult to decide whether love for him, the ideal projection of the *rasika-sahṛdaya,* is a surrender of emotional autonomy (*qua* self-dedication to the Radiant Female) or a detached savoring of affect, both in himself and in the woman who arouses his interest. Ultimately it is a question about *kāvya's* human meaning.

2. The Woman in the Garden

I have to start by recalling certain passages from the literature in poetics that bring *kāvya* more directly in line with the *līlāvāda* we have already discussed. First we may mention *Nāṭyaśāstra* 1, in which the gods, desirous of a Veda for the Kali Age, seek a 'plaything' (*krīḍanīyaka,* 1.11; cf. 1.104 [KSS ed.]) that will serve as an instructive model of life in the triple-world. There is nothing in this innocent use of the term that need detain us. It is basically a formulation of the dual pleasure-instruction (*prīti-upadeśa*) function of poetry mentioned in surviving Indian texts first by Aśvaghoṣa (2nd C. AD)[20] and familiar as well in the Western classical tradition. But when Dhanaṃjaya uses the play-paradigm in *Daśarūpaka* 4, the application is more significant: 'Like children playing with clay elephants and the like, hearers of poetry, playing with characters like Arjuna, etc., savor their own energy (*utsāha*).[21] These lines come just after the theoretical discussion of *rasāsvāda,* which follows the teaching of Bhaṭṭa Nāyaka,[22] and just before the descriptive treatment of the individual *rasas.* Thus it summarizes the doctrine of the subjective nature of aesthetic delight (consciousness savoring itself through real appearances[23]) in a trope that gives emphasis to the 'hearer's'—i.e., the *rasika's* or *sahṛdaya's*—imaginative autonomy.

To fill out the meaning of this aesthetic 'child's play' we must move to Mammaṭa and Ānandavardhana. Let me take Mammaṭa (late 11th C. AD) first, despite the anachronism, because *Kāvyaprakāśa* 1.1 gives us a cosmic perspective on the poetic playworld without immediately introducing us to the *śṛṅgāra* theme.

> Triumphant is the word of the poet,
> which creates a world devoid of Fate's restrictions,
> consisting only of delight,
> utterly autonomous, and radiant with the nine *rasas.*[24]

Mammaṭa paints here the picture of a world of pure enchantment. Poetry is triumphant because it succeeds in delivering us from all the restrictions we associate with the law of *karman* but not at the price of banishing the sensuous manifold. The actual world undergoes a sea-change: bondage becomes freedom, and painful emotions (fear, disgust, sorrow, etc.) are transmuted to *rasas,* whose essence is delight. Thus Mammaṭa explains his own verse:

> Such is the world created by Brahmā: essentially restricted by the power of fate; consisting of happiness, unhappiness, and delusion (*moha*); dependent on material and auxiliary causes such as atoms and activity (*karman*); having only six *rasas* (tastes), not all of them agreeable [the reference is to sweet, sour, salty, bitter, astringent, and pungent]. The poet's world is without these characteristics: that is why it is triumphant.[25]

In poetry we transcend the workaday fate-bound world of the Vedic creator-figure Brahmā and distill from its experience what Rāmānuja calls the 'savor of play' (*līlārasa*). Thus we are put on the plane of God or the liberated soul in Rāmānuja's Vedānta and Kashmir Śaivism.

So too in a frequently cited passage of Ānandavardhana some

200 years earlier (c. 875 AD):

> In the boundless universe of poetry, the poet is the sole creator,
> and as it pleases him, so does this world come forth.
> If the poet is a man of passion (*śṛṅgārin*), the world in poetry
> is full of *rasa*.
> But if he is passionless (*vītarāga*), that world is devoid of *rasa* altogether.[26]

The poet creates the world according to the pleasure-principle. If we combine this statement with Mammaṭa's the implicit connection between poet and *rasika* becomes obvious. If the only law is that of *rasa*, then there can be no essential difference between the poet's and listener-spectator-reader's *experience* of the poetic universe.[27] But something else surfaces here. In metaphysical *līlāvāda* we have noted the inevitable ascetical accent, the reduction of play to a modality of self-savoring for a consciousness which remains fundamentally transcendent. Ānandavardhana's *rasika,* however, must already be a man of passion, i.e., he is not ideally disengaged from the world. He creates a new world in order to give play to already-existent feeling, to receive the surfeit that finds no adequate expression in his actuality. The model is perhaps the poetically familiar one of Prajāpati's creation of a beautiful woman out of the longing of his heart, through meditation or by bringing a picture to life, a woman who embodies the disparate world's potential for ravishing charm.[28] Here, though, is where the *līlā*-ideal of autonomy begins to erode. If the *rasika*-poet is already a man of feeling for whom the world as it is insufficient, is not the new creation the echo of a desire for emotional fulfilment *in* life? In other words are we talking here about entering a rarified world of aesthetic (self-) savoring or is the poetic universe an attempt to realize a potential presence?

We can determine the nature of this presence by attending to certain metaphors that describe poetic charm. Here first is Mammaṭa again, verse and commentary:

> *Kāvya* gives glory, attainment of wealth,
> knowledge of the world, an end to the inauspicious,
> sudden bliss, and counsel sweet
> as from the lips of a beautiful woman.

> Bliss is its (poetry's) chief purpose and is immediate; it derives from the savoring of *rasa* and makes fall away all other objects of cognition. Poetry (*kāvya*), i.e., the activity of the poet skilled in depicting the supranormal world [cf. *KP* 1.1 *supra*], is different from learned texts (*śāstras*) such as the Vedas, whose words are like those of a master, and from epic and Purāṇa, which is like the advice of a friend—different by virtue of its prevalent function of rendering word and content subservient to *rasa*. Poetry renders the poet's appropriate instruction—such as 'One should act like Rāma rather than Rāvaṇa'—to the *sahṛdaya* in the manner of a beautiful woman, addressing him directly and producing a state of being with *rasa*.[29]

Passages like this, which convey a standard trope, should convince us to what extent the *rasika* in general is assumed to be male. The metaphorical association of poetic and erotic seduction is not dismissable as a pedagogical device, the self-effacing vehicle of a purely intellectual principle, but gives us essential information about poetic reception in the Indian cultural context.[30] Any extensive reading of *kāvya* will establish beyond doubt that the poetic playworld must have the Radiant Female, a Śri-like principle of charm, at its center. It is by her magic that one enters into the poetic universe, which is to feel oneself and the world transformed by *rasa,* to feel suddenly free (Mammaṭa 1.1) in an atmosphere whose *raison d'être* is the elicitation of an emotional response described as both a melting (*dravaṇa, druti*) and an opening or sprouting (*vikāsa, aṅkurībhāva*) sensation.[31] The 'state of being with *rasa'*—as in the use of that term in non-technical language—is in the first instance a state of erotic excitement or captivation.[32]

Thus Abhinavagupta describes the inception of *rasāsvāda* (savoring of sentiment) in such a way that we cannot really distinguish the *rasika* outside the poem from the hero within it:

> The savoring of *rasa,* whose essence is a more-than-ordinary delight/thrill (*alaukika camatkāra*), is different from memory or inference (of an emotional state) or ordinary self-consciousness. Thus one does not apprehend a beautiful woman, etc.,[33] in a state of indifference, as he would in ordinary inference, but rather in a state of germinating *rasa*-savoring soon to reach fullness, because he is a *sahṛdaya,* which means that his heart is attuned (to such objects). He does not need to climb the ladder of inference, memory, etc., because the experience is essentially

> a savoring (*carvaṇā*) befitting utter absorption (*tanmayībhāva*) (in her *qua* object).[34]

This passage reveals that the hero's (*nāyaka's*) response to the *pramadā* (woman of intoxicating beauty) within poem or play enacts a paradigm of aesthetic response in general.[35] The *rasika* is both in the poem as the woman's admirer, savoring his response to her, and outside savoring his response to the poem itself.[36] To extract some purely aesthetic essence from the total aesthetic-erotic response, as most critics have tried to do, is to deny the suggestive principle (*dhvani, vyañjana*) that Indian theory itself enshrines. Let us again cite the dictum of Bhaṭṭa Tauta: 'The hero, the poet, and the listener (i.e., *rasika*) all have the same experience' (*nāyakasya kaveḥ śrotuḥ samāno' nubhavas tataḥ, DhĀL* 1.6+). The *rasika* enjoys the playworld of poetry as a *participant* who surrenders himself to it, as to a beautiful woman. In the passage cited above we have a much more vivid and telling use of *tanmayībhāva* (identification, absorption) than in the abstract generalisation of the famous definition of the *sahṛdaya* in the *DhĀL*.[37] Who else is this ideally seductive woman, then, but the generic heroine of all Sanskrit poetry?[38]

And where do we find her if not in the floral paradise that typifies *kavya* as a whole? Even if the garden were not her actual setting, she would create it around herself, like a seasonal Śrī, in metaphor or suggestion. In the 3rd Act of Bhāsa's *Pratijñāyaugandharāyaṇa* this is precisely what occurs: Vāsavadattā creates a pleasure-garden out of Udanaya's prison cell, casting a spell over his imagination. Instead of lamenting his fate Udayana basks in the magical aura of the Radiant Female and devotes himself to the 'royal sport of love.'[39] The garden-aura that surrounds the *pramadā* heroine is nothing other than the mise-en-scene of the sprouting sensation (*aṅkurībhāva*) of *rasāsvāda*.[40]

But there is a further dimension as well, which invests the aesthetic-erotic paradigm of The-Woman-in-the-Garden with the suggestion of a venerable religious idea and gives special symbolic significance to the courtly ambience in which the erotic *līlā* of *kāvya* usually takes place. This is Śrī-concept, to which we have several times alluded. In Srī-Lakṣmī seasonal fertility, wealth, and happiness are personified precisely in the figure of the voluptuous garden-world *pramadā*. The king as ideal representative of the human community is regarded as wedded to the goddess (mythologically the consort of the god Viṣṇu), whose worship goes well back into Vedic times.[41] She is thus not only the goddess of seasonal beauty, fertility, etc., but the personification of victory and the sovereignty itself.[42] The monarchy therefore becomes a conduit of divine radiance, representing or embodying the paradisal playworld of divinity on earth. Notions of magical correspondence between the person of the king and the state of the kingdom—often remarked on in studies of Indian kingship[43]—make it possible for the king's dalliance with beautiful women, all auspicious representatives of the Śrī-principle, to be taken as a 'magical' inducement to social prosperity. We see similar auspicious symbolism in the *mithuna* motif in Indian art: the auspicious male-female pair (sometimes engaged in sexual intercourse, *maithuna*) that adorns religious structures ubiquitously.[44] The union of hero and heroine and the luxuriant heightening of erotic atmosphere in drama and poetry cannot be understood adequately without reference to these notions. The garden-world of poetry with its synaesthetic allure (soft breezes, fragrant scents, low hums and warbles, etc., amid the opulence of florid vegetation) is thus the locus for the epiphany of Śrī and the auspicious transformation of her hero-consort and his world.

Let us recapitulate the themes of this section before moving into the *Śakuntalā* in the next chapter. We have seen that the poeticians celebrate poetry as a world constructed according to the demands of *rasa*, an aesthetic parallel to *līlāmokṣa*. We have likewise seen that the central element in this playworld is encounter with the Radiant Female who embodies its power (*śakti*) to captivate or entrance. Without her there would be no world nor any *rasa* for it to enshrine. And finally we have noted how the dream-woman of poetry wears the aspect of Śrī, thus becoming a communal symbol of auspiciousness. The questions we posed at the end of the last section are still unanswered, but now we can better appreciate their implications. In the Abhinavagupta paradigm cited two pages back, aesthetic and erotic perspectives mix, but in such a way that love is transformed into a connoisseur's savoring of *rasa*. In other words, it is a solipsizing *līlā:* the *rasika* enters into the poetic universe only to savor the rarified emotion aroused by stimulating images. This is not far from what on the purely secular plain would be a refined courtly hedonism. In Ānandavardhana's model, however, we seem to find something more poignantly human: the longing for love, for the utopian world that mirrors the heart's demand for sentimental response. For in both his and Mammaṭa's praise of poetry as ideal universe we glimpse a shadow of disappointment in the real world, which does not offer sufficient opportunity for that mingling of hearts that *kāvya* holds up as its ideal.[46] Yet the more *kāvya* takes on the dimensions of wish-fulfilment the less playlike it becomes. *Līlā's* delicate balance of immanence and transcendence tilts here towards immanence. Courtly (or mystical) aestheticism begins to seem like a screen separating the *rasika* as lover from the dream-woman who would deliver his heart from its isolation. Which version is correct? Or are both?

Notes

1. Ch. 6, 'Paradise in a Prison Cell.'
2. Alexis Sanderson, who has generously commented on an earlier version of this chapter, has noted that Kashmiri Vaiṣṇava non-dualism is more pertinent to Kashmiri aesthetics than Rāmānuja's *viśiṣṭādvaita*. I include Rāmānuja primarily as a check on Śaṅkara, whose version of Vedānta was and still is unduly generalized, to show that even within the sober Vedāntic tradition there is an 'aesthetical' understanding of play. The relation of both to Indian aesthetics is quite indirect, despite S.K. De and others who have read Śaṅkara into Abhinavagupta's theory. Here they (the Vedāntins) serve as foils, and to underline the Upaniṣadic roots of *līlā*.
3. *Lokavat tu līlākaivalyam:* 'Play only, as in the world.'
4. Śaṅkara, *BSBh* 2.1.33:

   yatra loke kasyacid āptaiṣaṇasya rājño rājāmatyasya vā vyatiriktam kiṃcit prayojanam anabhisaṃdhāya kevalaṃ līlārūpāḥ pravṛttayaḥ krīḍāvihāreṣu bhavanti, yathā cocchvāsapraśvāsādayo'nabhisaṃdhāya bāhyaṃ kiṃcit prayojanaṃ svabhāvād eva saṃbhavanti, evam īśvarasyāpi anapekṣya kiṃcit prayojanānantaraṃ svabhāvād eva kevalaṃ līlārūpā pravṛtti bhaviṣyati/

   Rāmānuja's commentary is very similar.
5. *BSBh* 2.1.33:

   na ceyaṃ paramārthaviṣayā sṛṣṭiśrutir avidyākalpitanāmarūpavyavahāragocaratvād brahmātmabhāvapratipādanaparatvāc cetyetad api naiva vismartavyam/
6. As in *Śrī-Bhāṣya* 2.1.15.
7. Śāṅkara, *BSBh* 4.4.6:

   pratiṣiddhaṃ hi brahmaṇo'nekakaratvaṃ na sthānato'pi parasyobhayaliṅgam ityatra [*BS* 3.2.11]/ *ata eva jakṣaṇādisaṃkīrtanaṃ duḥkhābhāvamātrābhiprāyaṃ stutyartham ātmaratirityādivat/ na hi mukhyānyeva ratikrīḍāmithunānyātmani śakyante varṇayitum dvitīyaviṣayatvāt teṣām/ tasmān nirastāśeṣaprapañcena prasannenāvya-padeśyena bodhātmanābhiniṣpadyata ityauḍulomir ācāryo manyate/*
8. *Śrī-Bhāṣya* 4.14. (For the notion of *satyasaṃkalpa* see *ChU* 3.14.2, 8.1.4-6.) The principal Rāmānuja texts on *līlā* are his commentaries on *Brahmasūtra*

1.4.27, 2.1.15, 2.1.33, 3.2.12, and 4.4.13-14. These are discussed by Baumer, *Scchöpfung als Spiel,* as are all the Upaniṣadic passages and much more. See also Lacombe, *L'Absolu selon le Vedānta* and Thibaut's translations of the *Brahmasūtra* with Śaṅkara's and Rāmānuja's commentaries.

9. *ChU* 7.25.2:

athāta ātmādeśa evātmaivādhastād ātmopariṣṭād ātmā paścād ātmā purastād ātmā dakṣiṇata ātmottarata ātmaivedaṃ sarvam iti sa vā eṣa evaṃ paśyann evaṃ manvāna evaṃ vijānann ātmaratir atmakrīḍa ātmamithuna ātmānandaḥ sa svarāḍ bhavati tasya sarveṣu lokeṣu kāmacāro bhavati/atha ye'nyathāto vidur anyarājānas te kṣayyalokā bhavanti teṣāṃ sarveṣu lokeṣvakāmacāro bhavati/

There is an echo of this passage in *MuU* 3.1.4. See Baumer, pp. 13-23, for all Upaniṣadic passages.

10. *ChU* 8.12.1-3 (trans. Hume, *Thirteen Principal Upanishads,* p. 272:

maghavan martyaṃ vā idam śarīram āttaṃ mṛtyunā tad asyāmṛtasyāśarīrasyātmano'dhiṣṭhānam ātto vai saśarīraḥ priyāpriyābhyāṃ na vai saśarīrasya sataḥ priyāpriyayor apahatir astyaśarīraṃ vāva santaṃ na priyāpriye spṛśataḥ/ aśarīro vāyur abhraṃ vidyut stanayitnur aśarīrāṇyetāni tad yathaitānyamuṣmād ākāśat samutthāya paraṃ jyotir upasaṃpadya svena rūpeṇābhiniṣpadyante/ evam evaiṣa samprasādo'smāc charīrāt samutthāya paraṃ jyotir upasaṃpadya svena rūpeṇābhiniṣpadyate sa uttamapuruṣaḥ sa tatra paryeti jakṣat krīḍan ramamāṇaḥ strībhir vā yānair vā jñātibhir vā nopajanaṃ smarann idam śarīraṃ sa yathā prayogya ācaraṇe yukta evam evaiyam asmin charīre prāṇo yuktaḥ/

Of the numerous passages one could compare, the most important are *ChU* 8.1.4-6; *BĀU* 2.1.17-20; 4.3.7-38; 4.4.22; 4.5.15. The *mokṣa* doctrine of *BĀU* 4.3-5 supports a Śaṅkaran *advaita* interpretation relegating the *līlāvāda of ChU* to the level of figurative meaning. See also Śaṅkara's treatment of *Brahmasūtra* 4.4.8 ff. as teaching only 'lower knowledge' (*aparā vidyā*).

11. In Vibration Doctrine (*spandavāda*), adopted by AG in his Trika synthesis of the monistic stranis of Tantra, self-knowledge is an orgasmic ecstasy. The *ābhāsa-* or appearance-world is mediated by the feminine *śakti,* and Śiva's relation to it calls to mind the iconographic representation of the Androgyne Śiva (*ardhanārīśvara*), in which orgasmic experience is fully internal and constant. This experience is ritually reduplicated in the *kulayāga,* in which the initiate achieves gnosis through sexual intercourse amid the—in part antinomian—delights of wine, meat, incense, flowers, etc. See *Vijñānabhairava* 69-75; AG, *Tantrāloka* 29.115-16 (and throughout Ch. 29); AG, *Parātriṃśikā-* or *Parātrīśikāvaraṇa* in Gnoli, *Il Commento,* pp. 201-03. Also, L. Silburn, *Kuṇḍalinī,* pp. 177-205; Maheśvarānanda's *Mahārthamañjarī,* pp. 54 ff.; Pandey, *Abhinavagupta,* Ch. 7 (pp. 542-732). On the general subject of *spandavāda* see Dyczkowski, *The Doctrine of Vibration,* which among other things is an invaluable bibliographical guide. The most concentrated treatment of Trika's orgasmicism can be found in Sanderson, 'Trika Śaivism'; see also Sanderson, 'Purity and Power among the Brahmans of Kashmir,' esp. pp. 203-206.

12. *Śivasūtravimarśinī* 3.9-11 (*sūtras* marked off by double lines beginning paragraphs):

nartaka ātmā// nṛtyati, antarnigūhitasvasvarūpāvaṣṭambhamūlam tattajjāgarādinānābhūmikāprapañcaṃ svaparispandalīlayaiva svabhittau prakaṭayatīti nartaka ātmā/ . . . bhaṭṭanārāyaṇenāpi [*tad uktam*]—

visṛṣṭāśeṣasadbījagarbhaṃ trailokyanāṭakam/
prastāvya hara saṃhartuṃ tvattaḥ ko'nyaḥ kaviḥ kṣamaḥ//
raṅgo'ntarātmā// rajyate'smin jagannāṭyakrīḍāpradarśanāśrayenātmanā iti raṅgaḥ . . . . tatra hi [i.e., *dehāpekṣayā antare jīve*] *ayaṃ kṛtapadaḥ svakaraṇaparispandakrameṇa jagannāṭyam ābhāsayati/ . . . prekṣakāṇīndriyāṇi// yoginaś cakṣurādīni indriyāṇi hi saṃsāranāṭyaprakaṭanapramo-danirbharaṃ svasvarūpam antarmukhatayā sākṣāt kurvanti, tatprayogaprarūḍhyā vigalitavibhāgāṃ camatkārarasasaṃpūrṇatām āpādayanti/*

13. In *spandavāda* knowledge is essentially feeling. Cf. AG's comment on *NŚ* 6.33: *asmanmate saṃvedanam evānandaghanam āsvādyate/ tatra kā duḥkhāśaṅkā/ kevalaṃ tasyaiva citratākaraṇe ratiśokādivāsanāvyāpāraḥ/ tadudbodhane cābhinayādivyāpāraḥ/* 'In our teaching, consciousness itself, all full of bliss, is what is savored. And in this what suspicion of unhappiness could there be? The functions of the *vāsanās* of love, sorrow, etc., are solely to effect a marvelous variation of this consciousness. The function of the *abhinayas*, etc., is to awaken it.' Trans. after Gnoli, *Aesthetic Experience*, p. xxxvi. Thus we can under stand AG's compression of Bhaṭṭa Nāyaka's *bhāvaka* and *bhojaka* functions of language: perception and enjoyment merge when self consciousness is the highest form of relish (*camatkāra*): Gnoli, *Aesthethic Experience*, pp. 10-11.
14. I am speaking here of consciousness of self in the objective genitive sense. Śaṅkara's Ātman can not even be aware of itself: it is pure, objectless awareness.
15. The difference is one of degree. Aesthetic experience is *tātkālika*, i.e., temporally limited to the duration of aesthetic stimuli (*AEAG*, p. 20). Nor does it completely eliminate the *saṃskāras* (traces of desire and action) that bind us to the karmic world. The *locus classicus* is *IPVV*, vol. 2 (KSTS 62), pp. 178-79, which is extracted in full by Pandey, *Indian Aesthetics*, pp. 631-32, and in part by Masson and Patwardhan, *Śāntarasa*, p. 44. For translations see the latter, pp. 44-45, and *AEAG*, pp. xlii-xlv. I cite the final sentences in Gnoli's trans.:

    The so-called supreme bliss [*paramānanda*, i.e., mystical experience], the lysis [*nirvṛti*], the wonder [*camatkāra*], is therefore nothing but a tasting, that is, a cogitation, in all its compact density, of our own liberty. This liberty is *realissima* (that is to say, not metaphorical [*anupacaritasya*]) and inseparable from the very nature of consciousness. We must not, however, forget, that in the tasting of a juice of sweet flavor, etc., there is between this bliss and us the separating screen [*vyavadhāna*], so to say, of the exterior reality. In poetry, in drama, and so on, this screen is actually missing [since the aesthetic world is virtual or irreal], but it remains in a latent state. Also in these forms of limited bliss, however, those people whose hearts are carefully devoted to cancel out the part which performs the function of a screen, succeed in reaching the supreme bliss. 'Supreme bliss,' it has been said, 'may even take place disclosed by drinking and eating.'

    'Those whose hearts,' etc., are the so-called *yogins* of the Tantra tradition, who cultivate the savoring of mystical bliss in complete *tanmayībhāva* (identification) with the world-appearance, i.e., complete identification with Śiva-consciousness itself, since the world is, as certain Buddhists say, 'mind only' (*vijñaptimātra*): see *AEAG*, p. xxiv. Cf. the Bhaṭṭa Nāyaka verse by which the *sahṛdaya* achieves bliss watching the cosmic drama created by Śiva, cited in Masson and Patwardhan,

ŚR, p. 23:

namas trailokyaniramāṇkavaye śambhave yataḥ/
pratikṣaṇaṃ jagannāṭyaprayogarasiko janaḥ//
Bow to Śambhu, poet of the triple-world,
from whom at every instant we savor
the performance of the universal play.
—*Abhinavabhāratī 1.1*

Gerald J. Larson, 'The Aesthetic (*rasāsvāda*) and the Religious (*brahmāsvāda*) in Abhinavagupta's Kashmir Śaivism,' makes useful distinctions, but fails to grasp (p. 382) the identity of *vikalpa* (varied) and *nirvikalpa* (unvaried or absolute) experience for enlightened consciousness in Trika Śaivism as opposed to Vedānta. (I thank my former colleague Donna M. Wulff for this reference—see her own 'Religion in a New Mode: The Convergence of the Aesthetic and the Religious in Medieval India').

16. Utpaladeva, *Śivastotrāvalī* 20.12:

duḥkhāny api sukhāyante viṣam apy amṛtāyate/
mokṣāyate ca saṃsāro yatra mārgaḥ sa śāṅkaraḥ//
Pains become pleasures, poison turns to nectar,
the world becomes deliverance: this is Śiva's path.

This conversion of pain into pleasure is one of the central elements of *rasa* theory, which must take into account how the aesthetic subject can experience delight in the representation of sorrow. Cf. BhN *apud* AG in *AEAG*, p. 10; *DhĀ* 1.5 (with *Locana*); Viśvanātha, *SD* 3.6-7.

17. Cf., e.g., AG's *Viśrānti* in *AEAG*, p. 15, with the reference to *spanda* of the preceding page. The notion that *rasāsvāda* is a repose of consciousness free of obstacles i.e., generalized (*sādhāraṇīkṛta*), is found earlier in Bhaṭṭa Nāyaka (*AEAG*, p. 10; for a discussion of the philosophical idea, see pp. xxxvi-xxxvii.)
18. See the interesting observation of Lacombe, *L'Absolu*, p. 253: 'Il y a comme une ascèse souriante et suave, une incantation salvatrice en ce thème du jeu magique du Seigneur.' He is speaking about Śaṅkara's doctrine here, but it applies to all monistic *līlāvāda*.
19. The case is not much better in Rāmānuja's system: the world as such is a charming playground, but no more. The only true affective relationship is between Īśvara and the *Jīvas* who are never fully absorbed in Him. One can love God but not man or woman.
20. *Saundarananda*, final two verses.
21. *DR* 4.41cd-42ab:

krīḍatāṃ mṛnmayair yadvad bālānāṃ dviradādibhiḥ/
svotsāhaḥ svadate tadvac chrotṛṇām arjunādibhiḥ//

22. BhN flourished c. 900 AD in Kashmir. To be more accurate it is Dhanika, Dhanañjaya's contemporary commentator (and brother, it seems) who uses BhN's *bhāvakatva* termninology. Dhanañjaya and Dhanika (living in Mālwā) were contemporaries of Abhinavagupta but seem not to have been aware of his work.
23. This doctrine is more typically associated with AG, who developed it in great detail after receiving it from BhN, doubtless through his own teacher Bhaṭṭa Tauta. BhN's only known work—*Hṛdaya-* or *Sahṛdayadarpaṇa*—has not survived. See *AEAG*, pp. 10-11 for a summary of BhN's position. For AG's own classical formulations, see *idem*, pp. 13-15, 20-23.
24. *KP* 1.1:

niyatikṛtaniyamarahitāṃ hlādikamayīm ananyaparatantrām/
navarasaruciraṃ nirmitim ādadhatī bhāratī kaver jayati//

AG too uses this trope in *ABh* 1.1: 'The poet is like Prajāpati from whose desire (*kāma*) the world is produced. He possesses the power (*śakti*) of creating the marvelous and unprecedented, a power which arises through the favor of the goddess Parā Vāc (Supreme Speech), termed *pratibhā,* and remains always in the expanse of his own heart' (*kaver api svahṛdayāyatana-satatoditapratibhābhidhānaparavāgdevatānugrahotthitavicitrāpūrvārthanirmāṇaśaktiśālinaḥ prajāpater iva kāmajanitajagataḥ).*

25. Here and in the *vṛtti* on 1.2 (cited later) my translation sometimes echoes that of Ganganatha Jha.
niyatiśaktyā niyatarūpā sukhaduḥkhamohasvabhāvā paramāṇvādyupādānakarmā-disahakārikāraṇaparatantrā ṣaḍrasā na ca hṛdyaiva taiḥ, tādṛṣī brahmaṇo nirmitir nirmāṇam/ etadvilakṣaṇā tu kavivāṅnirmitiḥ/ ata eva jayati/

26. DhĀ 3.42+
apāre kāvyasaṃsāre kavir ekaḥ prajāpatiḥ/
yathāsmai rocate viśvaṃ tathedaṃ parivartate//
śṛṅgārī cet kaviḥ kāvye jātaṃ rasamayaṃ jagat/
sa eva vītarāgaś cet nīrasaṃ sarvam eva tat//

It is difficult to know to what extent ĀV was relying on Tantric conceptions of *pratibhā.* Vasuguptá, author (ostensibly the discoverer) of the *Śivasūtra,* is earlier by some decades (early to mid 9th C AD), so there is no chronological difficulty in assuming his familiarity with Śaiva 'poetic' cosmogony. *Pratibhā* itself (or its synonym *śakti*) as cause of poetic creation goes back to Bhāmaha and Daṇḍin (both 8th C) and probably earlier; and in Daṇḍin, at least with regard to related Speech (Vāc), we have a cosmogonic dimension. The seminal source is Bhartṛhari's sublimation of *vāc* and *pratibha* (the relation between them is problematic, see Christie, 'Indian Philosophers on Poetic Imagination,' pp. 164 ff.) as cosmogonic principles, an idea already developed in the late *Ṛgveda* for Vāc. For passages on *pratibhā see ŚR,* pp. 17-20; Christie, *passim;* and K. Krishnamoorthy, 'The Sanskrit Conception of a Poet,' pp. 167-86. Cf. Gopinath Kaviraj, 'The Doctrine of *Pratibhā,*' and Gaurinath Sastri, *The Philosophy of Word and Meaning.*

27. As the poet is himself a *rasika,* so the *rasika's* imaginative capacity makes him a virtual poet. Cf. Rājaśekhara's elevation of the *rasika's* role to that of creative *pratibhā* (*bhāvayitrī* as distinct from the poet's *kārayitrī*) in *Kāvyamīmāṃsā* 4. Also AG's citation of his teacher Bhaṭṭa Tauta in *DhĀL* 1.6+: 'The hero (of a poem or drama), the poet, and the listener all have the same experience' (*nāyakasya kaveḥ śrotuḥ sāmāno' nubhavas tataḥ).*

28. E.g., Ś 2.10(9):
Did He paint her in a picture and then bring her to life
or create her by great power of mind from an amalgam of beautiful shapes?
When I consider the power of the Creator and her lovely form
she seems the new creation of the jewel known as Woman.
citre niveśya parikalpitasattvayogā
rupoccayena mahatā manasā kṛtā nu/
strīratnasṛṣṭir aparā pratibhāti sā me
dhātur vibhutvam anucintya vapuś ca tasyāḥ/

For the reading see my note on the stanza in the next chapter.

29. *KP* 1.2:

kāvyaṃ yaśase'rthakṛte vyavahāravide śivetarakṣataye/
sadyaḥ parinirvṛtaye kāntāsammitatayopadeśayuje//

. . . sakalaprayojanamaulibhūtaṃ samanantaram eva rasāsvādanasamudbhūtaṃ vigalitavedyāntaram ānandaṃ prabhusaṃmitaśabdapradhānavedādiśāstrebhyaḥ suhṛtsaṃmitārthatātparyavatpurāṇāditihāsebhyaś ca śabdārthayor guṇabhāvena rasāṅgabhūtavyāpārapravaṇatayā vilakṣaṇaṃ yat kāvyaṃ lokottaravarṇanānipuṇakavikarma tat kānteva sarasatāpādanenābhimukhīkṛtya rāmādivad vartitavyaṃ na rāvaṇādivad ity upadeśaṃ ca yathāyogaṃ kaveḥ sahṛdayasya karoti . . . . / Mammaṭa appears to be following AG (*DhĀL* 1.1 towards end), where the same analogies are made:

But pleasure (*prīti*) or bliss (*ānanda*) is the chief thing. For this is what makes poetry, which provides instruction (*vyutpatti*) as if coming from a woman, different from the Vedas, etc., which provide it as if coming from a master, and from a friend. For bliss is far and away the principal reward of poetry, more so even than instruction in the four ends of life.

tathāpi tatra prītir eva pradhānam/ anyathā prabhusaṃmitebhyo vedādibhyo mitrasaṃmitebhyaś cetihāsādibhyo vyutpattihetubhyaḥ ko'sya kāvyarūpasya vyutpattihetor jāyāsaṃmitatvalakṣaṇo viśeṣa iti prādhānyenānanda evoktaḥ/ caturvargeṣvutpatter api cānanda eva pāryantikaṃ mukhyaṃ phalam/

See also *DhĀL* 2.4, where he cites BhN to the same effect. The same image is present also in Ānandavardhana, who compares *dhvani* (suggestion), the soul of poetry (*kāvyātmā, DhĀ* 1.1-5, to the 'charm of beautiful women' (1.4 and commentary) and later (4.7+) quotes from one of his own poetic works to the same effect?

No limit is set for them, nor are they ever repeated:
the charms of beautiful women and the meanings of poetical expressions.
na ca teṣāṃ ghaṭate'vadhir na ca te dṛśyante katham api punaruktāḥ/
ye vibramāḥ priyāṇām arthā vā sukavivāṇīnām//
Sanskritized from the Prakrit.

30. Cf. what Derrida has called the 'materiality of the signifier.' The point is that images and analogies invoked in didactic explanation leave a residue and either become part of the meaning or disclose the fact that they always were part of the meaning. Note how the graphic language of modern science ('big bang,' 'black hole,' 'genetic code,' etc.) tells us more about the limits and mythic assumptions of our intellectual understanding of objective truth than tomes of analytical discourse ever could. Our language reveals us willy-nilly.

31. It seems to have been BhN who codified the three facets of aesthetic response as 'melting, expansion and opening-up' (*drutivistāravikāsātmanā . . . bhogena: AEAG*, p. 10), but thereafter it is general. For *aṅkurībhāvā* (sprouting) see next quote and the passage of *DhAL* cited by Masson and Patwardhan, *Aesthetic Rapture,* vol. 2, pp. 37-38.

32. *Rasa* is often a word for love itself *qua* delicious feeling. It is no accident that the handbooks' treatment of *śṛṅgāra* (the 'erotic') is always the longest and most detailed: how could it be otherwise given the overwhelming importance—and ubiquitous presence—of the erotic theme in *kāvya?* It is doubtful that the *rasa* aesthetic could have evolved in any other circumstances, since it is only when a fictional subject—a necessary feature of *rasa* theory—is in love that we get the slow nuanced build-up of emotion with full attention to landscape, etc. (the *vibhāvādi*), that the theory demands for all *rasāvāda.*

33. The 'etc.' here refers to the full complex of aesthetic presentation demanded

by *rasa* theory. The woman herself is an *ālambana vibhāva* or 'basic cause' of an emotional response in a fictional character. Various elements of landscape, etc., such as sweet breezes, flowering vegetation, her jewelry, are 'excitatory causes' (*uddīpana vibhāva*). Certain effects (called *anubhāva*) such as horripilation or sighing show themselves in the hero gazing at her. And finally subsidiary emotional states (*saṃcāri-* or *vyabhicāribhāva*), such as joy or contentment, accompany the hero's basic emotional response, viz. love (*rati*). For the reader-spectator the whole complex taken together transmutes *rati* into *śṛṅgāra rasa* (the erotic sentiment). In practice, however, it is not so easy to distinguish fictional and actual subjects. The erotic hero of drama, such as King Duḥṣanta of *Śakuntalā*, is in fact a savorer of his own emotional state. Abhinava usually avoids the question of the status of characters within a play or poem, regarding them as mere vehicles of emotional response for the *rasika* spectator, though in at least one place (*AEAG* 89-90, 96-8) he speaks of 'identification' (*tanmayībhāva, āveśa*) in the sense in which we use the term today. Ordinarily, as in the passage being cited here, *tanmayībhāva* for him refers to the *rasika's* absorption in the fictional object (here the woman being apprehended by the hero) not the fictional subject (the hero himself).

34. *AEAG*, p. 21:

 tenālaukikacamatkārātmā rasāsvādaḥ smṛtyanumānalaukikasvasaṃvedanavilakṣaṇa eva/ tathā hi laukikenānumānena saṃskṛtaḥ pramadādi na tāṭasthyena pratipadyate, api tu hṛdayasaṃvādātmakasahṛdayatvabalāt pūrṇībhaviṣyadrasāsvādāṅkurībhāve-nānumānasmṛtyādisopānam anāruhyaiva tanmayībhāvocitacarvaṇāprāṇatayā/

 For the germinating sensation (*vikāsa, aṅkurībhāva*) as typical of *śṛṅgāra* see DR 4.43-44 (Adyar ed.) with Dhanika's commentary.

35. This passage contrasts with another famous example of aesthetic experience. In that passage (*AEAG*, p. 13) the aesthetic object (the deer pursued by Duḥṣanta in *Ś* 1.7) and the emotion (fear) that becomes universalized as the fearful sentiment (*bhayānaka rasa*) are in the same locus, while we share the point of view of the speaker, whose emotional response is one of detached wonder rather than sympathetic fear. (One could argue on this basis that the true *rasa* here is *adbhuta* rather than *bhayānaka*. This is one of many problematic areas of AG's thought that await careful exploration.) In the present case, our response is felt through a fictive subject who is himself a *rasika*, i.e., whose emotion is aroused by what is for him simultaneously an aesthetic and erotic object. Thus *tanmayībhāva* has to be understood in very different sense in the two cases. The deer cannot stand as a symbol of poetry the way the beautiful woman can, unless we are willing to argue that *adbhuta* is at the root of all *rasa*-experience. Some, indeed, have made such an argument, most notably Viśvanātha: see Raghavan, *Number of Rasas*, pp. 205-6. But this quasi-Aristotelian thesis misses the seductiveness of Sanskrit poetry. See the next chapter for a discussion of the deer's 'white-rabbit' function in leading the *rasika* into the full aesthetic-erotic playworld.

36. No truly critical analysis of Abhinavagupta's aesthetic theory has yet been made. Gnoli, Masson and Patwardhan, and Pandey (so far our best guides) are exegetes who avoid troubling theoretical inconsistencies in order to present an overall picture.

37. *DhĀL* 1.1 (towards end): 'The *sahṛdaya* is one who participates in a 'concordance of heart,' i.e., one who has a capacity identification with what is

described (in poem or play), an identification which takes place in a mirror-like mind made clear by familiarity with and practice of poetry' (*yeṣām kāvyānuśīlanābhyāsavaśād viśadībhūte manomukure varṇanīyatanmayībhavanayogyatā te svahṛdayasaṃvādabhājaḥ sahṛdayāḥ*). We should note that, although *tanmayībhāva* seems to have come into prominence as a theoretical concept only with AG (or BhN judging from the title of his lost work: *The Mirror of the Heart* [*Hṛdayadarpaṇa*]), it was already being used by Kālidāsa as a technical term in the 4th-5th C AD: see *Mālavikāgnimitra* 2.8 (*tanmayatvaṃ raseṣu*). For *tanmayībhāva* in the metaphysical context see *TĀ* 4.207-09, 3.240 (mistranslated by Masson and Patwardhan, *ŚR*, p. 49), and 28.373 ff., comparing the use of 'mirror' and 'heart' with the definition just quoted. In *PTV*, in a passage describing the yogi's susceptibility to mystical *camatkāra*, AG gives us another definition of *sahṛdaya:*

> Those who are not nourished by this force (*vīrya*), who do not experience the intoxicating bliss that consists of the arousal of such force, are like stones, and for them neither the sight of a beautiful woman nor the sound of the song that comes from her mouth results in complete bliss. *Camatkāra* is limited according to the degree of (presence or) absence of that which nourishes it i.e., *vīrya*). The complete absence of *camatkāra* indicates an insensate state, whereas a high degree of immersion/absorption (*āveśa*) in *camatkāra*—which is nothing but the arousal of *vīrya*—is termed the state of sensibility (*'sahṛdayatā'* being a *sahṛdaya*'). The person whose heart is noursihed by the infinite nourishing force (*vīrya*) and given over to (*niveśita*) constant practice in such enjoyments, such a person possesses *camatkriyā* in the highest degree. (KSTS ed., pp. 46-48 [= Gnoli, *PTV*, p. 202])

It is impossible to maintain there is no *intrinsic* connection in AG's thought between the three domains of aesthetic, erotic, and mystical experience. (N.B. *vīrya* is the ordinary term for male potency.)

38. Barbara Stoler Miller, 'Kālidāsa's World and His Plays, pp. 27-31, is certainly right to identify the heroine of drama in some sense with Vāc-Sarasvatī, the goddess of poetry, as well as with Śrī. ĀV's final verse in *DhĀ* identifies the sweet instructress as Sarasvatī, though he says nothing about the kāvyic heroine as such. Maria Christopher Byrski, *Concept of an Ancient Indian Theater*, pp. 76-90, also sees the heroine of drama as Vāc, for entirely different reasons. F.B.J. Kuiper, *Varuṇa and Vidūṣaka: On the Origins of Sanskrit Drama*, pp. 236-41, sees her as both Vāc-Sarasvati and Śrī from a cosmological-ritual point of view.

39. *PY* 3.5+: 'He has now imagined his cell as a pleasure-garden and is all ready for the royal sport of love' (*bandhanam idānīṃ pramadavanaṃ sambhāvya pravṛtto rāga-[or rāja-] līlāṃ kartum*).

40. Cf. the organic imagery of *DhĀ* 4.4: 'Inclusion of *rasa* makes the trite subjects of poetry seem new as trees in Spring.'

    dṛṣṭapūrvā api hyarthāḥ kāvye rasaparigrahāt/
    sarve navā ivābhānti madhumāsa iva drumāḥ//

41. I. Scheftelowitz, *Die Apokryphen des Ṛgveda*, p. 3, dates most of the *khilas* (including the *śrīsūkta* or Hymn to Śrī, 72 ff.) to the Yajurvedic period c. 800 BC. In general see Gerda Hartmann, *Beiträge zür Geschichte der Göttin Lakṣmī* and David Kinsley, *Hindu Goddesses*. Alf Hiltebeitel, *The Ritual of Battle*, has much to say about Śrī from a Dumézilian structuralist position. For some early Buddhist references see T.W. Rhys Davids, *Buddhist India*, pp. 216-19. See

John M. Rosenfield, *The Dynastic Arts of the Kushans* for iconographic information; likewise A.S. Altekar, *Catalogue of the Gupta Gold Coins in the Bayana Hoard.*

42. Vivid examples of this personification in *Mudrārākṣasa* 2 and 6. See also inscription such as the Junāgaḍh Rock Inscription of Skandagupta, pp. 299 ff. of Bhandarkar, Chhabra, and Gai (s. v. 'Inscriptions' in the Bibliography).
43. E.g., J. Gonda, *Ancient Indian Kingship from the Religious Point of View,* pp. 6-11. His treatment of Śrī (pp. 27, 46, 52, etc.) and the symbolism of wealth (pp. 13-5) is not very imaginative, however.
44. The *mithuna* is not only religiously auspicious symbol of this type. The bright and sinuous sensuality of Buddhist sculpture at such sites as Sānchī and Amarāvatī reveal that the *līlā*-world of the court in all its aspects itself functioned this way. The paradox of intoxicating sensuous depiction of the charms of embodied life in the context of a religious message which denies its validity is a commonplace of Indian art history.
45. See Kālidāsa, *Malavikāgnimitra* 3.15, for example. Thus too the ideal of *gāndharva* marriage in *kāvya,* since only this presupposes mutual love.

CHAPTER 2

Aesthetic and Erotic Entrancement in the Śakuntalā

Kālidāsa, who probably lived in the 5th century AD and enjoyed Gupta partronage, is almost unanimously accepted as India's greatest poet.[1] His reputation in Sanskrit is comparable only to Shakespeare's in English,[2] and his play *Abhijñānaśākuntala* (*Śankuntala and the Token*), more commonly referred to as *Śakuntalā*, has a paradigmatic status for the whole of *kāvya*.[3] Thus the lyric recited by a Bengali *paṇḍita* to Sir William Jones, the pioneering Sanskritist and first translator of the play into any modern language:

> Drama is the best of poetry, and *Śakuntalā* the best of drama.
> In this the Fourth Act is best, in this four stanzas,
> and of these the best begins, 'She will leave today'.[4]

Edwin Gerow's comment on this is perceptive:

> Such traditional verses exaggerate a point that nevertheless deserves our attention: in discussing the Śakuntalā as drama, we are also at the center of the Indian poetic problem. By the judgment of the tradition itself, the Śakuntalā is the validating aesthetic creation of a civilization.[5]

I would argue that the reason the play holds this central place is because it gives us the most profound mythic rendition of the *rasika's* encounter with the Śrī of his imagination. Śakuntalā, a forest foundling, is the daughter of celestial nymph (*apsaras*) by a sage (Viśvāmitra) who straddled the two highest positions in the socio-religious hierarchy, Brahmin and King, with all that this entails vis-à-vis questions of knowledge, power, and authority. The action encompasses town and forest, pristine hermitage and palace compound. The heroine is virginal and protected by *tapas*, yet represented as the child of an Edenic (*kṛtayuga*) garden world laden with fructifying sexual promise, and in both capacities she reminds us of the primordial female creation of the world-father.[6]

A stanza in Act 2 that alludes to this dimension also makes us aware of her stature as the supreme aesthetic object:

> Did He paint her in a picture and then bring her to life
> Or create her by great power of mind from an amalgam of beautiful shapes?
> When I consider the power of the Creator and her lovely form,
> She seems the new creation of the jewel known as woman.[7]

No other heroine in Sanskrit drama is so profoundly enhanced as the object of aesthetic gaze, no other reveals herself in quite so marked an epiphany as the Woman in the Garden.

We will consider the implications of the love-encounter between the *rasika* King and the forest maiden, and its problematic aftermath, in three sections, followed by a conclusion. The first will study the *rasika* hero's aesthetic-erotic entrancement and trace its permutations throughout the play; the second will evaluate it in terms of the playworld paradigm we set up in the last chapter; and the third will address the important issue of the obstacle (*vighna, ghāta*) posed by the Ascetical Father. Besides the concept of *līlā* we will utilize the notion of *siddhi* as described in *NŚ* 27. We have already described 'human' and 'divine' success in the Introduction and remarked that the latter is reached when the *rasika* spectator achieves 'aesthetic rapture' (*rasāsvāda*). What we shall see in this chapter is that the *rasika* protagonist enacts this achievement in a dialectical movement: an initial state of breathtaking infatuation, followed by loss and confusion, and then a recovery which, however, must include an acknowledgment of an extrinsic power that makes the whole notion of aesthetic rapture in the Indian context problematic.

1. Aesthetic Rapture

The Prologue of the *Śakuntalā* (*Ś*) sets up a paradigm of aesthetic rapture that leads directly into the play itself. The Stage-Manager, having praised the intelligence and taste of the audience, has summoned the leading Actress to the stage to sing for the audience's delight a song evoking the summer season in which the first three Acts of the play are set. He himself begins with a lovely *svabhāvokti* description of long and drowsy summer days:

Days lovely in their ripeness,
of happy plungs into rivers and lakes,
of forest breezes fragrant with trumpet-flower
and leisurely naps in the shade of trees.[8]

The Actress answers with a charming portrait of young women whose ornamental ear-blossoms have their filaments kissed by buzzing bees:

Behold the beautiful women
as they ring their ears
with fine-tufted *śirīṣa*-flowers
instantly kissed by bees.[9]

The effect this has on the audience and the Stage-Manager himself is to put them in the kind of trance described in the *daivikī siddhi* verses of *NŚ* 27:

> Divine success may always be determined by the audience as abounding in purity and feeling.
> There is no noise, jostling, or ominous disturbance, and the auditorium is full.[10]

For observe the effect on both audience and Stage-Manager:

> Stage-Manager: Lady, that was beautifully sung. Behold, the whole audience, their minds ravished by emotion (or 'charm': *rāgāpahṛta*), look like a painted picture. But what play should we honor them with?
> Actress: But my lord, haven't you already announced the play called *Śakuntalā and the Token*?
> Stage-Manager: Thank you, lady, for awakening me. For a moment I forgot. You see—
> I was forcibly carried off
> by the ravishing charm of your song
> like King Duḥṣanta here before us
> carried off by the fleet spotted deer.[11]

There is much play in this short passage with notions of aesthetic rapture, illusion and reality, awareness and forgetting, and we cannot fail to notice its thematic import for a drama that has so much to do with these notions. The Prologue, which enacts captivation by aesthetic illusion and points the way to the dramatic illusion proper, is itself part of the dramatic illusion, part of the *rasa*-inducing process. The Stage-Manager's lapse of consciousness amounts to a forgetting of the task at hand, and so is very much like the critical mistake of Śakuntalā, whose beguilement by the memories and dreams of love is the cause of her failure to attend to the sage Durvāsas when he comes to the *āśrama* at the beginning of Act 4. It also reminds us of the King under the effects of the curse, when he cannot remember having seen Śakuntalā before.[12] I would also argue that it describes the state of the King before the curse: his infatuation with Śakuntalā in the garden world which muffles the claims of outside works and days. But if the Stage-Manager's awakening has as its intended effect re-entry into aesthetic illusion, the full drama now replacing its anticipation in the Actress' summer song, then to awaken is again to enter into a charmed sleep. The effect is vertiginous and insistently underscores the chief tension of the play, namely the conflicting valuations of the state of entrancement by beauty. Is it essentially negative: loss of awareness of one's surroundings and the *dharma* that they entail? This is the perspective that leads us to interpret the curse as moral condemnation of hedonism, for it has the effect of shaking the lovers from their complacency, restoring them to reality, and—in particular—forcing Duḥṣanta to face the consequences of his frivolousness. Or is entrancement itself positive, a fullness rather than an emptiness of perception, an access to a higher or more intense level of experience? From this perspective the curse will seem rancorous and philistine, and the King's loss of memory will seem an inversion caused by the ascetic's begrudgement of the *rasika's* aesthetic-erotic transport (which involves loss of memory in regard to mundane reality).[13]

Note the suggestive uses of *rāga* and derivatives of √hṛ in the cited passage. 'The whole audience, their minds ravished by emotion /charm (*rāga*), look like a painted picture'. But *rāga* also means 'color' and 'passion'. In the former sense the phrase underlines the synesthetic trope: the Actress' song become the coloric medium of the audience's hushed transformation into a work of pictorial art. In the sense of 'passion' it signals the erotic character of the aesthetic experience in question: contemplation of the charming gestures of beautiful young women (*pramadāḥ*) on a summer's day. The use of *hṛ* also contributes to the erotic suggestion, as is especially indicated by the transitional verse 1.4: 'I was forcibly carried off', etc. *Hāriṇā* as 'ravishing' (describing 'charm of song' *gītarāgeṇa*) echoes the earlier *rāgāpahṛta* ('ravished by charm'), as does *hṛtaḥ* ('carried off'). Here too the prime meaning of 'carried off' is figurative: the Stage-Manager explains that he was 'ravished' or 'enraptured' (*hṛtaḥ*) by the 'ravishing beauty of your song' (*gītarāgeṇa hāriṇā*). But the analogy in the simile is to the King being 'carried off' or 'drawn' by the spotted antelope. Drawn into what? Into the play, certainly, as the audiences was drawn into the picture created by the Actress' song, but in terms of the fiction it is into the *āśrama,* the paradoxical garden of delights, a sensuous *locus amoenus* which is at the same time a center of asceticism. The immediate parallel to the Stage-Manager's and *rasika* audience's entrancement by beauty is Duḥṣanta's captivation by the epiphany of Śakuntalā, the perfect embodiment of the hermitage's paradisal allure.

Thus, the deer, which is the direct counterpart of *gītarāgeṇa* as the instrument of ravishment or drawing-in (and there are certainly overtones in *hāriṇā* of *hāriṇa* with the meaning 'relating to a deer'), is a White-Rabbit figure leading the King across the threshold to an enchanted world. In the *āśrama* he will become first a *rasika* spectator of precisely that scene projected in the Actress' song, and the bee buzzing around Śakuntalā's ear-ornament (more fancifully, her lips) will be the pretext of his stepping forth from his audience-like position behind the trees into the midst of the charming spectacle.

If I seem to belabor this point it is only because criticism is still very resistant to the idea of erotic and aesthetic interpenetration despite *kāvya's* untiring celebration, unrivaled in world literature, of the sexual beauty of women. To put my analysis above in a nutshell: Duḥṣanta's entry into the vegetal paradise over which Śakuntalā presides like a virtual goddess (*sādhidaivata iva śakuntalayānumālinītiram āśramo,* 1.11.6*), an embodiment of Śrī-Lakṣmī, is the mythic enactment of the audience's captivation by the Actress' song, which functions as a model of *kāvya* in general. The audience first enters into a charming, erotically tinged picture of summer, incorporated as it were into the world of poetic fantasy. It then, almost imperceptibly, finds itself sharing the point of view of Duḥṣanta, its idealized *rasika* projection, as he lurks in the shade of the trees watching and listening as the Śrī of the poetic universe makes her entry attended by two lovely companions. The women of the Actress' song-portrait now become characters in the drama of the *rasika-sahṛdaya's* aspirations, as does the *rasika-sahṛdaya* himself. With and through the King, therefore, the spectator in the audience contemplates and savors her beauty as she exhibits to him amid the lush, fragrant flora of a primordial paradise a sexual ripeness deliciously enhanced by innocence and the promise of the ecstatic fruition of desire, so often evoked in poetry, to him the long-awaited Lover and Prince Charming of this precious fairy-tale. To enter the charmed world of poetry—and thus to achieve the 'divine success'—is in this play to enter the charmed world of feminine beauty. But is this not always the case in *kāvya?* The woman in the garden, as we saw in the last chapter, is the privileged theme of Sanskrit poetry generally. The point argued at great length would only serve to prove the obvious. Thus in Ānandavardhana, Abhinavagupta, Mammaṭa, and so many others, the beautiful woman is the only adequate analogue of symbol of poetry. When the *rasika* hero enters the flowering garden with its synesthetic allure (murmuring cuckoos, fragrant breezes, beckoning boughs, etc.) and beholds Radiant Female who epitomizes its luxurious charm, he comes to the mythic core of the Indian poetic experience.

But though the play begins on this high, rapturous note and develops it through three Acts, it cannot sustain it. We noted briefly above that Śakuntalā's absent-mindedness and the King's curse-induced oblivion are in their way as analogous as the love-revery itself to the aesthetic entrancement of audience and stage-Manager presented in the Prologue. We have likewise raised the issue of ambivalence regarding the aesthetic-erotic captivation, how it may be seen negatively (as an absence) or positively (as a more intense presence) according to the ascetic and aesthetic perspectives respectively. Before focusing on this double significance, however, we need to sketch in the development of the entrancement-theme. First, there is the entrancement of Duḥṣanta, extended over the first 3 Acts. He is captivated by the vision of Śakuntalā, and while he does not actually forget the outside world and his dhārmic role in it, he is virtually indifferent to it, as many critics have noted. Most, following Tagore, have regarded his attitude as indicative of a shallow, exploitative hedonism, whereas our argument has been that it is as serious as the ideals of Indian aesthetics, wherein eros occupies the central place. Duḥṣanta acts normally for a *nāyaka* in his position; we can hardly imagine a *dhīraialita* ('steadfast-and-gallant) hero who would not be taken with Śakuntalā precisely as he is.[14] It behooves the romantic hero to be swept off his feet and to seek clandestine union.[15] This is not to deny the predatory aspect of the King's behavior, which is adequately symbolized by the aggressive manner in which he appears on stage (a hunter with drawn bow). But he is as much the 'ravished' (*hṛtaḥ*) as the ravisher.[16]

The audience entrancement in the Prologue is followed by the King's entrancement by Śakuntalā. First he is the tantalized spectator in the audience (behind the trees). When the bee begins to buzz around Śakuntalā's ear-flower (like the bees in the Actress' song), and the maiden-in-distress calls for help, the *rasika* protagonist hears his cue to enter into the scene and become a full participant in the action. Flirtation ensues, and the King learns of her marriageability to a *kṣatriya.* But the scene ends with a disturbance, an elephant loose from his hunting party, that temporarily ends the idyll. The disturbance-theme is constantly sounded even in the first three Acts. We have not mentioned it yet, because we will deal with it fully in the 3rd section, but the King's initial entry on stage in his chariot, aggressively pursuing a hermitage deer, is a kind of assault on the peace and innocence of the primordial paradise. He is confronted then, vicariously, with the ascetical power of the sage Kaṇva that requires him to put away his weapons; but by the end of the Act the note of aggressive sexuality is again sounded in the alarm over wild elephant.

The 2nd Act shows the King at a crossroads. He commands his army to keep its distance, but has no pretext for remaining in the *āśrama.* Meanwhile he idealizes Śakuntalā in the most exalted terms to his friend, the Vidūṣaka. She is like the new moon at whose beauty the world can only gaze from afar with wide unblinking eyes.[17] The creator must have painted her in a picture and brought her to life or assembled her from the most beautiful objects in the universe (see note 7).

> An unsmelt flower, a shoot the nails have not snipped,
> a jewel unworn, new wine as yet unsavored,
> the undiminished fruit of past merits: this faultless beauty—
> whose lot will it be to enjoy it in this world?[18]

Then, as in the fantasy that it is, the problem of how to approach her is solved when the hermits beseech him (in panegyrical terms) to protect their sacrifice from the onslaught of demons, while their monastic 'father' Kaṇva is absent (he is away on a pilgrimage praying for Śakuntalā's 'adverse fate' to be lifted). Thus he gains access in the posture of a hero, standing in the place of the distressed maiden's father. The disturbance no longer seems to come from himself, but from scapegoat demons. The army is sent back to the capital, and the King remains in the world of paradisal promise, safely insulated from the prosaic duties and distractions of the outside world.

In Act 3 he is again the rescuing hero, delivering the distressed maiden not from the minor annoyance of an impertinent bee but the paralysis of love-fever.[19] Her very friends, assured by stated intent to make her his queen, leave the lovers alone and the seduction begins.[20] It culminates in a moment of erotic contemplation of Śakuntalā's face, held up by his fingers that he might blow pollen from her eye:

> Her lower lip so soft and tender,
> so beautifully throbbing,
> seems to give me leave
> to satisfy my thirst.[21]

But before the kiss, he gently blows into her eye, and suddenly—another disturbance. Gautamī, the head female ascetic, her arrival announced off-stage by Śakuntalā's vigilant companions, has come to collect Śakuntalā for the evening prayers. The King, left alone, bemoans the missed opportunity, but soon he is summoned once again to his heroic duty as preserver of sacrifice.

When Act 4 opens, the King has already departed. The love-union has taken place, and Śakuntalā is in a state of distraced revery, reliving the happiness of love. Her lover has left her with his ring, inscribed with his name. Someone will arrive to escort her to his palace before she can count a day for each character in the inscription (there are 3). But a curse intervenes. The irascible ascetic Durvāsas arrives in the hermitage, and Śakuntalā, in charge of receiving guests with the usual offerings, fails to notice his presence. Therefore, he says, she must suffer in kind:

> That person of whom you were distractedly thinking
> when you failed to notice me, a treasure of austerities,
> will not remember you even in his waking,
> like a careless man who forgets what he has said.[22]

But though the punishment falls nominally on her, it is Duḥṣanta who suffers the obliviousness, which is entrancement emptied of *rasāsvāda,* the negative inversion of aesthetic-erotic rapture. It is not that Śakuntalā herself does not suffer, but as we shall see in the next two sections she is not so much the victim of *tapas* (indeed it protects her) as of an affective gap in aestheticized love.

In the midst of oblivion, however, the King, at the beginning of Act 5, falls spellbound to a song which, with its bee-motif, recalls the Actress' song of the Prologue and also the bee-scene of the First Act, when the King stepped from the bushes onto center stage with Śakuntalā. As the King chats with the Vidūṣaka, one of his queens sing off-stage in the *dhvani* style of a bee that once favored the mango-blossom and now makes the lotus his haunt.[23] The verse is a *tour de force* because, though sung by Haṃsavatī to reproach her husband for new loves such as Śakuntalā (about whom she, of course, knows nothing in particular—she has, ironically and suggestively, mistaken the King's curse-induced oblivion for the entrancement which effectively set it off), we feel it as the plaint of Śakuntalā herself and the foreshadowing of her rejection. Śakuntalā will herself become a Haṃsavatī, this is her inevitable destiny in a polygynous system. Indeed her father Kaṇva's realistic instructions in Act 4 do not expect that she will continue to captivate her husband's heart, only that she be treated with respect.[24] Her role as the Radiant Female whose sexual magic creates an erotic paradise around her is only a temporary one, lasting as long as she can embody the principle of erotic auspiciousness (Śrī).

But the verse does more than balance the poignancy of her loss and inevitable passage into the condition of wife and mother against the fullness of an earlier state. It introduces an aesthetic response—a sudden pensiveness whose object remains mysterious—which acknowledges that fullness as an ever-present though hidden reality in the oblivious hum-drum of the day-to-day. Moreover it sets up the paradigm of art or poetry as the vehicle of a *déjà vu* whose function is to vindicate the reality of a truer state of affairs than can be lived in ordinary life. In that truer realm lovers remain united and separation is the illusion. Thus the perspective of *saṃsāra* that makes the verse spoken by the King in response so hauntingly beautiful:

> One glimpses beauty unexpected or hears a chance song
> And all at once one becomes filled with a wistful longing.

> Can this be other than the dim recollection of past lives
> Whose loves still linger undisclosed at the core of feeling?[25]

Coming as it does in this Act, with its principal focus on mutual accusation set in the mundane atmosphere of the place (as opposed to Act, 6 which takes place in the pleasure-garden, here we are in the chambers of state with their atmosphere of routine duty), this verse has a calming, consolatory force. And it effectively reverses the terms established by the curse, in which aesthetic-erotic rapture was a dangerous forgetting. Now it is everyday reality, the world of practical engagement with *dharma,* that is a forgetting, while the aesthetic moment delivers a near-awakening.

It is at this point that we approach the profoundest aspect of the issue, a fact no doubt signified by Abhinavagupta's marking the verse as an example of how *rasāsvāda* or *carvaṇā* ('aesthetic relish') may also function as *smaraṇa* ('recollection').[26] Here, for instance, we can see the connection between an ideal eroticism cursed into oblivion and the ring that is at this moment in the play still in the belly of a fish, a golden brilliance apparently lost to the world forever, yet with the power to dispel the darkness that envelops it. We also glimpse, for the first time, a significance for aesthetic experience in the Indian context that we might not have expected, what we would have to call an ethical perspective by virtue of its capacity to effect a change of attitude. The *rasika* approaches a work of art with a certain complacency (*sukhito'pi jantuḥ*). He knows all the rules of the aesthetic game, all the figures of speech (*alaṃkāra*) and fine turns of diction (*guṇa, rīti*), the subtle logic of suggestion (*dhvani*), and the soothing and titillating predictabilities of *rasa.* But in the conventional artform is the hidden jewel, the spark of life[27] that awakens him to a strange transformation: complacency gives way to an indefinable longing (*paryutsuko bhavati*) that can only be articulated, in the Indian context, as a dim remembrance of ideal love in a former life. Art, then, seems to promise the fulfilment of the deepest longings for love in the recovery of a primal sweetness that has been left behind in the process of living.[28]

Perhaps a sociological reminder is not out of place here. Though princes and other wealthy partrons of the arts did have the opportunity of marrying and taking concubines according to their desire, for the majority of *rasikas,* involved in arranged marriages, this would have been an unusual situation. 'Play' with courtesans also had its limitations, as the *kathā* literature constantly reminds us. But art was able to disclose an ideal world in which a ravishing and naively sweet child-woman might appear to one virtually in the role of a suppliant, inviting him, the *rasika,* who is uniquely sensitive to the many facets of her appeal, to pose as her hero-lover. In drama, marriage takes place only on the basis of a meeting of hearts, which causes problems, but eventually earns the full approval of society and its Brahmanical authority. It is not to diminish the haunting beauty of this moment in the play that I call attention to *kāvya's* wishfulfilling role in affirming basic erotic fantasies, because there is nothing trivial about the erotic promise. The matter has more than an Indian scope. Art has the ability to connect adult desire with our earliest hopes and aspirations, the innocence of childhood and the poignancy of adolescence, and project a social vision that does not betray and hopefully educates the private dream: what Ernst Bloch has called art's 'utopian' function.[29] What we see here, then, is the *rasika* in his Everyman dimensions.[30] Beneath the turbulence (the angry outbursts of Act 5) and boredom of everyday life, the *rasika* believes in the persistence of an ideal level of experience to which one is now and then all-but-awakened.

The need to awaken fully to this promise and the paradoxically illusory quality of aesthetic intimations are the dominant concerns of Act 6. It is surprising, given the importance of the ideas of awakening and illusion in Indian culture, how little attention the epistemological conceits in this play have received.[31] Yet Acts 6 and 7, the play's finale, are saturated with them.[32] I will enumerate the instances here precisely because they have not received critical treatment. In 6.7 the King's heart, formerly 'asleep while waking' (*pratibodhyamānam api suptam*), now 'awakens to the misery of remorse' (*anuśayaduḥkhāya . . . vibuddham*). In 6.8 his 'mind is freed from the darkness that blocked [his] memory' (*smṛtirodhinā . . . muktam idaṃ tamasā manaḥ*). In 6.11(10) he asks himself whether Śakuntalā had been 'a dream or an illusion a trick of the mind or a reward for merit whose account has run out' (*svapno nu māyā nu matibhramo nu kliṣṭaṃ nu tāvatphalam eva puṇyam*).[33] In 6.17(16) he compares his rapture before the painting of Śakuntalā to a traveler's paradoxical feeling of thirst before a mirage (*mṛgatṛṣṇikāyām*), which was not felt when passing a flowing river.

In Act 7, when Śakuntalā finally stands before him, he has become one 'whose darkness of delusion has been dispelled by memory' (*smṛtibhinnamohatamaso*), 7.22. In 7.24 he begs her to understand the 'powerful confusion of his mind' (*manasaḥ sammoho . . . balavān*) and includes himself in the category of the 'benighted' (*prabalatamasām*), using the example of a blind man who shakes away a garland thinking it to be a snake (cf. the snake-rope paradigm of Indian epistemology). Again, in 7.25 he begs forgiveness for his 'delusion' (*mohāt*), while in 7.31 he compares himself to one who doubts (*saṃśayaḥ*) the existence of an elephant when it passes before his eyes, but becomes certain of it (*pratītiḥ*) after examining its tracks. Finally, in 7.32 Mārīca explains to Śakuntalā that she was rejected because her husband's mind was 'coarsened by obliviousness due to a curse' (*śāpād . . . smṛtirodharūkṣe*), but that now, with 'the darkness removed' (*apetatāmasī*), she is queen over his heart again (*bhartary . . . prabhutā tavaiva*). He too uses an example from idealist epistemology: The image does not take shape in the dusty mirror, but once the mirror is cleansed, the image stands out in all its brilliance.

The outcome of this series is a full awakening expressed in terms of a perfectly clear image of the beloved. The analogy of the mirror, however, not only signals the dispersal of the darkness that had enveloped the world intimated by Haṃsavatī's song, but intimates that the final disclosure retains an aesthetic aspect, i.e., we are still in the realm of images, of epiphanies. The mirror conveys representations, as poetry itself does. One wonders if Abhinavagupta did not frame his classical definition of the *sahṛdaya* under the unconscious influence of this verse (7.32) with its mirror trope. '*Sahṛdayas*: those who in a mirror-like mind made clear by constant familiarity with the practice in poetry share in a sympathy of heart by virtue of their capacity to become identical with what is represented'.[34]

But let us return to Act 6, where the King's confusion is not yet dissolved and his resort to aesthetics leads again to conflicting valuations of entrancement: ideal reality or emptiness? I am referring specifically to his attempt to lose himself in his own artistic recreation of the hermitage and its principal attraction Śakuntalā (the whole passage extends from 6.13 to 6.24+). Here again we find the bee-motif, the fourth time it has occurred in the play. Now it is the occasion of what is apparently a sad irony. In lovingly recreating the paradisal atmosphere he had once enjoyed, Duḥṣanta has focused on precisely that moment when circumstances conspired to draw him into the aura of Śakuntalā's charm, itself the mythic realization of the promise in the Actress' song. In Act 6, however, we seem to have a foreclosure of the promise. Reacting to the bee in the portrait just as he had reacted to it in Act 1—i.e., with jealousy and quaint bravado—he betrays his full captivation by the aesthetic illusion. He seems to think he is in the charmed world of the portrait, like the audience with regard to the Actress' song-portrait (*ālikhita iva raṅgaḥ*) in the Prologue. So that when the Vidūṣaka 'awakens' him to his actual surroundings, he finds himself marooned in the so-called real world without her. Truth or illusion: what is the *rasika's* hope? The irony is particularly effective because the scene takes place in the palace pleasure garden which seems itself an artificial attempt to recreate the natural lushness of the pre-societal garden-hermitage.[35] We are clearly invited to see the incident as an exposure of the ultimate emptiness of aesthetic intimations, and yet the further irony is that this is a false conclusion.

Acquiescence in the apparent reality of Śakuntalā's absence is itself delusion. It is exactly at this moment when Miśrakeśī (or Sānumatī), the *apsaras* who observes him in secret, declares that he has atoned for his earlier mistake.[36] In other worlds by giving in to the aesthetic illusion, by allowing himself to be captivated by its promise of paradise regained, he has revealed the depth of his sentiment, the sincerity of his love. The *apsaras* does not even need to understand the mechanics of his earlier rejection of Śakuntalā: the disclosure of the hero's essential *rasa* is enough to win her over.[37] Again we glimpse the fantasy-character of the play, for it shows us clearly the *rasika's* longing to believe in the saving power of sentiment. Sentiment nurtured deep in the heart is truer than outward action. This is what we have already learned from the *déjà vu* paradigm of Act 5. Thus, at the close of the passage showing the King both as a paragon of sympathetic generosity and as an object of pity, the same *apsaras* remarks that there is a light beyond the veil which he cannot yet see—again the suggestive epistemological-idealistic language that elevates the King's plight to metaphysical Everyman status.[38]

The painted picture has not disclosed a falsehood after all, and the King will be transported (*hṛtaḥ*) to an *āśrama* that is even more wondrous than the first, once he has demonstrated his heroic grandeur—an *āśrama* whose authority is not the conveniently absent Kaṇva, but Mārīca, a sagely father-figure raised to the ultimate power of wisdom and benevolence. In the final Act, then, society in the person of this dazzling sage (7.27) gives its full endorsement to the love that began with the epiphany of Śakuntalā in Act 1—or even earlier, with the Actress' song. In Act 6, then, the series of attempts to evoke and enter the charmed world of ideal erotic encounter comes to a head in the image of the *rasika* desperately trying to recapture its happiness in a work of art, and eventually, though obliquely, succeeding. If we cast our eye back over this whole series of evocations beginning with the Actress' song, we see that its object is to bring the aesthetic promise to life. The *rasika* is a would-be Prajāpati trying to give life to his portrait.[39] One may enter the poetic universe and find oneself in a Śakuntalā's paradise, but at the same time to remain there is to be marooned in an aesthetic dreamworld. How can the *rasika* translate the utopian hope into the real world? How, at least can he imagine doing so?

2. Love and the Playworld

We have not yet addressed the issue of what goes wrong in the poetic fantasy-world of the first three Acts. We have spoken of the curse, but not examined its significance. It is an obstacle to the lovers' progress, at least ostensibly, but what kind of an obstacle? We have found the notion of 'divine success' (*daivikī siddhi*) relevant to the aesthetic experience and its mythicization in this play. Equally useful is the passage in *NŚ* 27 that immediately follows the description of dramatic success: the discourse on the obstacles (*ghātas*) that impede it. These are divided into two general categories, those that arise from the actor or author ('self-originating' *ātmasamuttha,* 27.23) and those that come from outside ('employed by an other/enemy' *paraprayukta,* 27.22).[40] We can use these categories in our own way to understand the two types of problem that afflict the *sahṛdaya* in his construction of a poetic dream world. In this section we look only at the internal conflict, the kind of obstacle created by aestheticized love itself. We also need to refer back to the discussion of *līlā* in the preceding chapter, particularly to the matter of its solipsizing tendency.

The erotic excitement of the first three Acts of *Ś* is heady stuff: the *rasika* has entered the enchanted world of poetic promise, led to the threshold by a wondrous animal that metaphorically embodies the charm of song. Once inside he finds himself in an ideally feminine atmosphere of lush vegetation and synesthetic sensuous allure, with the nubile child-woman Śakuntalā as its focus, the virtual tutelary goddess of the place (1.1+*). His first glimpse of her sends him into shudders of ecstasy: innocent and ripe for the plucking, her breasts pressing with the sap of youth against the confines of her barken garment. This last detail could stand as a symbol of his expectations, for he wishes either to ignore as much as possible the ascetical character of the place or see it as a source of charm.[41] In his imagination it is the paradise he, as *rasika,* has encountered many times in poetry and song. His own palace pleasure-garden is but an imitation of this lush primordial grove (1.16[15]). Here is the Golden Age (*kṛtayuga*) in all its alluring freshness, untainted by the vulgarity of hunting or farming economies. Śakuntalā seems to him like the embodiment of its vegetal abundance;[42] a 'new creation of woman' in the imagination of a *rasika* Prajāpati (2.10[9]); 'an unsmelt flower, an unsnipped shoot, an uncut gem, new honey/wine yet unsavored, the full fruit of past lives' merit—whose lot will it be to enjoy her faultless beauty in this world?'[43] The final question is the crux of the matter, but we know without a doubt that the lot is his, the *rasika's.* Poetic theory is unanimous on this point. Only the *rasika-sahṛdaya* has the cultivation (*vyutpatti, abhyāsa*) and imagination (*pratibhā*) capable of enjoying the Śrī of the poetic universe.[44] What could an 'oily-head ascetic'[45]—think of the poeticians' scorn for the insensitive pedant (*ahṛdaya paṇḍita*)—do with beauty of such resonance? Duḥṣanta's lyrical asides, which translate her charm into the figural language (*alaṃkāra*) of poetry, are the only adequate response, for they alone present her in her imaginative dimension as an object of *rasāsvāda.* Sexual intercourse, which takes place off-stage between Acts 3 and 4, must have its way prepared by poetic incantations of this sort. Sexual love as envisioned by *kāvya* is not merely physical,[46] but sensuous and imaginative, encompassing that whole area in which sensation drifts into aesthetic savoring. It is only not so for those without the aesthetic capacity (*sahṛdayatva*).

Yet, in the terms we have set up, we can see a drift here towards the solipsistic consciousness of aesthetic hedonism: love paradoxically reduced through aesthetic enhancement to sensation. Śakuntalā has become simply the vehicle of her own ravishing charm, which the *rasika* can savor as a modality of his own subjective consciousness. In the terms of Kashmiri Śaivism she is the play-manifestation (*ābhāsa*) whose *raison d'être* is the savoring subject's 'sport of self-vibration' (*svaparispandalīlā*). Even the glimpses we have into her mind in the first 3 Acts, as desire disturbs her girlish innocence, seem designed to make her more erotically appealing, as fantasy object, to the *rasika*. We could almost say that she is really no more than the concretization of a dreamily erotic atmosphere, an aphrodisiac to a refined, contemplative onanism. But in the end there is something terribly one-sided and unsympathetic about such a view, which distorts the *rasika* consciousness by stripping it of its psychological resonance. We have referred before to the principle of the 'materiality of the signifier' and it applies here as well. Śakuntalā cannot be the merely transparent vehicle of a subjective experience. If the Radiant Female is necessary to the aesthetic-erotic consciousness, then she is an irreducible Other. This otherness, which is at bottom a subjectivity resistant to the *rasika's* narcissism, can be suppressed but not overcome in *rasa*-savoring. There is a trapdoor in aesthetical idealism. Śakuntalā attracts because she represents a promise, a promise that can never be fully defined or attained without ceasing to attract. Here is the abyssal pseudo-logic of Lacan's 'Imaginary' level of consciousness: one seeks to appropriate the radiant fullness of the Other only to find that it can only reside elsewhere. The solipsizing aesthetic ideal contains an inescapable contradiction.

The fact is that the hero of the aesthetic-erotic playworld *needs* the Śrī-presence whose magic conjures it into existence. However pronounced the tendency to narcissistic appropriation of the heroine as savor-bearing appearance, there is an equally strong tendency toward submission to her transformative power. With the King's first appearance on stage we see him as a hunter who is being lured (*hṛta,* 1.5) by his prey into the garden-world of the hermitage which will soon disclose Śakuntalā as its 'virtual goddess'. He is, in other words, as passive as he is active, captivated by a principle of female beauty that demands a response of him. Is there no symbolic resonance in the fact that he enters as a devotee—nominally to salute Śakuntalā as her father's proxy, but his 'devotion' (*bhakti,* 1.12+) soon acquires more suggestive meaning—even divesting himself of the insignia of his wordly rank? The note of awestruck devotion and pained craving, maintained in numerous verses of Acts 2 and 3, is of course a conventional feature of *kāvya,* but does this fact rob it of its content? Does not the convention itself require explanation? I do not suggest that the awestruck, devotional posture is inconsistent with a narcissistic tendency (erotic idealization can easily be a form of domination[47]), but the very fact that it takes the form of an implicit plea makes us realize that the Other is a force undermining the autonomy of the subject's play-fantasy. It is virtually inevitable on these grounds alone that the erotic tone of the first three Acts will shift to one of pathos (*karuṇa rasa*), most prominent in Acts 4 and 6, but underlying the anger (*raudra*) of Act 5 and the wonder (*adbhuta*) of Act 7 as well.

I think that we can best understand this pathetic accent in terms of the remarks made in the final section of the last chapter on the implications of Ānandavardhana's model of the aesthetic playworld, viz. that it is not created out of some spontaneous play-impulse as in the 'theological' paradigms, but rather to realize or fulfill a desire for something that is lacking in the real world. Thus in the latter part of *Ś* the hero is in the position of having somehow to translate the elation of the first three Acts into the actual world of the court, where despite panegyrical salutes which perpetuate the fiction of his charismatic dominance the pleasure-principle is in fact subordinated to the reality-principle. In Act 5, in his *déjà vu* reaction to another wife's off-stage song, it strikes him forcefully that aesthetic response discloses a disturbing gap in ordinary emotional experience (see 5.9 [2] quoted *supra*), which can only be bridged, as he comes to understand in Act 6, by bringing the woman epiphanized in poetry—for him, Śakuntalā—to life. In the portrait scene of Act 6 he tries to re-enter the illusory aesthetic-erotic paradise, but he finds he cannot go backwards. Śakuntalā must now be brought into his world, not the other way around. But this is precisely where he reveals his lack of autonomy. To enter the kāvyic dreamworld there are only two requirements: enchantment (*pratibhā, rasa*) and a cultivated sensibility (*sahṛdayatva*); but to bring its promise to life one must submit to certain demands that have their source outside oneself, demands that accentuate the hero's vulnerability.

In the 6th Act Duḥṣanta, the *sahṛdaya* hero, is reduced to making a sentimental display of himself in order to attract sympathy. He is on stage before a hidden observer, specifically Miśrakeśī (or

Sānumatī), the *apsaras* from Mārīca-Kāśyapa's hermitage who represents the lost female presence. In demonstrating his hurt confusion before her he is surreptitiously pleading for female understanding.

The Śrī of his imagination is not after all his to conjure up at will. Rather, he appears in his pathetic posture like a disconsolate child. It is, I think, significant that the female presence has a distinct maternal aspect: Miśrakeśī's solicitous attitude and the fact that she has been sent by Śakuntalā's mother. But if we reflect on the nurturing feminine atmosphere of the hermitage in Act 1, as it presented itself to the hero's imagination, we may realize that even as a love-object Śakuntalā has held the promise of maternal shelter. The gentle teasing laughter of three female companions, highlighted by a lushly sensuous world with its soft humming sounds and warm fragrant breezes, might be the muffled echo of voices heard long ago in the 'maternal cosmos' of infancy,[48] where the females of the extended family—mother, aunts, older sisters, cousins—had maintained an enveloping atmosphere of benign solicitude and indulgence. In entering the paradise of Acts 1-3 the hero was in a sense re-entering the pre-dhārmic playworld of early childhood, bringing its diffuse, subliminal eroticism into sharp adult focus in the image of a beautiful young woman whose sexual awakening is to him alone, a beautiful-and-distressed fairy-tale princess (Indian style), whose savior-hero he was always meant to be.[49] The curse that has exiled him from this paradise is, in this perspective, the fundamental No to the pleasure-principle, the renunciation which is at the root of all Law and which marks the first stage of entry into the adult world of responsibility.

But why must there be a plea, and why, further, must it be conveyed indirectly through dramatics, i.e., by making a spectacle of oneself? The answer has both ethical and psychological dimensions, both of which undermine the erotic-aesthetic autonomy of the play-ideal. It is hard to avoid the impression that the curse is in some sense a concretization of a betrayal. Despite the numerous epistemological tropes in Act 6 that seek to ennoble the hero's confusion by placing it in a quasi-metaphysical context (the *māyā*-bewilderment of the Indian Everyman), it is clear enough that the hero needs to expiate a sense of guilt. We could see this betrayal with Tagore as a simple matter of sexual exploitation of innocence. But this, I think, is too literal. The betrayal is structural, a matter of intrinsic disposition rather than act. The aesthetic-erotic idealization of woman creates a barrier to love as an affective relationship. The *rasika* hero oscillates between two idealizations of the heroine, neither of which leaves him any room for a genuine understanding of and with her. On the one hand she is the aesthetic-erotic object with all its solipsistic implications, on the other the sole access to a lost world of nurturing affection. But where is she herself, as subject in her own right? The problem is not exclusively a women's issue. The *rasika* himself does not escape the isolation that results from the failure of mutual engagement on a personal level. Ultimately one cannot love, or even bask in, an image or an atmosphere. One needs the vitality of another consciousness.

Whether the hero (or the *rasika* he represents) ever reaches such a realization is impossible to decide, since the play never represents the issue as his conscious concern. Nevertheless, we see him attempting to demonstrate the authenticity of his feeling for her across the abyss that separates them in Act 6, dramatizing for the *apsaras* who functions as Śakuntalā's representative the pathos of his situation without her. While he thus displays his vulnerability—which comes to a peak first in the episode of the portrait, and then again in his shame over his childlessness—she remains a hidden spectator, the female *rasikā* whose sympathetic response will validate his innocence and good faith. Is this a genuine call for recognition or a ploy by which the (male) *rasika* relieves himself of any sense of responsibility for the gap which divides him from his idealized beloved? Let us remember that the theme of a hero's betrayal of his wife is a major one in Sanskrit literature. We have only to think of Nala and Rāma. The former abandons his wife in the forest, leaving her to deal with wild animals, rape, bandits, etc., while he seeks to comprehend the dark forces that inhabit him (he is literally possessed by a gambling demon). The latter humiliates Sītā (more than once) and makes himself miserable for the same reason he had gone into exile many years earlier, because he cannot choose pleasure over duty, personal inspiration over collective demand. None of these situations—Duḥṣanta's, Nala's, or Rāma's—is easy to judge. The texts that present them invite sympathy for both parties while—overtly, at least—insisting on the inevitability of the dilemma, thus establishing a tragic perspective on life in the world.

Nevertheless, we can see different levels of meaning here. In the context of *dharma*, the wife is in most respects the last one to whom the householder has any obligations. The emphasis is all the other way around: she is to serve him, take him as her *guru*, etc., while he fulfills his debts to the sages, the gods, his ancestors, guests, and even creatures at large (the *pañcayajña*). Even the intimacy of sexual life is invaded by the dhārmic *obligation* to have monthly intercourse, since constant pregnancy better ensures male offspring to perform the required rituals (some authorities regard an unfertilized ovum as equivalent to abortion). The wife is on the whole a means, an instrument, of the householder's fulfilment of essential obligations, rather than an object of his moral attention in her own right. If family disharmony develops, the overt blame is likely to fall on her (cf. the role of Kaikeyī in the Rāma story). Yet on the other hand, she is terribly idealized. She is held up as the Śrī of her husband's world, the locus and inspiration of his emotional life, even though she may be little more than a stranger to him.[50] Servant, mistress of his soul, and nurturing mother: how can she be all these things? And how can he bridge the gap on his side of the dilemma? How can he remove the veil that separates him from her, a veil for whose existence he denies personal responsibility, while nursing a sense of guilt and needing forgiveness?

What I am getting at here, obviously, is the way literary representations of love-separation become mythic nuclei of real-life feelings. In the context of arranged marriage (and let us remember that most *rasikas* were in fact not princes) there is a greater barrier to the intimate sharing of emotion than there would otherwise be, greater potential for awkwardness between husband and wife, for a certain stiff formality that may well remain throughout the marriage. In these mythic paradigms—the stories of Nala, Rāma, Duḥṣanta—the male demonstrates his good faith, shows himself to be at the mercy of destiny, and yet discloses the hidden existence of his love. He can have it both ways, in other words. The 4th and 5th Acts of *Ś* show a genuine sensitivity to the plight of women. The former's almost cloying tenderness combined with the latter's insults and accusations points not only to an awareness of the shock that awaited most Indian girls of high birth but an uneasy conscience about it. And not only about sending a precious daughter out into a colder, more impersonal world—all Kaṇva can really hope is that Śakuntalā will be treated with respect, the rest, he says, depends on fate, 4.19(17)—but about receiving her as a wife. Duḥṣanta betrays Śakuntalā in Act 5, and in Act 6 he acts out his incomprehension of the deed and the anguish he feels about it, all the while seeking to disclose a truer emotional self that defies appearances. 'This is the real me', he says to the woman behind the barrier, which he cannot remove though he has acquiesced in its construction. 'Please do not withdraw your love from me'. If I have suggested that this might be a ploy, it is because it is difficult to avoid seeing such dramatizations as self-pitying evasions. But the truth is that here we are at the limits of Sanskrit poetry and perhaps classical Indian culture itself. We wish that it were possible for the hero to raise this problem explicitly to consciousness. We wish both he and the heroine could be more than idealized types, that they could think as well as feel. We wish the demand for *rasa* did not exclude a moral problematics *on the conscious level.* This would mean, however, an ideal of love that was something more than either quasi-mystical intoxication or dharmic partnership.

For the *rasika* the dilemma—sentimental longing kept veiled by emotional reserve—is more charged than for the ordinary man, because he is naturally a sentimentalist. He cannot regard a world which does not place the demands of the heart first as a good world (see last chapter, esp. remarks on Mammaṭa 1.1). Yet he is forced to expiate an implicit sense of guilt for the gap that exists between his actual relations with women and their sentimental idealization in poetry and the further gap existing within the idealization itself, viz. the mutual incompatibility of autonomous aesthetic-erotic *līlā* and the 'cry from the heart' for mutual love and understanding. The dilemma is the tension between the first three Acts of *Śakuntalā* and the final four. In the former, *kāvya* is the playworld of the erotic imagination; in the latter—like the portrait in Act 6—it is a vehicle of pathos. Thus we see that something like a curse is needed to mythicize a gap that already exists between the desire of the heart and the poetic dreamworld that represents it. The *rasika* knows that his poetry contains a promise of a true emotional breakthrough, but he cannot achieve it in a poetry of idealized sentiment and high formal polish. the very conventional limits of *kāvya* ensure that it will always need to make the romantic hero a man of tears and swoons, seeking to demonstrate by self-display what he cannot communicate directly. By giving us the *rasika* as uncomprehending victim and soliciting a gush of sympathetic feeling on his behalf the play shifts from an ideal of aesthetic-erotic transformation to one of tragic self-portrayal: the man of feeling as beautiful, childlike soul, a hapless navigator of forces beyond his comprehension. If one can no longer find Śrī in her floral paradise, one can hope to attract her sympathetic smile from afar. The question is whether the appeal ever gets beyond self-pity.

The pathos works, to an extent, though the paradisal promise of the first three Acts (the utopian world of emotional release) is never realized. The hero succeeds in recuperating female sympathy: the eavesdropping *apsaras* acts the part of a mother impressed by her child's weepy protestations of innocence (Act 6). Śakuntalā herself, however, remains reserved though docile (Act 7). The bewitching goddess of the poetic imagination has become humble wife and mother, just as the hero is no longer the confident *rasika* but the chastened, obedient servant of destiny standing before the magnified Dhārmic Father Mārīca. The erotic magic of the first 3 Acts, in other words, is not a part of the conclusion. The magical atmosphere of the second *āśrama* rings with the emotional tone of wonder (*adbhuta rasa*). Thus we move from eros to pathos and finally, as the great paternal figure of Mārīca is revealed, to awe.

3. The Dhārmic Father

So much for internal problem (*ātmasamuttha ghāta*) inhibiting the 'success' of the initial model of the *rasika's* playworld. We must now examine the external problem (*paraprayukta*), which I would describe as the *sahṛdaya's* confrontation with authority. There is a major difference between the metaphysical or theological model of the playworld and the *rasika's* poetic universe, and that is that the divine subject is truly his own authority, whereas the *rasika* lives in a real world outside the poetic revery. Śiva is both *rasika* and ascetic, but at least on first impression the worldly *rasika* cannot make the same boast.[52] He lacks the power that the god's transcendent renunciation conveys, his *tapas*. The critical incident in *Ś* is the curse, considered now not as the symbol of the gap between love and its poetic idealization, but as the sign of ascetical anger. What does Durvāsas represent in the *rasikas's* imagination? We ended the last section with an allusion to the great paternal figure of Mārīca, but he is not the only father-figure in the play. To understand this role and what it means to the poetic playworld we have to go back to the beginning of the play.[53]

When the King crossed over the threshold into the wondrous world of the *āśrama* in Act 1, he was not immediately greeted with the epiphany of his dream woman. He initially suffed a rebuff to his autonomy. He had been engaged in a favorite form of *līlā,* the hunt,[54] which had turned into something magical because of the *adbhuta* quality of the deer, when suddenly two ascetics appear and command him to put up his weapon.

> Hail King! This deer belongs to the hermitage.
> Let not your arrow fly into its tender body
> like fire in a bed of flowers.
> What have the hard shafts of arrows to do
> with the tremulous life of deer?
> Therefore quickly sheathe
> the dart you have put to your bow.
> Your weapon should rescue the distressed
> and not assail the faultless.[55]

The phallic implications of the arrows suggest that the deer is a symbol of Śakuntalā and that the King's erotic *līlā* is implicitly aggressive and exploitative. Śakuntalā needs protection, which is institutionalized in *dharma. Dharma* is itself backed by the ascetical power of *tapas.* Thus the curse can be seen as retribution against the King, coming from the sphere of Vedic authority (an angry Brahmin), because the King has not sufficiently tempered his aggressive instincts. His so-called sport has camouflaged a transgression against a young woman, helpless but for the authority behind the law. Yet if this were the whole story (as it certainly is part of it), Tagore would be right, and we need go no further. But the deer is not a univocal symbol.

The ostensibly casual remark of the Charioteer made before the ascetical interruption opens up a whole area of meaning that has never been explored. The Sūtradhāra in the Prologue speaks the lines that liken the swift deer to the charm of the Actress' song (*gītarāgeṇa hāriṇā = sāraṅgenātiraṃhasā*), and immediately, as the chariot-mounted King appears on stage, the Charioteer exclaims:

> Longlived!
> As I cast my eye on the deer
> then on you with arrow poised on string
> I seem to see Lord Śiva
> in person pursuing the stag.

This is an allusion to a well-known incident in Hindu mythology. The great Prajāpati Dakṣa held a sacrificial assembly to which all the gods except Śiva, the husband of his daughter Satī, were invited.[56] Śiva then, in some versions at Satī's urging, bursts in on the assembly firing arrows from his great bow Pināka. The sacrifice itself, clearly a stand-in or 'allomorph' of father Dakṣa himself, takes flight in deer-form, and in different versions Śiva pierces or beheads it. Also, behind this story lurks the older account of primordial incest: the gods call in Rudra, the archer god, to stop the father from having intercourse with his daughter.[57] Even in the Dakṣa-version, where Śiva is already the daughter's husband, we can sense the oedipal tension between the male antagonists: Dakṣa's denial of sacrificial participation to his son-in-law being the echo of the more rudimentary denial. The invocation of the myth makes perfect sense in the play, where the hero's main concern in the first 3 Acts is possession of the daughter of asceticism. Virginity itself can be seen in oedipal terms as possession by the girl's father. This, in part, explains the paradoxical nature of the hermitage as a place of sacrifice and penance on the one hand and burgeoning sexual innuendo on the other (Śakuntalā's ripening nubility reflected in the surrounding vegetation). Śakuntalā's auspicious sexuality needs to be released from the paternal enclosure in order to benefit the hero, as the representative worldling. In terms of communal symbolism he makes bold, as culture hero, to harness the feminine *śakti* or Śrī-principle for the good of the world. [58]

Thus the King enters the scene with oedipal bravado, but immediately encounters representatives of the absent father who force him to sheathe his phallic arrows. The direct encounter, in psychological terms, makes him doubt himself. He submissively relinquishes the Śiva-stance, and we see him several times in the course of this and the next Act worrying about making a disturbance of their ascetical peace.[59] It is not just that he has become humbly pious: he himself admits that he is afraid of the ascetics' *tapas.* In Act 2 he puts it to the Vidūṣaka in the suggestive imagery of fire:

> There is a burning energy hidden in tranquil penance–groves.
> Though harmless to the touch sunstones burn when countered
> by another's fiery brilliance.[60]

In the apparent paradise of piety and sexual innuendo lurks a deadly fire waiting to assault the lover who makes a careless move. The sunstone may stand as the symbol of the hermitage as a whole, for the image of an inviting surface concealing a deadly threat reminds us of the paradox of fire among flowers that finds expression more than once in the play. The fire that was initially identified with the desire of the phallic intruder (arrows like fire among flowers) is already part of the *āśrama* (the sunstone). Thus when, in Act 3, we find Śakuntalā lying in fever on her couch of flowers, we cannot be sure whether the fire that wracks her body (itself often compared with flowers) is the fire of desire or its opposite i.e., the *tapas* which will eventually punish desire. Or rather, it is surely both at once: Śakuntalā's love-fever, so in line with the *rasika* lover's hopeful desire, nevertheless contains a danger for him.[61] Jewel or flower inviting to the touch, she will before long make him feel the sting of *tapas*. For that is precisely the form the curse takes, even to the use of fire-imagery.[62]

Though the curse falls nominally on Śakuntalā it is really aimed at the *rasika* hero. Act 5 with its confrontation of royal and ascetical powers (*tejas* vs. *tapas*) seems to bear this out. No sooner does the ascetical party arrive in the capital than the two leaders show disdain for the King's worldliness. Again we have significant use of fire-imagery:

> Though he is a King of great fortune and unvarying constancy
> and keeps the castes firmly on the path of righteousness,
> nevertheless to this mind ever intimate with solitude
> the crowded palace seems like a house engulfed in flames.[63]

In one sense these are the flames of desire (*kāma*) and worldly majesty (*tejas*), but in another they belong to the curse itself (*tapas, kopa*). Oblivion has already overspread the hero's mind: he has been, without knowing it, rendered impotent by the superior potency of ascetical wrath (cf. *tapaso vīryam*, 3.2). So that, although the King seems to win the showdown that shortly takes place, he has already lost. Śakuntalā is squeezed out of the picture. Caught in the middle of a covert struggle for power, the disputed object is lost sight of. But in effect she is retained by ascetical authority, although in new form, for she is transferred to the marvelous *āśrama* of Mārīca-Kāśyapa, not to be released until the King drops his surreptitious hostility to the disposing ascetical power.

We can better understand what is going on here if we see

that the play really contains two versions of paternal authority, which from the *rasika's* point of view may be called Good and Bad Father. The Good Father is initially the absent one, namely the complaisant Kaṇva, who has always intended his foster-daughter (in reality the daughter of the Durvāsas-like Viśvāmtra, an ascetical straddler between Kṣatriya and Brahmin positions) for such a suitor as King Duḥṣanta. Kaṇva shows his amenability by accepting the divine voice in the fire-room that declares the *rasika's* claim on the dream-woman to have sacrificial legitimacy (4.6[4]), and sends his treasured daughter off with wistful blessings. This is the image of paternal authority generated by the *rasika's* confidence and fond hope. But while Śakuntalā and her friends wait for this benign figure to return from his pilgrimage (undertaken to allay Śakuntalā's bad fortune—see note 61), the Bad Father makes his appearance instead, the projection of the *rasika's* fear. There is no understanding or sympathy in Durvāsas, only outrage for having been ignored—the subliminal issue being the Gāndharva marriage, as Tagore knew.[64] In oedipal terms the curse is an act of paternal revenge, and the King's obliviousness a form of impotence or figurative castration. But the 'proof' of Durvāsas' role as stand-in father is the fact that the ascetics who take Śakuntalā to the capital are actually extensions of Durvāsas' anger, though nominally representing Kaṇva. It is only toward the end of Act 7 and in Act 7 that the Good Father begins to re-emerge, no longer as Kaṇva, but as the all-wise Father-of-Creatures (Prajāpati), who has the dimensions of a destiny figure, manipulating appearances from behind the scenes. Though it is specifically Indra who sends his charioteer to test the hero's mettle, Indra's power and authority pale next to that of the great Brahmin Father. Mārīca's is the omniscience that has governed all, and appear as children before him. Though an ascetic he sparkles with the splendor of the sun itself (7.27): where before the hero had seemed to absorb the paternal role (note 61) now the ascetic appears with dazzling Kinglike majesty (cf. royal *tejas*).

Thus everything culminates in the aura of wonder that surrounds this magical, benign Father, who pronounces his blessing on the united family (assigning them allegorial identities, 7.29) and reveals the mystery of the curse (7.32), thus delivering the hero from guilt and confusion. The hero has relinquished all confrontation with authority. He has felt the sting of his impotence in the form of bewildered remorse, and, significantly, the depth of his humiliation comes not with pangs of longing for Śakuntalā but with the imagined disappointment and disapproval of his ancestors (6.27 [25]). The conciousness of virile failure in the spectral presence of his male forbears cripples him. But in his pathetic nadir comes salvation—or, we might say, because of it. By presenting himself as completely helpless, but at the same time lovable and well-meaning he has stirred the Father in his soul. What he was unable to accomplish by force and confidence, he now accomplishes by his very weakness. The passive, pathetic display succeeds in rousing the hidden paternal spectator to action. A messenger is sent to administer a loyalty test, which the *rasika* hero passes with flying colors. He takes up his bow against a fully surrogate demonic Other (the ever-available scapegoat),[65] showing himself full of mettle in his officially authorized dharmic role. No ambivalence or ambiguity now with regard to paternal authority: he is its splendid (if entirely nominal) champion. He has again become the Noble Child in his hidden father's eyes. We are never in doubt about where the real power lies, about who pulls the strings of destiny, etc. But—and this is the important point—the paternal power is no longer hostile. It has become sensitized to the *rakika's* plight. It makes its own *rasa* response to the hero's displays of grief and noble courage. It grants him its favor. And, as a result, grateful respect and awe of the sagely Superfather cast their glow over the final scene.[66]

Thus, to frame this within the context of *siddhi* and obstacles from outside, we may say that in Durvāsas the outside world seems to say: In me there is a dangerous power that you must respect. You cannot have your dreamy aesthetic-erotic transcendence in a flowery feminine paradise with impunity. It is correct enough to say that *dharma* impinges here on *kāma,* as so many critics following Tagore have done, but we must insist at the same time that the point of view remains that of the *rasika.* In the person of Durvāsas *dharma* appears negative, cantankerous, a force to be reckoned with, but only reluctantly. Behind this portrayal of the dharmic imperative is a puritanical, anti-sensual spirit at war with the *rasika* practice and temperament. The lover's mistake is to assume that *tapas* can be neutralized in the aesthetic transformation of the hermitage into the poetic garden-world backdrop for *śṛṅgāra rasa.* But it is too powerful a force in the Indian cultural psyche to be fantasized into submission. In Durvāsas' curse the flame of *tapas* leaps forth from its lurking place among the shadows in the lush shrubbery of the poetic paradise. The lovers, therefore, must learn to deal with Brahmanical authority. 'Success' (*siddhi*) cannot be achieved by ignoring the unpalatable or disruptive but only through an act of inclusion.

Again we find a suitable mythical pattern, this time in the aetiological first chapter of the *Nāṭyaśāstra*, the earliest dramatic handbook. The sage Bharata has acquired the new artform drama from Brahmā-Pitāmaha, but the first production before the gods is thwarted by attacks from demons who personify 'obstacles' (*vighna*). Indra beats them down with his banner-pole numerous times, but they always spring back to inhibit the performance. Finally the gods ask Pitāmaha to intervene, and he, after consulting with the demons, stipulates that they have a legitimate place in dramatic representation. Once that place is acknowledged the drama may proceed (though it does not seem to do so until Ch. 4). We cannot press the analogy too closely, but the point is clear. The real obstacles in the *Śakuntalā* are not the demons, who are pure scapegoat figures, but the internal and external forces weighing against aesthetic-erotic entrancement: the insufficiency of aestheticized love and the power of ascetical authority. In the *NŚ* myth the gods take the case to the great father-god, and in the *Śakuntalā* the lovers take theirs to the Prajāpati Mārica Kāśyapa, who represents wisdom and benevolence.

Yet Mārīca's benedictory, forgiving role has already been anticipated in the pivotal 4th Act of the play in the figure of Kaṇva.[67] We have referred many times in the preceding paragraphs to the significance of fire-symbolism in this play, but we have not yet mentioned the sacrificial fire which dominates Act 4. It is in the fire-room while preparing for sacrifice that Kaṇva hears the divine voice informing him of Śakuntalā's pregnancy and its rightness:

> Know, Brahmin, that your daughter
> bears the seed of Duḥṣanta
> for the world's well-being,
> as the *śamī*-wood bears the seed of fire.[68]

The word for 'seed' is *tejas,* which also means 'fire, brilliance, heat', a standard means of designating royal majesty and also ascetical *tapas* (cf. 2.7). *Śamī*-wood, a hard wood supposed to contain seeds of fire, was used to kindle the sacred fire. Kaṇva has also used fire-imagery in his words of forgiveness to Śakuntalā (4.5+): 'My dear, fortunately the offering has fallen into the fire, though the sacrificer's eyes were blinded by smoke'.[69] The King, in other words, was blinded by his own bravado, nevertheless he did the right thing. Later in the Act, Śakuntalā processes around the sacrificial fire, which Kaṇva adjures to protect her.[70] All these references to the ritual fire may be seen as establishing the primacy of a form of heat that contains within itself all of its other significations: the sacrifice, which in the Brāhmaṇa texts symbolizes the recurring cycles of the cosmos, includes the fires of asceticism, desire, and majesty, as well as the heat of remorse (*anutāpa*) that emerges in the King's lamentations in Act 6.[71] After the curse episode, Act 4 opens with several verses (2 ff.) that establish a cyclical perspective (dawn supplanting night, sun replacing moon), which prepare us for the prominent position of sacrifice in the play. Thus in the course of the play the summer heat of the first three Acts (symbolically reflecting the war between *kāma* and *tapas*) yields by Act 6 to the mildness of spring and its promise of abundance and prosperity. All things have their place in this broad inclusive perspective. And it is against this understanding that we must view the stanza spoken by Mārīca in Act 7, which allegorizes the roles of the two lovers and their child.

> I congratulate the three of you,
> noble Śakuntalā, your good offspring, and yourself,
> the assembled triad
> of Faith, Prosperity, and Order.[72]

Through the emphasis on sacrifice, which is a middle ground between his own pretensions and the paternal authority he fears, the *rasika* is able to pose a counter-image of *dharma*. It is no longer the paternal No to the pleasure-principle, but a formula which gives all elements of life their due. Not that the *rasika* has moved away from wish-fulfilment: being unable to wish away the negative force of Brahmanical authority, he now settles for its conversion into the comforting figure of a benevolent omniscient sage, in whose ritual he (the *rasika*) plays the leading symbolic role (personification of *vidhi*). Thus obligation becomes a part to play, an impersonation. This is where *dharma* intersects with *nāṭya*. But in playing the dharmic role the *rasika* is by no means led beyond the sentimental register. On the contrary, he is able to make a virtue of necessity and translate Brahmanical prescription into narcissistic posture. But even this—the aestheticization of the external demand through role-playing—is not complete. What reminds us pointedly of this is the disturbing figure of the ascetic whose presence functions as a landmark of Mārīca's magical world.

> Half-merged with an anthill, his sacred cord a snakeskin,
> his neck strangled by an old dry vine, birds nesting
> in the tumble of matted locks reaching to his shoulders,
> there, facing the sun like a motionless pillar, behold a sage.[73]

In this figure the ascetic's utter alienation from the domain of the senses becomes a threat merged with the landscape like the *tapas* in the first three Acts. His very designation (*sthāṇu*) suggests the power of Śiva, who has the word as an epithet. We can appreciate the significance of such a landmark, when we consider that Śakuntalā herself, by means of a pun to which attention is called within the same Act, is entangled in his hair, an idea which point to her original condition in Kaṇva's *āśrama* where *tapas* seemed a hostile force threatening to keep her back from the hero's possession.[74]

The play performs an act of inclusion with the dangerous outside force, but, despite the comforting figure of Mārīca, the danger remains, resistant to aesthetic conversion. In terms of *rasa,* the wondrous (*adbhuta*) conclusion—a conventional feature of drama—contains a hint of the grotesque and repulsive (*bībhatsa*) attached to the paternal ascetical figure.

4. Conclusion: The Ambiguous Playworld

But exactly what is the outcome for the *rasika*? Viewed positively, the conclusion represents reconciliation with male authority and the recuperation of female indulgence. It is the stuff of all romance. We can even say that the shift from esctatic eroticism to familial tenderness—the movement from Śakuntalā's breathtaking sexual allure to her chastened dignity as wife and mother—is all for the good, since it seems to represent a more balance ideal of love between man and woman. But, the problem is not so much with the outcome itself as with its implementation, which makes us suspicious about the value of the ideal. What we lack is a sense of *rasika's* conscious engagement of and dialectic with the larger-than-life male and female powers that dominate his imagination. Instead he succeeds through psycho-drama, i.e., through self-display, the taking of postures. While this is natural in an artform that depends so much on posture to stimulate *rasa,* it nevertheless evades the substantial issues that the artform raises. The hero never comes—nor apparently does the *rasika* in the audience—to any moral or intellectual insight into his situation. We might say that the issues are only accidentally invoked, but I think this is wrong. We are missing the point of the mythic paradigm we have explored if we think it is not fundamentally about the hope of realization of the love-ideal and the tensions that surround it. There is nothing accidental about subliminal meaning: quite the contrary.

We have seen that the paradisal model of love incorporates many different facets of the *rasika's* aspiration. First there is the intensity of longing for aesthetic transformation of the real world into something shimmering with intensified feeling, a feeling that Ānandavardhana identifies as *śṛṅgāra.* We find here a yearning for escape from the strictures of life in the world, especially from the ascetical spirit of *dharma* with its characteristic frown on desire—an escape readily invested with the emotional intensity of the longing for *mokṣa.* Thus the aptness of the aesthetic model of world-experience as *līlā* with its transcendental implications. Beyond this there is the socio–religious idea of Śrī, an idea which valorized the fulfilment of desire as an auspicious force percolating through the whole society. Against the ascetical ideal of *dharma* as self-restraint (the impersonal ritualization of *pravṛtti* according to *nivṛtti* values) is set the model of an ordered society infused from within by a divine radiance: charismatic happiness vs. depersonalized calm. Included in this idea is the valorization of the courtly and aristocratic environment in which *līlā* was a lived ideal. Then there is the psychological dimension of the recaptured Golden Age, the bliss of play in the 'maternal cosmos' of early childhood. But to achieve this multifaceted paradise one must evade reality—not only the paternal No to the pleasure-principle, but even the genuine needs of the heart. No art, no wish-fulfilling dream, can really evade reality, since only in reality does the fantasy desire has a chance of being satisfied. Even for the most radical escapist the ideal leads surreptitiously back to the real. Thus one is brought to the point of psychological, ethical, even ontological revelations concerning the subjectivity of the Other. The very intensity of longing creates a paradoxical effect, and *kāvya* moves in two directions at once: towards a purely autonomous world of 'sport' insulated by the coy excellences of poetic form (*alaṃkāra, guṇa, dhvani,* etc.) and towards an epiphany which holds out the promise of happiness for which an autonomous aesthetic world is an inadequate vehicle, a *de facto* constraint.

In section 1 of the last chapter I argued that the paradox of play is precisely its indecision between transcendence and immanence. What we have found after examining the poetic playworld, I believe, is what Śaṅkara seems to have known when he rejected *līlā* on the level of the Absolute, viz. that play inevitably tilts towards the immanent because of its necessary erotic component,[75] which contains *sub rosa* a humanizing plea. The aesthetic-erotic ideal of *kāvya* as thematized in the mythic framework of the *Śakuntalā* seems to prove that any flirtation with Eros inevitably subverts *līlā's* transcendent claims. A curse hangs over the solipsistic garden-world of the first three Acts, which can be lifted only when the *rasika* seeks to translate the Śrī of his imagination into the real world with its social and practical limitations. The *Śakuntalā* moves to the side of desire for *fulfilment* of the promise enshrined in the erotic paradise: the utopian hope of happiness in love supported by a social system that honors the sentimental ideals of the heart. It has to be this way, or else even erotic play becomes paradoxically ascetical by virtue of its solipsistic detachment from affect. The question is whether or not the hero has actually learned that this must be the case. If there were an Act 8 to this play, would we not find the hero again dazzled by another Śakuntalā, with the original reduced to the off-stage role of Haṃsavatī? Will the hero know, when he hears her plaintive offstage song, that the woman of his dreams resides in the now-familiar wife and mother of his children? Or will he look again to the horizon for the new epiphany of the elusive Śrī, the 'new creation of the jewel known as woman' (*strīratnasṛṣṭir aparā,* 2.10[9])? But this is really a rhetorical question. The lure of the playworld paradigm of emotional release never lost its force in *kāvya,* or religion for that matter. Nevertheless, this play of Kālidāsa's (and it is emblematic rather than unique in this regard) gives us reasons for doubting the psychological viability of the ideal. The hero as self-possessed connoisseur of emotion, sporting in the feminized garden of Eros, becomes a child pleading for understanding from hidden authorities who, he fears, may be indifferent to his affective needs.

Notes

1. The debate over his date cannot conclusively be settled, though the *termini* are fixed as 2nd century BC (the reign of Puṣyamitra, who figures in the *Mālavikāgnimitra*) and the Aihole inscription of AD 634, which mentions him. The tradition that he was the court poet of a legendary Vikramāditya, who inaugurated the Vikrama age in 56 BC, has led some Indian critics especially to place him earlier than Aśvaghoṣa (1st or 2nd century AD). But there is little real evidence here. See D. C. Sircar's note on the Vikrama age on p. 125 of *Age of Imperial Unity,* ed. by Majumdar *et al.*, and compare Majumdar's excursus on the problem pp. 154-57; see also Raychaudhuri, *Political History,* pp. 465-66. Others would like to cite the *Mālavikāgnimitra* as 'proof' that Kālidāsa lived in the 2nd century BC. But by this logic we would date Viśākhadatta to the Mauryan period, except that we are prevented from doing so by the attribution of the fragmentary *Devīcandragupta* to him (see Ch. 5). See the discussions of Krishnamachariar, *History,* pp. 100-113; Upadhyaya, *India in Kālidāsa,* pp. 352-360; and Ingalls, 'Kālidāsa and the Attitudes', p. 15. For my part I favor the period covering possibly the latter part of Candragupta II's reign (who had the epithet Vikramāditya), the reign of his son Kumāragupta (the likely honoree of the *Kumārasambhava*), and at least part of the reign of Skandagupta, who defeated the Huns (like Raghu in *Raghuvaṃśa* 4) c. AD 460. See the inscriptions in Chhabra *et al.* and Fleet, and the historical data in, e.g., *The Classical Age,* ed. Majumdar *et al.*, pp. 18-28, and 35. This would give him a quite plausible lifespan of c. 385-465. Those who say that Kālidāsa's poems do not reflect a consciousness of decline had better reread the last canto of *Raghuvaṃśa.*
2. He also seems to have been the last major figure to have excelled at both drama (*nāṭya, nāṭaka*) and narrative poetic forms (*mahākāvya* and *laghukāvya*). If the *Ṛtusaṃhāra* is his, he also composed a collection of individual lyrics on the seasons. That the critics never quote from the latter, however, is a plausible argument for the spuriousness of the attribution: see the tabulation of citations in Hari Chand, *Kālidāsa et l'art poétique de l'Inde.*
3. I have listed a number of books on Kālidāsa in the bibliography (representing only a small portion of the 'Kalidāsa industry'), all of which praise him lavishly however much they differ in emphasis. Only Indu Shekhar and A.K. Warder in my recollection offer what might be considered faint criticism of his work: see Ch. 8 of *Sanskrit Drama: Origin and Decline* and *Indian Kāvya Literature,* vol. 3, pp. 123-26, 129, 148-49.
4. Introduction to Jones' translation, first published in 1789.
   kāvyeṣu nāṭakaṃ ramyaṃ tatra ramyā śakuntalā/
   tatrāpi ca caturtho'ṅkas tatra ślokacatuṣṭayam/
   yāsyatyadyeti tatrāpi padyaṃ ramyatamaṃ matam/
5. 'Plot Structure', Part I, p. 564.
6. See Section 3 *infra.*
7. 2.10 (9):
   citre niveśya parikalpitasattvayogā
   rūpoccayena mahatā manasā kṛtā nu/

strīratnasṛṣṭir aparā pratibhāti sā me
dhātur vibhutvam anucintya vapuś ca tasyāḥ//

The text of this verse is truly vexed. I am convinced for aesthetic reasons (namely its correspondence to the thematic pattern studied in this essay) that the reading should be *citre*, as in the Devanāgarī and related recensions, and not *cittle*, which seems to be the reading of all the Bengali Mss. (*Citre* is not acknowledged by Pischel in the apparatus, not does Jha list it in any of the related Maithili manuscripts. Kanjilal gives it as a reading in the 'Mithila ed.', apparently Jha's, though I do not find it, and in any case there seems to be no Ms. support for it in his apparatus.) Variables in the rest of the quatrain do not significantly affect the meaning, if *citre* is accepted. Also interesting is the Maithili commentator Śaṅkara's observation that *strīratna* could be interpreted as an epithet of Śrī (see Jha edition, p. 200).

I have throughout this chapter used as my basic text the edition of Pischel, referring also to Kanjilal and Jha (Maithili) and the Godabole edition of the Devanāgarī recension (to which the South Indian recensions are related). In my numbering of verses I have followed Gerow's practice in 'Plot Structure': the number outside brackets is that in Pischel's ed., while that inside the brackets is the equivalent in the Devanāgarī recension of Godabole. An asterisk indicates that the verse does not occur in the Devanāgarī. While favoring the Bengali text (I do not regard the expanded third Act as spurious, though even if it were it is perfectly in keeping with the rest), I have not relied for my interpretation on anything that is not common to all recensions.

8. *Ś* 1.3:

śubhagasalilāvagāhāḥ pāṭalisaṃsargasurabhivanavātāḥ/
pracchāyasulabhanidrā divasāḥ pariṇāmaramaṇīyāḥ//

9. *Ś* 1.4:

kṣaṇacumbitāni bhramarair ūhata sukumārakesaraśikhāni/
avataṃsayanti sadayaṃ śirīṣakusumāni pramadāḥ//

It will be my practice to give Sanskrit equivalents in place of the original Prakrit.

10. *NŚ* 27.16-17:

sā sattvātiśayā jñeyā bhāvayuktā tathaiva ca/
nāṭye samprekṣakair jñeyā nityaṃ siddhis tu daivikī//
na śabdo naiva ca kṣobho cotpātananidarśanam/
sampūrṇatā ca raṅgasya sā siddhir daivikī smṛtā//

The verses are not easy to interpret. *Sattva* may in fact refer to the *sāttvika bhāvas* ('natural emotions'), i.e., the 8 involuntary effects of emotion conveyed by skilled actors: horripilation, perspiration, blushing, paralysis, weeping, breaking of voice, trembling, and fainting. Likewise *bhāva* may refer to the combination of *vibhāvas, anubhāvas,* and *sthāyibhāvas.* These would be markedly present in a play when the focus was on producing *rasa.* the only difference this would make in the translation is in the world 'purity', for which we might substitute something like 'natural effect'. Again, the lack of noise and jostling may refer to what is happening in the drama rather than in the hall. In the description of 'human success' which preceds this, we have the impression of drama concerned with action more than feeling, though the situations indicated have *rasa* correlations (mirth, wonder, heroics). I lean towards the opinion, however, that the reference is to audience behavior and that Kālidāsa's designation of the audience's response to the Actress' song is his rendition of its 'divine success'.

11. *Ś* 1.4.1-1.5:

Sūtradhāra: *ārye/ sādhu gītam/ asau hi rāgāpahṛtacittavṛttir ālikhita iva bhāti sarvato raṅgaḥ/ tat katamaṃ prayogam āśrityainam ārādhayāmaḥ/*

Naṭī: *nanu prathamam evāryeṇājñāptam abhijñānaśakuntalaṃ nāma apūrvaṃ nāṭakam abhinīyatam iti/*

Sūtradhāra: *ārye/ samyag avabodhito'smi/ asmin kṣaṇe vismṛtaṃ khalu mayaitat/ kutaḥ/*

tavāsmi gītarāgeṇa hāriṇā prasabhaṃ hṛtaḥ/
eṣa rājeva duṣyantaḥ sāraṅgeṇātiraṃhasā//

Note especially *rāgāpahṛtacittavṛttir* and compare the classical definition of yoga in *Yogasūtra* 1.2: *Yogaś cittavṛttinirodhaḥ.* For suppression of mental processes Kālidāsa has substituted their captivation by beauty, the difference between ascetic and aesthetic versions of trance. We will see later that the ascetic trance finds its counterpart in Duḥṣanta's imageless oblivion.

12. The very text of the curse strengthens this connection. Durvāsas says that the lover on whom she dotes will fail to remember her 'even though awake, like the careless man who forgets what he has said'. *Ś* 4.1:

vicintayantī yam ananyamānasā
taponidhiṃ vetsi na māṃ upasthitam/
smariṣyati tvāṃ na sa bodhito'pi san
kathāṃ pramattaḥ prathamaṃ kṛtam iva//

(There is no need to take *pramattaḥ* as 'drunk', as many translators have done, though there is probably no harm in it either. Rāghavabhaṭṭa, commentator on the Devanāgarī recension, admits both.) The Stage-Manager is already the paradigm of such a man, having forgotten his announcement of the play, just as Duḥṣanta will have forgotten his pledge to Śakuntalā.

13. See Kunhan Raja, *Kālidāsa,* pp. 142 ff., for a good example of the positive valuation in modern criticism. Kunhan Raja, Mainkar, Bhat, and Sri Aurobindo Ghose are part of a select few who have resisted Tagore's moralizing interpretation.

14. For Śaṅkara (Maithili ed, pp. 167-68) he is *dhīralalita,* for Rāghavabhaṭṭa (Devanāgarī ed., pp. 15-16) a *dhīrodātta* ('steadfast-and-exalted'). The designation will depend on which aspect, amorous or heroic, one chooses to exphasize, for in fact he is both.

15. *Gāndharva* union—a recognized 'marriage' between consenting adults without elders' approval—is a staple of Sanskrit drama. The epic source for *Ś* admittedly leaves the issue morally ambiguous, but the ideal pattern of a romantic relationship in classical Tamil poetry—regarded by Hart as reflecting a Deccani prototype which was also a major influence on *kāvya*—requires clandestine union despite its socially illicit character. See K. V. Zvelebil, *Literary Conventions in Akam Poetry,* and George Hart, *The Poems of Ancient Tamil.* In Act 3 the King will argue dharmic precedent for their sexual union as *gāndharva* marriage, 3.28 (20). Cf. *Manusmṛti* 3.20-26 and *MBh* 1.67.1-14. The *Kāmasūtra* notes that the *gāndharva* form of marriage is the only one which assures happiness: see the whole 5th chapter of book 3 (with its appeal to the example of Śakuntalā).

16. Thus the verses opening Act 3, conventional but obviously meant to be persuasive within the rhetoric established by the conventions, depicting him as the prey of another bowman-hunter, the love-god Kāma.

17. 2.8*:

nirākṛtanimeṣābhir netrapaṅktibhir unmukhaḥ/
navām indukalāṃ lokaḥ kena bhāvena paśyati//

18. 2.11 (10):

anāghrātaṃ puṣpaṃ kisalayam alūnaṃ kararuhair
anāmuktaṃ ratnaṃ madhu navam anāsvāditarasam/
akhaṇḍaṃ puṇyānāṃ phalam iva ca tad rūpam anaghaṃ
na jāne bhoktāraṃ kam iha samupāsthāsyati bhuvi//

The Devanāgarī version has minor variations. *Madhu,* here translated as 'wine', may also be 'honey'. Cf. the cognate 'mead'.

19. In the conventions of Sanskrit poetry this leads inevitably to death if love remains unrequited. See the 'ten stages of love' schema in e.g. *NŚ* 24.160 ff. or *Kāmasūtra* 5.1.5. The lists always vary in detail, though the last two conditions are constants. I cite the version in the *Kāmasūtra:* love by sight (*cakṣuḥprīti*), mental attachment (*manaḥsaṅga*), preoccupation (*saṃkalpotpatti*) sleeplessness (*nidrāccheda*), loss of weight (*tanutā*), indifference to the outer world (*viṣayebhyo vyāvṛtti*), loss of shame (*lajjāpraṇāśa*), madness (*unmāda*), unconsciousness (*mūrcchā*), death (*maraṇa*). The *NŚ* list substitutes 'sickness' (*vyādhi*) for 'madness' in the 8th position, which puts Śakuntalā very close to death. We need hardly mention that the King exemplifies many of these conditions.

20. It is my belief that the Devanāgarī version of the play has truncated this act rather than that the Bengali and related recensions have amplified it.

21. *Ś* 3.36*:

cāruṇā sphuritenāyam aparikṣatakomalaḥ/
pipāsato mamānujñāṃ dadatīva priyādharaḥ//

Cf. Devanāgarī recension 3.21:

aparikṣatakomalasya yāvat kusumasyeva navasya ṣaṭpadena/
adharasya pipāsatā mayā te sadayaṃ sundari gṛhyate rasó' sya//

22. 4.1:

cintayantī yam ananyamānasā
taponidhiṃ vetsi na mām upasthitam/
smariṣyati tvāṃ na sa bodhito'pi san
kathāṃ pramattaḥ prathamaṃ kṛtām iva//

23. 5.8 (5.1):

abhinavamadhulobhabhāvitas tathā paricumbya cūtamañjarīm/
kamalavasatimātranirvṛto madhukara vismṛto'syenāṃ katham//

Again the forgetting theme (*vismṛta*), and the echo (*paricumbya*) of *cumbitāni* in 1.4.

24. 4.19 (4.16):

asmān sādhu vicintya saṃyamadhanān uccaiḥkulaṃ cātmanas
tvayyasyāḥ katham apyabāndhavakṛtāṃ snehapravṛttiṃ ca tām/
sāmānyapratipattipūrvakam iyaṃ dāreṣu dṛśyā tvayā
daivādhīnam ataḥ paraṃ na khalu tat strībandhubhir yācyate//

25. 5.9 (5.2):

ramyāṇi vīkṣya madhurāṃś ca niśamya śabdān
paryutsuko bhavati yat sukhito' pi jantuḥ/
tac cetasā smarati nūnam abodhapūrvaṃ
bhāvasthirāṇi jananāntarasauhṛdāni//

26. *AEAG,* pp. 14, 60.

27. Cf. *DhĀ* 4.4:
    Even conventional situations in poetry
    seem as new with the touch of *rasa*
    as all the trees in spring.
    dṛṣṭapūrvā api hyarthāḥ kāvye rasaparigrahāt/
    sarve navā ivābhānti madhumāsa iva drumāḥ//
28. Plato's *anamnesis*, triggered initially by the experience of the beautiful, was not so different, *mutatis mutandis*.
29. Bloch, *Das Prinzip Hoffnung*. For Eros as the affective glue that binds individuals together in large social networks, see Freud's *Civilization and Its Discontents*. Cf. Marcuse's now guite quaint-seeming *Eros and Civilization*, a kind of paean to the utopian potential of libido.
30. For Duḥṣanta as an Everyman see T. G. Mainkar, *Kālidāsa*, pp. 108-12, 143-7.
31. Treated, to my recollection, only by Dimbeswar Sarma, An *Interpretative Study of Kālidāsa*, pp. 247 ff.
32. They are anticipated in the play by the Stage-Manager's words to the Actress in the Prologue and the terms of the curse, both quoted *supra*.
33. He could also be referring to his state of mind in rejecting her.
34. *yeṣām kāvyānuśīlanābhyāsavaśād viśadībhūte manomukure varṇanīyatanmayībhavanayogyatā te hṛdayasaṃvādabhājah sahṛdayāḥ/ Dhvanyālokalocana*, commentary on *kārikavṛtti* 1.1.
    The image is, of course, common enough in Indian philosophy.
35. The nature-artifice contrast has already been invoked early on in 1.16 (15):
    Such beauty is rare even in the harem.
    If it belongs to this hermit-girl,
    then the cultivated vines of the pleasure garden
    are outdone by the virtues of forest-vines.
    śuddhāntadurlabham idaṃ vapur āśramavāsino yadi janasya/
    dūrīkṛtāḥ khalu guṇair udyānalatā vanalatābhiḥ//
36. This scene is anticipated by an episode towards the end of Act 3 in the Bengali and related recensions. Śakuntalā has broken free of the King's grasp and left the bower, but remains to eavesdrop on him. His soliloquy proves to her that his love is genuine and she finds a pretext to return.
37. Compare her words in the following passages. 6.22. 4*: *dhīram api janaṃ raso vikārayati/*6.24.1-2(6.22.1): *sarvathā vayasya saṃmārjitaṃ tvayā pratyādeśaduḥkhaṃ priyasakhyāḥ śakuntalāyāḥ pratyakṣam eva sakhījanasya/ Rasa*, the vehicle of an illusionary *vikāra* in the hero, is the element that has enabled him to pass this test in front of the invisible examiner.
38. 6.27.1 (6.25.3-4): *sati khalu dīpe vyavadhānadoṣenāndhakāram anubhavati rājarṣiḥ/* It is at this point in the plot that Śakuntalā suffers a diminishment in erotic allure and becomes primarily the mother of the hero's child. (Tagore is right, for all his reductive sentimentality, to underline this transformation of the heroine.) *Vipralambha śṛṅgāra* thus fades into a sense of guilt (a version of *karuṇa*) before male ancestors who demand offspring to perpetuate the *śrāddha* rites. It is only by means of a full analysis of *vīra* and *karuṇa* themes in the play that we would understand this shift and gain insight into the psychology represented by the hero. Here and below I confine myself to sketchy remarks on the subject.
39. See 2.10(9) quoted at the beginning of the chapter.
40. The former category includes such things as an actor's forgetting lines or poor

plot-construction; the latter sabotage by hostile member of the audience and the like, but also accidents such as an attack of ants or a thunderstorm.

41. 1.19 (17):

    The lotus is lovely though wrapped about with moss,
    the moon's spot is pretty though a smudge,
    and this slender girl is so charming in her barken garment:
    What is not an ornament to a graceful form?
    sarasijam anuviddhaṃ śaivalenāpi ramyaṃ
    malinam api himāṃśor lakṣma lakṣmīṃ tanoti/
    iyam adhikamanojñā valkalenāpi tanvī
    kim iva hi madhurṇaṃ maṇḍnaṃ nākṛtīnām//

42. 1.20 (18):

    Her lower lip is red as a shoot,
    her arms are like delicate branches,
    like a blossom her gorgeous youth
    spread throughout her limbs.
    adharaḥ kisalayarāgaḥ komalaviṭapānukāriṇau bahū/
    kusumam iva lobhanīyaṃ yauvanam aṅgeṣu saṃnaddham//

43. 2.11 (10), already quoted *supra*. Note the emphasis on Śakuntalā as aesthetic-erotic object, esp. *rasa* in the 2nd *pāda*.
44. These are actually the 3 requirements for being a poet, but they apply just as much to the *rasika*, as argued in section 2. See J. Nobel, *The Foundations of Indian Poetry*, pp. 43-77, for collected passages.
45. 2.11 (10)+: *tena hi laghu laghu gacchatu bhavān/ mā tāvat sā tapasvinī kasyāpiṅgudītailacikkaṇaśīrṣasya haste nipatiṣyati/*
    (Sanskritized from the Vidūṣaka's Prakrit)
46. See Gerow's reference to a 'good lay', 'Plot structure', Part 1, p. 568.
47. As indicated, for example, by 3.27*, where the King soliloquizes a cynical impatience with Śakuntalā's perceived coquettery. Though this is one of those conventional kāvyic verses that emblematizes a typical or universal sentiment, in its immediate dramatic context it shows the King lacking any appreciation of what Śakuntalā has to lose by yielding to him.
48. The phrase is that of Sudhir Kakar, *The Inner World*, chs. 3 and 4 especially. Kakar's attention to Indian childrearing practices and sensitivity to human dilemmas (particularly his treatment of women) make his more interesting and complex than other psychoanalytic culture-and-personality studies (e.g., Spratt and Carstairs).
49. His mother's little prince and savior. It is interesting to see Śakuntalā as a maiden in distress. Her 'bad fate' (alluded to as soon as her name is mentioned in the play, 1.12+) is, in one reading, the ascetical condition from which the hero comes to rescue her. Act 3 invokes the theme of her impending death (through love-sickness), a prospect which sets her friends thinking about how they can engineer an occasion for the two lovers to be alone. We can even see the fight with demons (off-stage after Acts 2 and 3) as an echo of dragon-killing or the like. And, as Northrop Frye suggests for the Andromeda-type myth that he sees informing all such tales (*Anatomy of Criticism*, ch. 3), the demonic presence is an oedipal substitution for the weakened father (here Kaṇva). The real dragon of this tale, however, is the angry ascetic Durvāsas, who embodies the negative paternal aspect and whom the hero confronts only indirectly in the abortive shouting-match with Śārṅgarava

and Śaradvata in Act 5: see the next section.

50. In fact, though, it may be that the wife—rarely married for love as in poetry—never achieves this position even in fantasy. The magical feminine aura is retained exclusively by the mother, while the explicitly erotic ideal is lived either fleetingly with courtesans or through poetry or even religion. See again Kakar, *Inner World*, chs. 3 and 4.
51. See the first verse quoted in this chapter, which singles out the 4th Act of the play as the epitome of all *kāvya.* Thus the problem we are addressing here is, in Gerow's apt phrase, 'at the center of the Indian poetic problem'.
52. We study this question, however, in Ch. 5 in relation to Cāṇakya's authorial role.
53. I doubt whether there is any play in the Sanskrit corpus, or any *kāvya*, whose opening is so pregnant with thematic implications for the rest of the work.
54. The other three major royal sports are love, gambling, and drinking: all a legacy from the heroic period.
55. 1.10*-11 (10):

bho bho rājan/ āśramamṛgaḥ khalvayam/
na khalu na khalu bāṇaḥ saṃnipātyo'yam asmin
mṛduni mṛgaśarīre puṣparāśāv ivāgnih/
kva bata hariṇakānāṃ jīvitaṃ cātilolaṃ
kva ca niśitanipātāḥ sārapuṅkhāḥ śarās te//
tad āśu kṛtasaṃdhānaṃ pratisaṃhara sāyakam/
ārtatrāṇāya vaḥ śastraṃ na prahartum anāgasi//

56. For Vedic and Epic-Purāṇic references to this and the earlier incest-myth, as well as to secondary literature, see Wendy Doniger O'Flaherty, *Hindu Myths*, pp. 25-26, 29-31, 117-25, 313-14, 323-25. Also O'Flaherty, *Śiva: The Erotic Ascetic*, pp. 30, 128-30, and *passim.*
57. Cf. Freud's primal-horde supposition, in which the primordial father is murdered by his sons (or, in literary remembrance, a hero who represents their interests) in order to supplant their tyrannical power and enjoy the females that had been under his exclusive control: *Totem and Taboo*, Part 4.
58. See the discussion of Śrī symbolism in section 2 above.
59. The disturbance at the end of Act 1—his elephants wreaking off-stage havoc in the paradisal grove—incidentally shows us that he has not truly relinquished the phallic role in which he entered the play, but only modified it to avoid overt confrontation with ascetical authority.
60. 2.7:

śamapradhāneṣu tapovaneṣu gūḍhaṃ hi dāhātmakam asti tejaḥ/
sparśānukūlā api sūryakāntās te hyanyatejobhibhavād dahanti//

The word *tejas* here refers both to the power inherent in Kings—often translated as 'majesty'—and the stored power of asceticism, more usually called *tapas.* The king's *tejas*, despite the analogy (in which he stands in the place of the sun), is no match for ascetical energy, as we know from numerous sources. Another significant verse expressing fear is 3.2, where the expression *tapaso vīryam* is used ('the virile power of asceticism) to indicate the paternal authority that holds Śakuntalā at arm's length from him. The oedipal implications seem unavoidable.

61. Note the false confidence of 1.27(23), whose imagery directly anticipates the sunstone:

Be bold, my heart, for now all doubt is resolved.

What you thought was fire is a jewel you may hold in your hand.
bhava hṛdaya sābhilāṣaṃ samprati saṃdehanirṇayo jātaḥ/
āśaṅkase yad agniṃ tad idaṃ sparśakṣamaṃ ratnam//

The reference is to Śakuntalā. The King had feared that she was a Brahmin, which would have made her above his station for marriage; but he has just learned that her real father was Viśvāmitra, a Kṣatriya ascetic who had not attained Brahminhood at the time Śakuntalā was conceived. The King's hopes rise and fall several times in the course of the first three Acts. The height of presumption seems to be reached at the end of Acts 2 and 3, when, besought by the ascetics, he is able to step into his heroic role as protector of sacrifice against demonic hordes. The ascetics implore him specifically 'because our father is absent' (*kulapater asāṃnidhyād,* 2.16[15]+). This sign of paternal impotence makes it seem plausible that he is the romantic Perseus-figure who will rescue Śakuntalā-Andromeda from the dragon: see note 49. Śakuntalā has indeed been introduced to us as a maiden-in-distress, as it were, whose father sought to free her from a 'bad fate' (*daivam asyāḥ pratikūlaṃ śamayitum somatīrthaṃ gataḥ,* 1.12+). In Act 3, as she lies near death (conventionally the final stage of lovesickness) on her couch, the hero is besought by her friends to rescue her. Another convolution comes at the beginning of Act 3 in with allusions to the fieriness of the love-god's arrows. Kāmadeva is thus the play's third archer, behind the King (entrance to Act 1) and Śiva (disrupter of sacrifice). We easily see the King in Kāmadeva's role in bringing the disturbance of desire to the *āśrama*, but here in Act 3 it is the King who is the victim. This points again to the paradoxical nature of the hermitage, whose internal heat is not only *tapas* (cf. the sunstone symbol) but *kāma*; and the proof of this is its sensual allure which comes to breathtaking focus in Śakuntalā's nubility (cf. the example cited from the *Matsya Purāṇa* in O'Flaherty, *Śiva*, p. 169). The King has fallen under the spell of this primordial paradise. The incest pattern in the mythical background is a way of symbolizing the withholding of the heat of female desire under paternal protection. This is especially valid in a culture in which ascetics/sages (who are the dharmic fathers) are regarded as sexually super-potent. The conflation of *kāma* and *tapas* is basic to Indian thought, as in the Vedic creation hymn *ṚV* 10.129. Cf. O'Flaherty, *Śiva*, throughout, for their interchangeability, esp. ch. 5.

62. Just after the curse is uttered Śakuntalā's two companions speak of Durvāsas' ascetical anger (*kopa*, typically identified with *tapas*) as the source of the curse, saying gnomically, 'what other than fire has the power to burn? (*ko'nyo hutavahād dagdhuṃ prabhavati,* 4.1+, adding that the sage is 'anger personified' (*śarīrīva kopaḥ*)). Shortly thereafter, believing that they possess the antidote to the curse, they agree not to tell Śakuntalā of her mishap, saying it would be like pouring hot water on a tender jasmine plant (*kas tāvad uṣṇodakena navamālikāṃ siñcati*).

63. 5.11 (10):
mahābhāgaḥ kāmaṃ narapatir abhinnasthitir asau
na kaścid varṇānām apatham apakṛṣṭo'pi bhajate/
tathāpīdaṃ śaśvatparicitaviviktena manasā
janākīrṇaṃ manye hutavahaparītaṃ gṛham iva//

64. See note 15. Although Tagore frequently deplored the dour Brahmanical restraints on romantic love in his other writing, in his reading of Ś he is on the side of the sages.

65. There is little difference between the pseudo-demon (actually Indra's charioteer, Mātali) who attacks the Vidūṣaka and the cosmic enemies of the gods in this respect. The point is the heroic demonstration of loyalty to the dharmic system.
66. We should not overlook the continued menace of the Father's power—cf. the grotesque asceticism of *Ś* 7.11.
67. For this pivotal status I quote note 27 of Gerow, 'Plot-structure', Part 1, p. 572:

    Sanna Deutsch [in an unpublished paper] suggests another interpretation of the plot of the Śakuntalā based on the acts (seven) rather than the *saṃdhis* (five). It has much to recommend it .... She notes particularly the *parallelisms* of acts 1 and 7 [entrance into an enchanted hermitage approached via chariot], 2 and 6 (penance grove/pleasure grove turned into its other [also musings with the Vidūṣaka]), 3 and 5 (seduction and rejection; forest and city): which parallelisms serve to highlight the centrality of the fourth act: the transition and parting.

68. 4.6

    duḥṣantenāhitaṃ tejo dadhānāṃ bhūtaye bhuvaḥ/
    avehi tanayāṃ brahmann agnigarbhāṃ śamīm iva//

69. *vatse diṣṭyā dhūmoparuddhadṛṣṭer api yajamānasya pāvakasya mukha eva nipatitāhutiḥ/* (Sanskritized from the Prakrit)
70. The circumambulation of the fire is a feature of the Hindu wedding ritual: Kane, *HDS* 2.1. pp. 528 ff.
71. There is very little that the Brāhmaṇa texts (including parts of the Upaniṣads) do not bring into the sacrificial formula. The appeal of ritual is its symbolic all-inclusiveness as the quintessential act (*karma*). In Tantra the same mentality, finding the Vedic symbols obsolete, veers off into magic.
72. 7.29:

    diṣṭyā śakuntalā sādhvī sadapatyam idaṃ bhavān/
    śraddhā vittaṃ vidhiś ceti tritayaṃ tat samāgatam/

    Notice the inclusiveness in the use of grammatically masculine, feminine, and neuter words for the family members in both actual and symbolical personae. The word *vidhi* (which I have translated as 'order') has ritual significance: it is any ritual prescription, but metonymically ritual (sacrifice) *en masse*. It is also, significantly, one of the typical words for 'Fate', as the '(fore)ordained'. In the ritual conception there is no distinction between sacrificial formula and cosmic order. Thus, the *rasika*, having tried to replace the Father in Acts 2 and 3, now symbolically personifies the Father's ritual order, which is *dharma*, while Śakuntalā is its/his inspiration, and the child is the resultant material well-being. For a study of *śraddhā* as used in various religious texts see K. L. Seshagiri Rao, *The Concept of Śraddhā*.

73. 7.11:

    valmīkārdhanimagnamūrtir uragatvagbrahmasūtrāntaraḥ
    kaṇṭhe jīrṇalatāpratānavalayenātyantasaṃpīḍitaḥ/
    aṃsavyāpi śakuntanīḍanicitaṃ bibhraj jaṭāmaṇḍalaṃ
    yatra sthāṇur ivācalo munir asāv abhyarkabimbaṃ sthitaḥ//

74. *śakuntanīḍanicitaṃ bibhraj jaṭāmaṇḍalam. śakunta* is 'bird'. The other passage punning *śakunta* with *śakuntalā* is 7+: the child Bharata mistakes the word for his mother's name.
75. Indian thought, by designating *kāma* as the third *puruṣārtha*, has always recognized that Desire is the basis of all pleasure.

CHAPTER 3

Dākṣiṇya and *Rasa* in the *Vikramorvaśīya*

priyavacanaśato'pi yoṣitāṃ dayitajanānunayo rasād ṛte/
praviśati hṛdayaṃ na tadvidāṃ maṇir iva kṛtrimarāga yojitaḥ//

If a lover's conciliation is without *rasa,* though it contain hundred sweet words, it will not enter a woman's heart.
For women are connoisseurs of rasa, like jewellers, who cannot be fooled by an artificially colored gem.

This verse comes at the end of the 2nd Act of Kālidāsa's *Vikramorvaśīya* (hereafter *V*).[1] It is spoken by the royal hero Purūravas moments after his wife Auśīnarī has left the scene in a jealous pique, refusing to accept his *anunaya,* his attempt at conciliation. Auśīnarī had confronted him with evidence of his affair with the *apsaras* Urvaśī, a love-verse that the nymph had inscribed on a piece of birch-bark. Urvaśī had by then already left the lovely palace garden where she had appeared to him beyond his hopes (for how can a mortal expect a liaison with a divinity?), called back to Indra's palace to act the principal role in a play called *Lakṣmī's Svayaṃvara.*[2] The King had entrusted the piece of bark to the Vidūṣaka's safekeeping, but of course the latter—true to his name of 'spoiler'[3]—had dropped it, leaving it to be discovered by Auśīnarī and her maid. At first the hero tries to deny that the inscribed message has anything to do with him, but this is hardly convincing. Furthermore, the Vidūṣaka's attempts at camouflage only succeed in underscoring his friend's guilt. But 'No', Auśīnarī responds, 'you haven't transgressed. It is I who transgress with my disagreeable presence. I'll go!' With this she plays her trump card, and Purūravas can only play his. He admits his guilt, but only formulaically, only by invoking a gallant convention: he is and has always been her slave, and when the mistress is angry then surely the slave is guilty.[4] Saying this, he falls at her feet, but she turns her back on him and leaves. The Vidūṣaka remarks that this is all to his favor since he will no longer have to camouflage his affair, but Purūravas rejects this callous notion. His respect (*bahumāna*) for Auśīnarī is genuine. He does not want to hurt her and regrets that his gallantry cannot soothe her. Thus he utters the lines I have quoted above.

The king's poetic reflection, with the situation it so poignantly crystalizes, will concern us in this chapter for a number of reasons. Most obviously, perhaps, it opens up a perspective on what we might call the sociology of the harem, particularly with respect to the dilemma of the 'replaced woman'. That theme (the replaced woman) appears in all of Kālidāsa's plays, in Bhāsa's *Svapnavāsavadattā* (*SV*), and in many other plays with which we are not concerned; it is, in fact, one of the conventional subjects of *kāvya*. Thus, in the second place, the verse helps us appreciate the complex ethos of courtly love in the Indian context. A playful aristocratic etiquette (*dākṣiṇya*) must exist side by side with an ideal emotional intensity (*rasa*) which, however, exists only in a certain tension with it. Finally, and to me most interestingly, as we meditate on the verse's overtones (its *dhvani*), we glimpse the inextricable interconnection between this ethos and the poetics of *rasa*. I shall treat these three dimensions one at a time, as much as that is possible, for they can be separated only artificially. In conclusion, I shall raise questions about the psychological character of the true feeling or longing that is portrayed in *V* and other plays.

The Replaced Woman

Auśīnarī's dilemma is that, faced with sexual loss, she can do nothing about it except either withdraw herself, keeping a sarcastic and hurt silence, or submit to her fate. The only dignified course, however, is submission. As Irāvatī remarks in the 4th Act of the *Mālavikāgnimitra* (*M*), by continuing to be a *caṇḍī* or angry mistress, when she no longer has any true claim on her husband's erotic interest, a woman only makes herself ridiculous. This is not Greek tragedy with *femmes fatales* like Medea, Clytemnaestra, and Phaedra, women who suffer sexual humiliation with violent outbursts of vengeful resentment. Auśīnarī, therefore, makes a ritual act of accepting her husband's polygyny in Act 3, and it is telling that even in these circumstances the hero refuses to admit that her suspicions are justified: he still maintains the courteous fiction of devotion to her alone.[5] Urvaśī, who happens to be witnessing the scene in state of invisibility, is even taken in by his protestations, prompting her companion Citralekhā to chide her for her naivity: 'O you naive girl, urbane men (*nāgarikas*) are especially courtly (*dakṣiṇa*) when they have transferred their love to other women!'[6] Auśīnarī, however, is beyond deception. As verse 2.21 states it, like all women she is a connoisseur of *rasa* or *rāga*. She knows the difference between gallantry and passion. Henceforth her marital satisfactions will be limited to those connected with her status in the royal family and in society at large. She will be, we are to assume, like Dhāriṇī in the *Mālavikāgnimitra*, the chief wife in the household, enjoying the power and prestige that goes with that position (though, unlike Dhāriṇī, Auśīnarī has no male child to give her a sense of fulfilment).

One reason she cannot seriously resist her eclipse is more symbolic than psychological or sociological. The new beloved is the embodiment of Śrī, the sexual auspiciousness that comes like the magic of spring. The romantic heroine in *kāvya* is always metaphorically connected with flowering vegetation and always suggests the luxuriant fertility of nature upon which the prosperity of kingdoms is based. Thus it is essential for the king to have the woman who radiates such an auspiciousness, for it is only by virtue of his marriage to Śrī that any king can rule successfully. In other words, there is an ideological justification for polygyny that is rooted in Indian religious conceptions (the worship of Śrī goes back at least to the late Vedic period and probably has a more ancient popular base).[7] A queen who put up major resistance to a king's new passion would, symbolically, be attempting to exclude a new infusion of divine auspiciousness from the realm. The king must always be open to the renewing magic of the Radiant Female. It is hard to guess the extent to which the Śrī-idea sanctioned royal promiscuity in real life, but in poetry there can be no doubt of its importance.

But by the same logic the heroine is also vulnerable. Presently she enjoys her role as the vehicle of an overpowering sexual magic, but how long can this last? Irāvatī in *M* was once in the position of Mālavikā, the play's heroine. In fact, her motive for going to the Ocean room in the 4th Act of that play is to revisit the past, for there is a mural there which depicts her as the king's favorite. But, encountering the actual Mālavikā, her replacement, there instead, she must learn to become a Dhāriṇī, i.e., a wife who may think no more of being a sexual favorite. Part of what makes the *Śakuntalā* (*Ś*) so poignant is the establishment of the perspective of sexual loss for the heroine. The song that is sung offstage by one of Duḥṣanta's wives early in Act 5, the song chiding him in the symbolic language of *dhvani* poetics for his roving erotic interests, can not fail to remind the audience of the imminent rejection of Śakuntalā. We feel the song as if it were sung for Śakuntalā rather than about her (who is in the song's thematics the new love that has taken him away from the old). In the *SV*, likewise, Vāsavadattā, against whose erotic magic King Udayana can set only his *bahumāna* (respect) for the hapless Padmāvatī, finds herself nevertheless provoked to jealous anger by the mention of one of her husband's earlier flirtations with a maidservant. (This occurs, significantly, in the middle of the poignant dream scene of Act 5.) And, by the time Harṣa took up the Vāśavadattā story, her hour had already passed.[8]

The woman's position as beloved is never secure, since sexual magic is by nature a matter of come-and-go inspiration. In writing *V* Kālidāsa was trying, on one level at least, to sentimentalize the old myth of the divine female who makes her-self inaccessible to the mortal she had once favored.[9] In his version Urvaśī is the deeply devoted beloved whose involuntary absence hurts her as much as it does Purūravas. Nevertheless, if we look closely at the text, we see that the pathetic separation of Act 4 is triggered by sexual jealousy. Urvaśī had come upon Purūravas absorbedly watching another woman, a Vidyādharī (a kind of demi-divinity of lower status than an *apsaras*), from his hidden vantage, as she amused herself on a river sandbank. Even a goddess is not immune to the stinging effect of a lover's roving eye. The text exonerates Purūravas' behavior by portraying Urvaśī's reaction as excessive,[10] but it is not difficult to see her anger and the resulting absence as motivated by a desire to punish him for entertaining the thought of replacing her in his desire.

The difference between the power of Urvaśī and the power of Auśīnarī is what the king has called *rasa*. When Auśīnarī absents herself as the *caṇḍī* she merely allows him greater scope for his interest in Urvaśī. He is sorry to have hurt her feelings, but he is also eager to throw himself into his new affair. When Urvaśī goes, however, he is drained of life and wanders about frantically seeking her. He has no substitute *rasa* to defend him against the loss. Or, rather, the sweetness of *saṃbhoga śṛṅgāra* has turned to the anxiety of *vipralambha,* the intensity of idyllic happiness has shifted to that of frenetic longing without warning. When *rasa* is involved, there is no equanimity. Urvaśī has, and exercises, the power to hurt him by withholding herself. She takes the intoxication of the Śrī-presence out of his life. The normally gardenlike atmosphere of the woodland grove in *kāvya* becomes Act 4's mockingly indifferent, phantasmagoric forest. The normal pathetic fallacy has collapsed, leaving only the echoes of a possible madness, as the hero whom we are wont to think of as the privileged child of nature, hub of the dhārmic wheel, the cynosure of all eyes, suddenly becomes a desperate loner in a wilderness that knows no charismatic focus. But what is the cost to Urvaśī? If he must trek through a kind of inferno, she inhabits a limbo. She can do nothing but patiently wait for him to find her, deprived of splendor and even of motion (she has been transformed into a flowerless vine) until he finds and embraces her. She has, indeed, the satisfaction of having witnessed his dismay and knowing that she is the *sine qua non* of his mental stability, but she has no efficacy apart from that. As Kālidāsa has rewritten the myth, the goddess needs the mortal husband in order to retain her aura. Like Śakuntalā in her limbo without Duḥṣanta, Urvaśī is not in the real world without Purūravas.

One way to see Kālidāsa's version of the story, then, is as woman's fantasy of retaining the Śrī-principle within herself, thus holding on to her sexual power and enjoyment, her dominance over a charismatic lover's imagination.[11] For, as we see Purūravas in the 5th Act, he is fully chastened, ready even to isolate himself in the forest again rather than face life in the capital without her. The specter of the Vidyādharī has evaporated, and Urvaśī is comfortable in her ascendancy. She has tamed her lover by means of the threat of disappearance, a theme that is prominent in the 5th Act itself. She is able to retain his devotion (and stop the philandering cycle) by structuring the shadow of absence into their relationship, although it is the privilege of the divine wife alone to withdraw with impunity. But the crucial ingredient is *rasa.* The sexual magic has to be there in the first place. Auśīnarī, the replaced woman, is no longer able to excite *rasa* in her husband: all she gets is a show of *dākṣiṇya,* i.e., a polished ritual that presents only the facade of passion. Urvaśī has it, and resorts to symbolic suicide to retain it.

Courtly Love

In the preceding section I mentioned briefly the scene in which Auśīnarī formally renounces her jealousy, while Purūravas maintains the gallant pretence of a slave's devotion to her alone. His elegant language is so convincing, so full of aplomb and apparent feeling, that it fools the eavesdropping heroine Urvaśī, who is then scolded for her childishness by her companion. This is typical *nāgarika* behavior, she is told: all polite society behaves this way. In *M* something similar occurs. Though she herself was not taken in by the hero Agnimitra's protestations of true devotion to Irāvatī, Mālavikā pointedly chides the king for his apparently cowardly behavior before his importunate wife. It is the 4th Act, and Agnimitra is trying to coax Mālavikā into compliance with his desire now that they are alone in the Ocean room, pleading with her not to be afraid of physical love. She reminds him that she just emerged from underground imprisonment because of their last rendezvous, and that he had hardly been her defender when Irāvatī had caught them together earlier (Act 3). Instead of apologizing, however, Agnimitra justifies his attempt to conciliate Irāvatī, even though he had to deny his love for Mālavikā in the process. His justification consists of a boast in his family's tradition of courtly refinement (*dākṣiṇya*):

> *Dāksiṇya,* my gourd-lipped lady, is the family vow of the Baimbikas,
> Nevertheless, long-eyed one, my very life hangs on the hope of your love.[12]

And, indeed, within a few minutes, when Irāvatī bursts again onto the scene, he will pretend distinterest in Mālavikā a second time in her very presence (4.16-7).

The hero—whether Agnimitra or Purūravas—is not ashamed of lying to a woman about his love for her, even in his beloved's presence. Western critics and many modern Indian ones have found this contemptible, but it was clearly not perceived as such by the contemporary audience of Sanskrit drama. In fact, this kind of behavior defined the hero as a *dakṣiṇa* (gallant) lover, rather than simply a *śaṭha* or *dhṛṣṭa.*[13] The latter two are, respectively, the secret deceiver and the man who callously disregards his wife's feelings. The distinction between the *dakṣiṇa* and *śaṭha* heroes is, in a sense, a matter of point of view. To Irāvatī, for instance, who is unimpressed by Agnimitra's *dākṣiṇya*, he is merely a *śaṭha* (*M* 3.19.43-4), but the audience, at least, is expected to admire his gallantry. We might put it best this way: when a *śaṭha* is detected, he can either prove himself to be a *dakṣiṇa* or a *dhṛṣṭa* hero. We would have no respect for the latter. He would show that he is really unqualified to play the game of courtly love, unworthy of the sophisticated ethos that *kāvya* loves to depict and of which *kāvya* is, in fact, an essential part.[14] The social atmosphere depicted in *kāvya* is one of graceful charm and refinement. It is social intercourse raised to the level of an art. Delightful conversation is virtually an obligation, yet it remains a form of play. This is the world of aristocratic *līlā*, where one revels in formal elegance because it marks one's freedom from the material vulgarities of cause and effect.[15] The rules of this aristocratic game are exactly homologous with the rules of the refined tongue (courtly Sanskrit), where, in *kāvya*, one constantly imbibes the spirit of detached playfulness in a formal elegance that never surrenders its distance even in the portrayal of the most poignant emotion.[16]

The art of social intercourse is not without its problems for lovers, however. Delicacy requires the hero to speak falsely when he no longer feels love for his wife. He has to retain the appearance of *rasa* (what in poetics is known as *rasābhāsa*) even though he does not feel it. Perhaps, though, it would be more accurate to say that what he feels is a watered down version of *rasa*: not sexual *śṛṅgāra* but a sort of friendship, an esteem (*bahumāna*), that has no formal place in the early versions of the *rasa-bhāva* schema.[17] And, besides this, there could be no charm in the etiquette of gallantry if it were not at heart infused with passion, the passion for graceful speech and manners it nothing else. But, then, what happens to the value of truth, and how is it communicated? Truth would seem to be wholly engulfed in the need to maintain the charming pose. The lines I have quoted at the beginning of this chapter give us the answer. Women *know*, they are connoisseurs of true emotion, they cannot really be fooled. Truth is communicated intangibly, by overtone or suggestion (*dhvani*), just as genuine emotion (*rasa*) is communicated in poetry. There is something beyond language itself that distinguishes verses such as those which Purūravas uses to conciliate Auśīnarī and those which—in the same imagery and turns of phrase—testify to his vital dependency on Urvaśī. In other words, every woman is a *rasikā* or *sahṛdayā*, a practiced receiver of elegant poetic messages who can distinguish the real thing from its imitation.

But a certain problem remains. Urvaśī was initially misled when she overheard Purūravas conciliating his wife. Not only that, she was unable to tell that his interest in the Vidyādharī girl was a mere trifle (what the text would overtly have us believe). Her passion makes her jealous and skittish. If the truth of an elegant statement is reduced to its implicit emotional value, then it is always subject to misinterpretation, for the recipient cannot fail to be emotionally involved in its meaning. Urvaśī has something at stake in the message she is trying to hear in Purūravas' words and actions. If we were to carry our analogy with poetics a little further, we would be led to say that a person in love cannot really be a *rasika*, i.e., cannot really determine the presence of *rasa* in an elegant statement of devotion. Paradoxically, only someone who can afford to keep a certain distance can be a connoisseur of emotion. There has to be a certain aesthetic detachment in the observer.

Auśīnarī already has that distance whether she likes it or not. In recognizing the artificiality or lack of genuine *rasa* in her husband's *anunaya*, she is merely acknowledging an already existing gap between the two of them. Urvaśī does not have that distance, but in sense this is just what she achieves by withdrawing from her lover in Act 4. The effect of Urvaśī's absence in Act 4 is to put Purūravas on stage to perform a pathetic mime for her benefit. All the while, the text tells us, she watches him from her invisible position in the shrubbery that forms a background to his performance. She has merged in with the background of action, becoming a secret watcher, part of an undefined sentience that gives meaning to the hero's tragic mime. She has become one of us, in other words, a member of the audience, whose task it is to judge the *rasa* value of the performance. If Purūravas convinces us, he convinces her as well. And, of course, he does convince; his performance is an aesthetic success. Urvaśī, the *rasikā*, has found the antidote to anxiety in an aesthetic distance whose fundamental purpose is to verify emotional truth. And Purūravas, the *nāyaka*, by virtue of his convincing performance before the *nāyikā* who has become his audience, is able to communicate a sincerity that is beyond the capacity of poetic language and all manneristic conventions.

The important point here is that in the courtly ethos of *kāvya* characters are so adept at taking the elegant pose and making the charming statement that they cannot really be sure of each other's emotional investment in the pose or statement. And what they do to correct the situation is not to cut through the formalism of speech and insist on direct confession. This would be altogether foreign to the manneristic spirit of *kāvya.* Rather they accentuate aesthetic distance by becoming observers of each other in private. Thus the countless occasions in drama when one character eavesdrops on another from the bushes, etc. It is in this way that Agnimitra in *M* finds out that Mālavikā really loves him. It is in this way that Duḥṣanta learns of Śakuntalā's passion and that Śakuntalā's proxy Miśrakeśī or Sānumatī (depending on your recension) tests the truth of Duḥṣanta's sentiment in Act 6 of *Ś.* It is only by observing another's behavior in private that one can determine the true presence of *rasa* in his or her disposition. One has to put the other on stage and make him or her perform.

So far we have looked at the 4th Act of V primarily from Urvaśī's psychological point of view, but it works just as well, perhaps better in some ways, from the hero's. Purūravas is in a position where he knows words alone will not suffice. Nor will the usual *anunaya* practice of *nipatana* (falling at he beloved's feet). These are standard devices which need signify no more than *bahumāna,* as we have seen. How can Purūravas show that when he falls at Urvaśī's feet his performance is full of *rasa* and not just an artful show of good grace and charismatic charm? He has to put her in the audience and become an actor in the performance of a tragic episode, showing that he cannot live without her, that she is destroying him by staying away, that her anger is unreasonable, etc. She hears him and grants her favor.[18] It is significant that her first words to him, when she emerges from her limbo, show *her* begging *his* forgiveness.[19] He has succeeded in making her feel that she feel has caused him unnecessary suffering, that she—not he—has transgressed. By exciting pity (*karuṇa rasa*), both in the audience and in the beloved herself, the hero establishes his authenticity as a lover.

It is in this way that the hero of *kāvya* can be simultaneously a virtuoso player of the sophisticated courtly game and a childlike innocent who wears his heart on his sleeve. We admire his aplomb, his faultless command of *dākṣiṇya,* his charm in the *līlā* of flirtation, yet we love and pity him for his emotional intensity, his sincerity, his sorrow. The delicacy of the balance he must maintain can perhaps best be shown by reference to Udayana's masterful performance in the 4th Act of *SV.*

Udayana is in the position of having to please two wives, both of whom have an active claim on his affections. Padmāvatī is no Auśīnarī or Irāvatī. There is nothing passé about her. She is, rather, a newly-wed touchingly in love with her husband, and we in the audience share her perspective of hopeful joy in her passage from maidenhood to marriage. But in the space of one dramatic scene she reaches a maturity far beyond her years, for she witnesses from a secret vantage her husband's confession of deeper love for another woman, Vāsavadattā, who is supposedly dead but is actually standing beside her. The emotional complexity of this scene is perhaps unmatched in all of *kāvya.* We feel simultaneously elated for Vāsavadattā (who has weathered the shock of seeing herself apparently replaced by a woman for whom she feels only bond of sympathy and sisterly affection) and sorry and even afraid for Padmāvatī. We feel also a certain comic exhilaration, for the scene in which Udayana makes his confession is one in which he and the Vidūṣaka have been bantering about their favorite queen. We also feel the poignancy of the moment for Udayana himself, who has almost succeeded in overcoming his feeling of loss when the game of pretend gets carried too far. He loses himself in the illusion of Vāsavadatttā's presence, only to be rudely awakened to the truth of her absence. And all the while we know that what he takes to be illusion is the truth after all.

When Udayana makes his confession of spellbound love for the ostensibly dead Vasavadattā and only affectionate *bahumāna* for his new young wife Padmāvatī,[20] the latter's maidservant feels outrage in her mistress's behalf. She accuses the king of *adākṣiṇya.* We are in a position to know precisely what she means, since we have already observed that the mark of *dākṣiṇya* is the graceful lie, the pretence of *rasa,* the care never to admit to a woman that one feels only *bahumāna* or sympathetic respect. And here the hero has—unwittingly to be sure—violated that code. In the need to convince the principal heroine that he loves her alone (by putting her in the audience and performing before her) he has had to finesse the *dākṣiṇya* imperative. But, of course, the fact that he makes this confession in private and with obvious distress makes him succeed on both counts. Vāsavadattā, like Urvaśī, can only forgive him for his interest in another woman, and Padmāvatī cannot second her servant's judgment. Indeed, she displays great tact in veiling her private pain with an elegant pretence: she says that his words have shown perfect *dākṣiṇya* with regard to his deceased wife. She means that he would have transgressed the code with regard to Vāsavadattā if he had said he did not love her alone, since this is the required fiction. We, and Vāsavadattā with us, know that she herself does not believe this, that it is her dignity and generosity of spirit that induce her to make such a statement. And later, when she comforts Udayana as he maintains the fiction that his tears are caused by wind-blown pollen, we react with an ironic understanding that belongs essentially to her. By contrast, the hero seems hopelessly naive when he confides to us that he can not tell her the truth because women are by nature frail.

Yet our ironic understanding in no way undercuts the hero's effectiveness. He is able to be polygynous and yet make us believe that his heart is essentially monogynous,[21] and he can do this without alienating the other woman in us (i.e., ourselves when we take her part). In the case of Purūravas and Agnimitra in their respective dramas the alienation of Auśīnarī and Irāvatī is temporary; Udayana shows the further virtuosity of managing not to alienate Padmāvatī at all. What had drawn her to him in the first place was his romantic devotion to his former wife.[22] If he were to forget Vāsavadattā as soon as he married Padmāvatī, he would seem shallow to both women and to every *rasika* in the audience, who has judged him a sympathetic romantic hero precisely as Padmāvatī and Vāsavadattā have done. Consequently, the *dākṣiṇya* he shows to Padmāvatī, when he speaks of pollen in his eyes, seems to her a *noble* pretence, an attempt to cover up his pain and save her feelings. It is a tactic she now uses herself. The truth remains a secret, however, a matter of the hidden observation of true emotion (*rasa*). On the overt level of social relations everything is nobel pretence: *dākṣiṇya. Rasa* has been communicated covertly, the two heroines becoming audience to the hero's pathetic mime. We sense that in this ethos there is a great faith in aesthetic reception of underlying emotion. The hero can be sure in displaying himself before the hidden observer that he will be understood and loved. I do not mean to say that he is represented as thinking this consciously, but it is an implicit assumption of the whole emotional constellation that is represented in his behavior. He is playing to an audience, and the stakes are understanding and indulgence.

The Aesthetics of *Dākṣiṇya* and *Rasa*

If we have not been able to avoid using aesthetic terminology in treating the courtly ethos, it is precisely because aesthetics is an essential part of the way the fictive characters within this ethos act, think, and feel. Udayana and Purūravas win their beloveds and their 'replaced women' over to themselves because they are able to take the poses and speak the words that evoke a *rasa* response. They also win us in the audience by the same means. This is partly because the ethos depicted within *kāvya* is largely an idealized version of the ethos within which *kāvya* itself is situated and of which it is an important part. Does not Kālidāsa make it very clear in the Prologue of *V* that the audience belongs to polite society, when he appeals to their sense of *dākṣiṇya* and *bahumāna* by name?

> Hear with attentive minds this play of Kālidāsa,
> either through the courtesy that one shows to friends,
> or out of respect for the hero of a noble table.[23]

The modest appeal also assumes, however, the capacity for sympathy (*sahṛdayatva*) or emotional responsiveness that marks the *rasika* as distinct from all other persons. It assumes, then, that both in manner and in emotional disposition the *rasika* spectator is very much like the characters within the play.

What this in turn suggests, therefore, is that it is artificial to separate aesthetic questions from thematic ones when dealing with Indian poetics. In other words, we should ignore neither the insights that *kāvya* itself gives us into the psychology of the *rasika* nor the bearing this has on the question of aesthetic taste. It is a standard practice in the various hand-books of Sanskrit literature to characterize the *rasika* on the one hand as an elegant fop, whether a courtier or one of the urban elite (*nāgarika*), and yet on the other a highly serious aesthetician alert to every linguistic nuance and ever ready to be transported to quasi-mystical heights of emotional detachment. In the former case the thematics of *kāvya*, in its dominant concern with the erotic, is trivialized; in the latter it is too easily ignored. What I think we need to see is that the *rasika* whom these plays assume as their ideal recipient is neither more superficial nor more unworldly than the *nāyaka* who is himself an idealized *rasika*, i.e., the *rasika* projected into a mythic frame. The courtly ethos is an ideal that includes a larger segment of society than the court itself or even the urban *goṣṭhī*. It also penetrates into the family library. It is a spirit of elegance and sentimental conviction modeled on courtly behavior rather than an exclusively courtly phenomenon. And as we have seen in the several plays we have discussed, it implicates serious thematic issues. In particular, the tension between the *dākṣiṇya* code and the *rasa* that infuses it suggests that the *rasika* too feels a disjunction between external behavior, however charged with elegance it might be, and the rather deeper concerns of emotional satisfaction, especially as they center around the question of erotic love. *Kāvya* is what it is thematically because it mirrors the *rasika*'s concerns.[24]

That this might easily be the case is suggested by what we know of marriage arrangements in the higher (and therefore more literate) strata of India society. That is to say, outwardly a certain type of *rasika* (e.g., a Brahmin *paṇḍita*) lives within a network of ritualistically formal relationships that includes marriage and the married life. The idealized elegance of the *dākṣiṇya* code as depicted in the plays we have looked at allows us to imagine that the *rasika* held as an ideal (on the level of fantasy, at least) the conversion of his own formal relationships into a kind of *līlā*. For it is at the level of *līlā* that formal obligation becomes something like a condition of freedom, like the rules of a game. But, as the plays again indicate, such a *līlā*, even in fantasy, is insufficient. It is, after all, too much a matter of controlled distance from the emotional object. Thus, inwardly, the *rasika* feels himself the potential hero of a great romance, for he sees his own cherished sentiments represented on stage and in other *kāvyas* in precisely that framework. Inwardly he is acting before such a beautiful *nāyikā* as Urvaśī, Śakuntalā, or Vāsavadattā. Of course, I do not limit the *rasika* experience to men, though one could hardly disclaim the dominance of the male erotic point of view in *kāvya*. I have already suggested that a play like *V* can be seen likewise as a woman's fantasy of erotic centrality. The essential point that I am arguing is that in divorcing aesthetic questions from the actual thematic content of *kāvya* we are depriving ourselves of any understanding of the emotional basis of the art, the resonant chords it strikes in the hearts of its natural hearers, readers, and spectators.

As we know, *rasa* was always considered the principal element in drama. It was the end for which perfect technique in the actors and perfect dramaturgical skill in the playwright existed. The ideal for the actor is so to infuse his or her role with authentic emotion that he gives life to illusion and draws the spectator into a world where he or she too takes on fictive personality. We can see this transforming process mirrored in one of those conventional scenes in drama the hero succumbs to the illusion created by wonderful painting of the beloved or some other artificial reminder (like the banter in *SV*) and believes that she stands before him. For a moment he becomes transported aesthetically into an illusory world created by *rasa*, i.e., his own memory-haunted desire. Such fictional representations of the aesthetic process are, in my judgment, important indications of the way *kāvya* functioned and continues to function for its audience. We become the *nāyaka* who stands in the shadow of trees witnessing the epiphany of the ideally attractive woman (*M* and *Ś*) or who saves her from demons and watches transfixed as she slowly emerges from a swoon in his aerial chariot (*V*); and the emotion that makes the illusion convincing is our own *rasa* or *bhāva*. In other words, it is our own desire that transports us into the poetic fantasy. The play is an enactment of that desire—and the problems that it entails.[25]

In this chapter we have been concerned only with the problem generated by the disjunction between emotional truth and courtly pretence. More broadly, this could be treated as a tension between feeling and form: and, indeed, I have suggested above that we see the dhārmic formalism of a high-caste Hindu's life at one end of the polarity. At best, from the aesthetic point of view, the ritualistic life becomes a species of *līlā*, where necessity is ideally transformed into a vehicle of charm. But, as I have said, this cannot be sufficient, precisely because *dākṣiṇya-līlā*, remains on the formal level. Its aesthetic counterpart is the *alaṃkāra* poetic, a highly sophisticated and charming formalism, that many (e. g., Kuntaka) have seen as the essential characteristic of *kāvya*.[26] But there is a reason for the historical intrusion of *rasa* on this poetic. To Ānandavardhana and others like him the *alaṃkāra* poetic remained superficial until it acknowledged *rasa* as its heart and soul. Thus Indian poetics after Ānandavardhana came to exemplify the famous dictum of Bharata (*Nāṭyaśāstra* 6.31+, KSS ed.):

> *na hi rasād ṛte kaścid apyarthaḥ pravartate/*
> Nothing significant happens without *rasa*.

The phrasing of this dictum reminds us, however, of the verse with which this chapter began:

> If a lover's conciliation is without *rasa* (*rasād ṛte*),
> though it contain a hundred sweet words,
> it will not enter a woman's heart.

In this way the aesthetic issue leads us back to the thematic perspectives that we have attempted to explore.

In particular it leads beyond a conception of *kāvya* as a refined linguistic or otherwise technical *līlā* (e.g. the actor's *abhinayas* or the author's dramaturgical devices, the *sandhi-sandhyaṅga* system, etc.) that finds its counterpart in the codified behavior of its characters. That *kāvya* remains a *līlā* is unquestionable. But it is a *līlā* that has a vital concern at its core, namely emotional need and aspiration: the longing for an ideal love, to be admired as a hero, to have one's authenticity vindicated. In other words, a thematic appreciation of *kāvya* leads to a conception of it as an enactment, in essence a wish-fulfilment. In this conception the conventional plot is more than a vehicle for highlighting lyric emotion. It provides an essential mythic shape for a specific emotional dynamic.[27]

Conclusion: The Love-Ideal

And with this idea of the *rasa* poetic as entailing a thematic enactment of emotional concerns there emerges a whole other question, which arises consciously only for the modern reader. The question has to do with the limitations of the emotional vision in question. We have seen that at critical junctures the elegant formality of poetic language fails the hero and heroine precisely because as *līlā* it is incapable of overcoming the distance between emotion and manneristic expression. What the characters want at this point is to know whether genuine feeling underlies the omnipresent formal adornment.[28] But instead of overcoming the aesthetic barrier to direct feeling they strengthen it. They step back from each other to become actor and audience. Communication, therefore, is achieved indirectly through posturing that is meant to arouse pity rather than desire. Purūravas, in order to retain Urvaśī's love, demonstrates his weakness without her, while she, the secret spectator, converts the apparently indifferent world that forms the backdrop to his emotional isolation into an indulgent sentience. But is this, at bottom, a real communication or is it a narcissistic fantasy? Is the heroine for the hero really anything more than a vehicle of sexual grace and mothering indulgence? And does he win her in any other way, finally, than by throwing before her the tragic spectacle of wounded innocence and lovability? In other words, we seem to have withdrawn from a sophisticated aesthetic code to a level of emotional enactment that seems childish, psychologically involuted. The hero is saved from whatever contradictions he is involved in by self-display: his true self is so lovable that there can be no indifference to his plight, there can be no No for him. But never having to endure a real No, he remains essentially a pampered child. He is always an actor confident of the presence of a sympathetic audience.[29]

The women characters, however, form a contrast to this pattern. The power of their self-display, though initially overwhelming in its sexual magic, is limited. Their allure does not belong to them by nature (as the hero's lovability belongs to him), but is only lent them for a time. When a new epiphany of Śrī occurs, the heroine must take up the role of the replaced woman. She loses her charisma, but she gains an adult perspective, like Padmāvatī in *SV* whose knowledge at the end of Act 4 ironizes the hero's childlike innocence. Urvaśī is able to retain her centrality only by keeping alive the threat of withdrawing herself (possible for a goddess, but not a married woman, in a patriarchal culture), a maneuver which is already an acknowledgment of the threat posed by time and circumstance to her charisma.

Yet, the last act of *V* shows the hero living the married life with the heroine with a bond of love between them. He no longer seems a pampered child, but a seasoned monarch ready to make way for the coming generation. Thus here we seem to have the recognition of an ideal of love that is based on the common understanding that grows out of living together. Of course, we learn that in the 14 years or so since the melodramatics of Act 4 Urvaśī has been keeping an important secret from her husband—thus, he still seems the relative innocent—but this does not seem to disturb the general impression we have of their domestic happiness. We also see that Purūravas still retains the traces of his former passion: he is ready to repeat his wandering in the forest, though we assume this time that his suffering would not be as histrionic as before. Thus, one may argue that this final portrait of mutual affection is meant to replace the immature and even narcissistic turbulence of the earlier erotic longing. This is something like the argument Tagore made about the sublimation of love in *Ś*. There may be something to this, but it doesn't really answer the question of how the transformation occurs. For Tagore, the lover's agony in the garden (for Purūravas it is a forest) is a genuine *tapas* that prepares him for a moral conception of love. But if that *tapas* is really a form of self-indulgence, as I have suggested it might be, then how can it lead to moral insight? How can the hero be simultaneously displaying his lovability and learning the consequences of his action?

The answer be that it is not an either-or situation. *Kāvya* does recognize both ideals of love. What it seems not to do is show us convincingly the link between them. Perhaps the very need to appeal to the beloved's sense of pity is enough of a shock to the narcissistic impulse to alter it fundamentally. In any case, the final emphasis on family and seasoned affection seems to tell us that the *rasika*'s abiding hope is for the ripening of erotic fantasy into domestic happiness. It still remains true, however, that in the lyrically erotic stage of love the lovers communicate in the indirect, aestheticized way I have discussed. And this seems to indicate that the *rasika* cannot imagine an erotic relationship that does not entail self-display and covert appeals, i.e., an implicit dramatics of sincerity. *Rasa* still depends, on posture and thus on the positing of a radical aesthetic and emotional distance between the lovers that at times seems to place each in a solipsistic emotional frame.

Notes

1. 2.21 in Velankar's edition, from which all citations in this chapter are taken.
2. The title of the play already indicates the heroine's character as a Śrī-figure.
3. The latest discussion of the meaning of *vidūṣaka* occurs in Kuiper, *Varuṇa and Vidūṣaka,* pp. 208 ff.
4. *V* 2.20

   aparādhī nāmāhaṃ prasīda rambhoru virama saṃrambhāt/
   sevyo janaś ca kupitaḥ kathaṃ nu dāso niraparādhaḥ//

   Just how little this means is revealed in contrast by a variant on the motif in 3.19:

   sāmantamaulimaṇirañjitaśāsanāṅkam
   ekātapatram avaner na tathā prabhutvam/
   asyāḥ sakhe caraṇayor aham adya kāntam
   ājñākaratvam adhigamya yathā kṛtārthaḥ//

   Purūravas here is speaking to the Vidūṣaka about his love for Urvaśī: 'My sovereignty, wherein a single umbrella is held over the earth and edicts are colored by (the rays of) my vassals' crest-jewels, does not satisfy me as much as beloved servitude at her feet, my friend!' The words of this verse will be vivified by the anguish of the 4th Act, in which the hero has indeed abandoned his kingdom and wanders half-crazed through the forest seeking his beloved. By contrast his protestations to Auśīnarī have no objective correlative. See also verses 4.26 and 55, which again use the language of mistress and servant during the forest-wandering soliloquy, and those cited in the following note, which occur in the 3rd Act. The point is: Sincerity or insincerity cannot be detected in the formulaic words themselves. Rather, they are only revealed by actions and emotional responses that can be verified by the audience.
5. 3.13-14:

   anena kalyāṇi mṛṇālakomalaṃ vratena gātraṃ glapayasyakāraṇam/
   prasādam ākāṅkṣati yas tavotsukaḥ sa kiṃ tvayā dāsajanaḥ prasādyate//
   dātuṃ vā prabhavasi mām anyasmai kartum eva vā dāsam/
   nāhaṃ punas tathā tvaṃ yathā hi māṃ śaṅkase bhīru//
6. 3.13.2-3: *ayi mugdhe anyasaṃkrāntapremāṇo nāgarikā adhikaṃ dakṣiṇā bhavanti/* My practice will be to give all Parkrit passages in their Sanskrit *chāyā.*
7. See Scheftelowitz, pp. 3-4, 72 ff.
8. A valuable sourcebook on the complete legend of Udayana and Vāsavadattā is Niti Adaval, *The Story of King Udayana.* The Harṣa plays (early 7th century) are *Ratnāvalī* and *Priyadarśikā,* which appear to draw heavily on Kālidāsa's *M.*
9. A theme studied in the *Ṛgveda* by Robert P. Goldman, 'Mortal Man and Immortal Woman'.
10. See the prologue to Act 4, in which her former companions are discussing the lovers' parting, esp. 4.2.19-20: *asahanā khalu sā/ dūrārūḍhaś cāsyāḥ praṇayaḥ/ tad bhavitavyatatra balavatī/* The theme is taken up numerous times by Purūravas in the course of the Act (e.g., 4.9, 4.26, 4.55, 4.66). Urvaśī's first words to him upon being released from her spell are a plea for forgiveness (cited *infra*). She also exactly echoes her friends' words earlier in the Act when she attributes her hasty departure to a mind clouded by a *guru*'s (Bharata's) curse (*guruśāpasaṃmūḍhahṛdayā,* 4.2.21 and 4.71.9).
11. Many critics have recognized Kālidāsa's sensitivity to women's emotions. For instance, Ingalls commends Ruben for sensing Kālidāsa's sympathy for Sītā

and lack of it for Rāma in the *Raghuvaṃśa*: 'Kālidāsa and the Attitudes of the Golden Age', p. 22.

12. *M* 4.14:
dākṣiṇyaṃ nāma bimboṣṭhi baimbikānāṃ kulavratam/
tan me dīrghākṣi ye prāṇās te tvadāśānibandhanāḥ//
Mālavikā had not been on stage when Agnimitra fell at Irāvatī's feet, etc. but we are obviously to understand that she knows all about it from what she says in this passage.
13. These and other of the hero's characteristics are conveniently codified in the first verses of *Daśarūpaka* 2. For an extensive list of sources see Rakesagupta, *Studies in Nāyaka-Nāyikā-Bheda*, pp. 385-94 (= Appendix A).
14. Duḥṣanta unconsciously slips into the *dhṛṣṭa* role in *Śakuntalā* 5.
15. Both Śaṅkara's and Rāmānuja's comments on *Brahmasūtra* 2.1.33 (*lokavat tu līlākaivalyam*) liken the free creation of Īśvara to the (ostensibly) unmotivated sport of a prince. (See Ch. 1).
16. The perfect example of this occurs in *V* 4, e. g., verse 4.49:
api vanāntaram alpakucāntarā śrayati parvata parvasu sannatā/
idam anaṅgaparigraham aṅganā pṛthunitamba nitambavatī tava//
O mountain, has the full-breasted woman of rounded limbs
taken refuge in your forest,
the abode of love, o broad-sloped mountain,
the woman of sloping haunches?
This is untranslatable in the intricacy of its verbal play, and yet it is intended, as far as *rasa* is concerned, to reveal the depths of Purūravas' anguish in love-separation. Also noteworthy is the fact that, despite Purūravas' great affliction, his words evoke nothing more than Urvaśī's, physical features (full breasts, rounded limbs and buttocks); also the expression *anaṅgaparigraham* surely refers to her, as well as the forest, as the 'abode of love'. We are kept on the level of sexual sport (mirrored in linguistic sport) even in its excruciating absence. Yet the two—emotional intensity and playful detachment—can exist simultaneously and infuse each other with greater value. This is precisely the paradox of *kāvya*'s effectiveness.
17. It is one of the great limitations of the *rasa* scheme that it does not acknowledge the emotional value of friendship even between men, though it is one of the more important themes of drama (e.g., the *sneha* theme of *Mudrārākṣasa, Mṛcchakaṭika,* and *Pratijñāyaugandharāyaṇa*). For the tradition's attempts to fill this obvious gap, see chapter 6 of V. Raghavan, *The Number of Rasas.* See also the Vaiṣṇava schematization of the *bhakti rasas* (*śānta, dāsya, sākhya, vāsalya,* and *mādhurya*), all versions of *śṛṅgāra* in effect, *apud* S. K. De, 'The Bhaktirasaśāstra of Bengal Vaiṣṇavism.'
18. The device in the play that makes this possible is the hero's finding of the gem-of-union (*saṃgamanīya maṇi*), derived from the dye (*rāga*) on Gaurī's feet. (It is interesting that *rāga* is often used as a synonym for *rasa,* as it is in the verse that heads this chapter and, for example, in *Ś* 1.4.1: *rāgāpahṛtacittavṛttir ālikhita iva bhāti sarvato raṅgaḥ.*) The jewel is delivered to him by an ascetic, who is also part of that vague sentience forming the background to the hero's mime. A full attempt at interpretation of this play would have to take into account the significance of the axis formed by the male authority figures associated with the curse and its resolution: Bharata, Kumāra, and the ascetic (who is a stand-in for Śiva), and (though of a

different type) Indra. Here I am only concerned with the direct relationship of hero and heroine. In a sense, Gaurī is the archetypal enhancement of Urvaśī. When Purūravas has suffered enough, when he has proven his case, he wins the favor of this larger feminine principle acting in concert with the male ascetical power which had intervened to separate Urvaśī from Purūravas in the first place. No longer needing to impose a *tapas* on her lover by withdrawing behind the veil of an ascetical curse, Urvaśī can appear as a sympathetic fellow victim in perfect correspondence with the hero's desires.

19. 4.70.1-2: *marṣayatu marṣayatu mahārājaḥ/ yan mayā kopavaśaṃ gatayāvasthāntaraṃ prāpito mahārājaḥ/*
20. *SV* 4.5:

    padmāvatī bahumatā mama yadyapi rupaśīlamādhuryaiḥ/
    vāsavadattābaddhaṃ na tu tāvan me mano harati//
21. Perhaps we should take Max Müller's lead ('henotheism') and coin the term 'henogynous'.
22. *SV* 1.12.47, 2.0.26.-7: Udayana is a romantic figure to the maiden Padmāvatī because his grief makes him *sānukrośa.* At this point in the play she has not even seen him: he is simply a hero in a romantic tale. For a full discussion see 'Paradise in a Prison Cell'.
23. *V* 1.2:

    praṇayiṣu va dākṣiṇyād athavā sadvastupuruṣabahumānāt/
    śṛṇuta manobhir avahitaiḥ kriyām imāṃ kālidāsasya//
24. Whatever the (e.g. ritual) origins of *kāvya*—and particularly *nāṭya*—may have been, whatever its original inheritance was, the form was perpetuated because it continued to appeal to the taste of the community of *rasikas* that stretched over many centuries. Its thematic invariance tells us not simply that it was a conventional poetry, but that its conventions corresponded to an emotional configuration that was likewise unvarying and which demanded mythic expression.
25. Within Indian poetics the notion of *sādhāraṇīkaraṇa* demands identification with the subject of feeling. More than this, it is understood to have practical effects on the *rasika*'s life: see Gnoli, *AEAG*, pp. 12-13, 52-53, who discusses the Mīmāṃsaka origins of the idea; and pp. 89-90, 97-98, where AG shows that the reader/spectator models his behavior on the characters he has identified with. In other words, despite the theory of impersonal aesthetic emotion, Indian aestheticians did covertly acknowledge identificatory links between fictive character and observer.
26. Gerow, *A Glossary of Indian Figures of Speech*, 'Introduction', offers an apologia for the *alaṃkāra* position which is in many ways a healthy, and realistic, corrective to the quasi-mystical poetics that modern scholars have tended to regard as exclusively characteristic of Indian aesthetics. My own antidote to the rampant idealism that pervades explanations of Sanskrit aesthetics is, as this essay indicates, the thematic understanding of tensions between formalism and emotion as they are mirrored throughout *kāvya.*
27. I need to make it clear that I am not arguing against the accepted judgment of Ingalls (*Anthology*, pp. 38-39) and many others that Sanskrit drama is really not dramatic but a spectacle-poetry (*dṛśya kāvya*) whose purposes are principally lyrical. See Introduction.
28. If I seem to harp on feeling, it is because *kāvya* portrays truth as a matter of feeling rather than thought. Thought would complicate emotion to a point

where the system of *rasa* aesthetics would break down. See esp. Ch. 5, 'The Divided World of Sanskrit Drama'.

29. I feel it is necessary to offer a partial defence of the much maligned Keith, who is seen as having no poetic sensibility and no appreciation of indigenous poetics, in his judgment of the insufficiency of Sanskrit poetry. I do not believe that the shibboleth of 'Indian standards' has really met Keith's objection that an essentially sentimental and melodramatic poetry cannot satisfy us on a profound level. As limited as he was as a literary critic, he nevertheless did not evade the question of *kāvya*'s moral and psychological impact and ability or lack thereof to transcend its own cultural conditions. On the whole I believe his attitude is healthier for its acceptance in the context of world literature than the opposite attitude of sheltering it from frank criticism. His objections have to be 'worked through' rather than dismissed as philistine. See Keith, *Sanskrit Drama*, pp. 276-88, vs. Ingalls, *Anthology*, p. 50.

CHAPTER 4

Kālidāsa's Metadrama

1. Introduction

Kālidāsa's metadrama, his drama about drama, is the *Mālavikāgnimitra* (hereafter *M*), named for its principal characters, the slavegirl/princess Mālavikā and the Śuṅga King Agnimitra who is enamored of her. The play is a comic delineation of the various intrigues whereby the King comes ever closer to achieving physical union with the heroine despite the jealousy of two of his wives. Dramaturgically it is unfailingly clever and compact, with no wasted scenes or excess poetic verbiage. Sociologically it provides us with a more intimate and realistic glimpse of court life than we get in the bulk of Sanskrit drama with its sentimental idealization of hero and heroine.[1] Historians also use it as a document on the Śuṅga period which gives us a picture of the political relations within the dynastic family as well as with rival kingdoms (including the Bactro-Greeks).[2] The play contains many fine touches, such as the rivalry between two dance/drama teachers (*nāṭyācāryas*) resident at the court, the alliance between the chief queen Dhāriṇī and her former rival Irāvatī against the newcomer Mālavikā, and the obscure reference to tension between the effete Agnimitra and his overlord father, who evidently preferred the brusque military title of 'General' to 'King'.[3]

Modern critics have not valued it highly, seeing it as at best a charming bagatelle, at worst a frivolous example of courtly decadence. But the disapproval is not entirely fair. There is very little difference in spirit between Agnimitra's infatuation for an ostensible slavegirl and King Duḥṣanta's passion for Śakuntalā: both are ostensibly entirely physical, with the aesthetic amplification typical of all *kāvya.* The difference is basically one of setting and scope. In the *nāṭikā* form the poet was allowed to treat a common kind of love affair at court, without the mythic idealization typical of the *nāṭaka,* even if it was necessary to make the heroine a princess incognito.[4] But what we lose in grandeur we gain in appreciation of the *realia* of court life, e. g. the precarious position of the servant who attracts the jealousy of her mistress. Dhāriṇī, it seems, has the power of life and death over her attendant. Such details as Mālavikā's underground imprisonment and Agnimitra's 'courtesy' (*dākṣiṇya*), which forbids his taking any overt steps to protect her, add poignancy to our understanding of courtly play (*līlā*) as it was actually practiced. And as for scope: critics tend to forget that it is love-in-absence (*viraha, vipralambha*) occuring after the initial sexual union (*saṃbhoga*) that provides whatever dimension of moral idealism a poem or drama may have. The 'fault' of this play is really generic: that it is 'realistically' set and treats only the initial stages of love.[5]

Not that the play is without idealistic features. One of its stanzas, in fact, is frequently quoted precisely to illustrate the high-mindedness of the classical Indian concept of love:

> I see no pleasure (*rati*) in a successful union
> if one is impassioned and the other is not.
> Better to share a mutual ardor
> and die in hopeless pining for its fulfilment.[6]

This could stand as a *rasika* credo, since it raises sex to the level of a shared emotional experience available only to the sensitive and cultivated.

Also idealizing, but in a different vein, are a verse exalting (and in a sense defining) drama and the *maṅgala* verse underlining the paradoxes of the patron god of drama:

> The sages consider it the lovely visual sacrifice to the gods;
> Rudra has divided it twofold on the body he shares with Umā;
> in it one sees the triple-stranded world as a source of exquisite savors (*rasa*):
> drama, though varied, is a single source of delight for an audience of manifold tastes.[7]

And:

> He is the sole Lord of the world, bringing many fruits to his votaries,
> yet he wears the elephant hide;
> his body is joined to his beloved's, yet he is the first among ascetics
> whose minds are devoid of sense-objects;
> he bears the entire universe on his eight bodily forms,
> yet has no self-conceit:
> may Lord Śiva rid you of benighted activity

so that you see the path of wisdom.[8]

Thematically both of these verses raise the play's *mithuna* motif (male-and-female couple) to a level of more than comic significance which critics and interpreters have not taken into account. And in fact one could point to much more: verses 1.5-6, which celebrate Mālavikā's skill as an actress-dancer; the technical assessment of her performance in Act 2 (2.8); the lovely descriptions of the pleasure-garden in Act 3 (3. 4-5) which signify the Śrī-like role of the heroine; the vegetal ritualism of Act 3 and the marriage celebration of Act 5.

The transmutation of the comically venereal, so as to exemplify an erotic playfulness that is universalized in the great god, is in keeping with a general thematic movement in the play. We can see this best in the character of the heroine, Mālavikā, who is simultaneously a slavegirl and a princess, the object of prey for the king's sexual sport, and yet one of the most clearly delineated Śrī figures among dramatic heroines and a consummate actress whose ability to effect the magic of *rasa*-transformation has real-life charismatic significance.[9] Viewed metadramatically, the play is about the hope or desire that art awakens in its audience, which signals the inextricably close connection between aesthetic experience and erotic fantasy in the Indian context. But, besides the charismatic aspect of *rasa*-transformation in its association with eros and burgeoning vegetation, the play also treats the strategic (*arthic*) side of the formula, thus making us aware of the link between dramaturgy, the schemes of the play's love-plot, and the overarching designs of fate. Thus the drama provides an interesting perspective on aesthetic reception and its relation to the real-life concerns and interests of the *sahṛdaya*.

2. Aesthetic, Organic, Erotic

The play's prologue segues into an introductory scene (*miśraviṣkambhaka*) that highlights the heroine's character as a symbol of aesthetic transformation with paradisal associations. Two maids, Bakulāvalikā and Kaumudikā, cross paths on their respective errands. Bakulāvalikā is on her way to Gaṇadāsa's dance-studio in behalf of Dhāriṇī, the chief Queen. Dhāriṇī is interested in the progress of her recently acquired slave, Mālavikā, in her study of dance/drama performance.[10] Kaumudikā, for her part, is on her way to Dhāriṇī from the palace jeweler's carrying a ring with a serpent seal, which will show up at a critical juncture later in the play. She is so absorbed in the beauty of the ring that she fails to notice her friend, who teasingly reproves her. After seeing the ring herself, however, Bakulāvalikā is not surprised that it had absorbed all her friend's attention: 'No wonder your gaze clung to it. With its burst of ray-filaments the ring makes your hand seem like a flower.'[11] Thus at the outset of the play we are confronted with a symbol that unites artifice with vegetal auspiciousness, a symbol that functions on various levels. It evokes *kāvya* itself as lapidary formal structure harboring the inner garden world of poetic revery. More particularly it is this very play with its special focus on the inflorescence of the Golden Aśoka tree (the vegetal-ritual counterpart of the King). Even more particularly it is the heroine, who combines art and auspiciousness in two ways. First, as the highly skilled performer, in both aesthetic and ritual contexts, who induces a mood of fertile enchantment (the King's fascination, the tree's blooming); and second, as the aesthetic-erotic object of the King's desire apart from her capacity as skilled artist. She is the gazed-at beauty, the Radiant Female, whose love fills the King with a special excitement that promises to lift him into the charismatic playworld of constant titillation and fulfilled desire. Thus, when the conversation between the two maids immediately turns to the painting of Queen Dhāriṇī's entourage through which Agnimitra has attained his first aesthetically mediated sight of the beautiful heroine, we know by the infallible logic of poetic suggestion (*dhvani*) that this epiphany will blossom into an auspicious love affair.

The most prominent motif in this play is that of burgeoning. The play shows us the effect of a Śrī in human form who makes of the hero's sovereignty a happy celebration of life's material and emotional abundance. The heroine is essentially a beautiful object, but female beauty in the world of Sanskrit poetry is a power which reveals itself in a series of epiphanies, through which the privileged beholder (the *rasika*) feels himself increasingly transported into a world in which desire itself and its aesthetic maximization are the vital forces. This world is none other than a fictive realization of the 'poetic universe' (*kāvyasaṃsāra*) celebrated by Ānandavardhana and other poeticians, because this state of transport cannot exist in anyone but the *rasika* who alone has the imaginative capacity to comprehend the power that discloses itself to him.

The initial symbolic incident, the carrying of the flower-like ring 'bursting with filament-rays', has its immediate counterpart in the portrait I have already mentioned. The King notices on a mural depicting the Chief Queen, Dhāriṇī, and her entourage a beautiful woman he has never seen before. He is immediately taken, and, after securing her name with some difficulty, sets the Vidūṣaka, his clownish Brahmin companion, to devise a means of circumventing Dhāriṇī's jealousy and meeting Mālavikā. In both of these incidents we have the impression of the potency of the still and silent object—gem and painted figure—casting its spell amid the routine bustle of court life. Soon we hear of the heroine's skill as a performer in the same terms:

> Whatever I teach her about the realization of emotion (*bhāvikam*) in performance
> the girl seems to reteach me by bringing it to perfection.
> The teacher's art placed in an excellent vessel becomes something more perfect,
> like the raindrop that falls into a shell in the ocean and comes to fruit as a pearl.[12]

The 'pearl-fruit' is, like the flowering ring, a symbol of the hidden organic nature of art, its fructifying promise. Gaṇadāsa praises Mālavikā as one of those rare artists who transforms technique into the means of disclosing something vital and essentially mysterious, like the process by which a drop of rain falling into the ocean (this was the poetic conceit) becomes a pearl in an oyster. In the formal terms of Sanskrit aesthetics she uses the formal acting techniques (the *abhinayas*) to convert *bhāva* (ordinary emotion) effortlessly to *rasa*, the transporting 'mood' or atmospheric 'flavor' of the 'poetic universe'.

So far the connection between bewitching aesthetic effect with organic overtones and the protagonist's desire for the heroine has been achieved by suggestive juxtaposition, but it soon becomes more explicit. The Vidūṣaka has strategically instigated a quarrel between Gaṇadāsa and Haradatta, dance teachers in the Chief Queen's and King's employ respectively. Each claims the superior knowledge of the dramatic art. Naturally this can only be demonstrated by their best students, and the King himself, with the aid of certain expert courtiers, must be the judge. So the King comes to behold Mālavikā in the flesh (scantily clothed to best exhibit her suppleness of limb) performing the part of a young woman passionately longing to arouse the attention of the man she desires. The presentation is perfect *double entendre,* because while the experts' assessment of it is impeccably technical, its true intent is to serve the desire of the King, whose own technical connoisseurship enables him all the better to savor the prize before him.[13] Not only this, but the ostensibly objective expert (*prāśnika*) acting as the King's chief adviser in the matter—the ascetical Brahmin widow Kauśikī—is an accomplice of the Vidūṣaka. Besides this (and the next Act reveals this conclusively) Mālavikā in fact acts out her own longing for the King in the performance. So we are a step closer to reality now: the picture has taken on lovely body and danced before the *rasika* King, acting out just the sentiments he would wish to find in her. The force of the heroine's beauty, like the winding shoot of a creeper, is reaching across the purely aesthetic boundary into the *rasika*'s vital emotional center.

We could say this is comedy, a lighthearted spoof of *rasa* aesthetics, and let the matter stand; but this, I think, would be a serious misunderstanding. Comedy it is, but not a spoof. There is indeed clever play with the 'comic sentiment' (*hāsya rasa*), which the *Nāṭyaśāstra* pairs with the erotic (*śṛṅgāra*). The kāvyic treatment of Eros especially in the initial courtship phase (*pūrvānurāga*) is always marked by a certain teasing, flirtatious play and benign irony. We frequently find it in poetry celebrating the loveplay of transcendent divinities.[14] It is comedy which enhances rather than undercuts the piquancy of the erotic mood, and—more importantly—it reveals that the classical Indian aesthetic experience was not the solemn, quasi-metaphysical experience many idealistic expositors have claimed it to be.[15] The idealist critics then write this play off as Kālidāsa's youthful indiscretion, as if its sportive erotic humor were a negligible feature of *kāvya.*

But it is the burgeoning theme, the heroine's obvious status as a Śrī figure, which should convince us that the play's comic conjunction of art and Eros is anything but peripheral. Can we even conceive of Sanskrit poetry without abundant floral imagery and the women who evoke it? The third Act not only applies imagery of vegetal growth to the King's growing desire for the young actress, but enhances it by mixing it in with fertility ritual. Mālavikā has stepped forth from a wall-painting into the aesthetic frame of a demonstrational performance, so becoming more concrete and all but tangible for her devoted *rasika.* Now she comes closer still. The third frame is not primarily aesthetic: she has been appointed by Dhāriṇī to perform the ritual of kicking the Golden Aśoka tree to bring it to springtime blossom. Her entrance in the Act is prepared for by pointed allusions to Śrī as the goddess of vernal inflorescence:

> Vidūṣaka: Look carefully, friend. Out of a desire to attract you the Lakṣmī of this pleasure garden has dressed herself in spring-blossoms that put young women's attire to shame.
> King: Indeed, it amazes me to behold—
> The brightness of the Red Aśoka outdoes the lac on gourdlike lower lips,
> the black, white, and red amaranth repudiates intricate facial paint,
> *tilaka*-blossoms thick with antimony-bees eclipse the application of forehead marks:
> so vernal Śrī seems to scorn the make-up on women's faces.[16]

It is as if the garden's beauty were now to concretize itself, for it is precisely at this point that Mālavikā enters, still unseen by the two speakers, soliloquizing her love for the King. When they do see her, the King decides to remain hidden in order both to savor her charms (*rasāsvāda*) and await the revelation of her feelings for his. The verses he speaks to register his sensitivity to her appeal are full of organic suggestion: she is water to thirsty traveler (*pathikasya pipāsataḥ salilam,* 3.6) and his very life (*jīvitam etad āyāti,* 3.7), she resembles a *kunda*-vine in spring (3,8), etc.

Most importantly the King sees the analogy between himself in his condition of unfulfilled longing and the Golden Aśoka that needs the touch of her foot in order to bloom.[17] A few verses after the one just quote he calls attention to the ritual streak of paint on Mālavikā's foot:

> Look, friend, at the moist (*sarasa*) streak of color (*rāga*)
> applied to the end of your friend's darling's foot,
> like the first burgeoning shoot on the tree of love
> that was destroyed by Hara's fire.[18]

In the next verse he sees the tree in the implied likeness (*upamālaṃkāradhvani*) of a penitent lover awaiting his mistress's foot on his bowed head[19]:

> The girl should kick two with that foot,
> with toes red as new shoots and nails brightly glittering:
> the blossomless *aśoka* out of regard for its longing
> and the lover with fresh transgression bending down his head.[20]

Later, when he has emerged from hiding, speaking to Mālavikā directly, he presses the comparison:

> I too for a long time have not borne the flower of happiness.
> Fulfill then my longing (*dohada*) with the nectar (*amṛta*) of your touch,
> for I can take no pleasure in others.[21]

And the culminating comparison is reached with the first verse of Act 4:

> Taking root with my desire when I heard her spoken of,
> sprouting red shoots when I first caught sight of her,
> budding in my gooseflesh when she touched me with her hand,
> may the tree of love end my pining
> with the taste of juice (*rasa*) from its fruit.[22]

There can be no questioning the idealizing intent of these comparisons. We are to regard, seriously, the hero's love as an organic fulfilment. The heroine is the means of his entrance into the paradise of burgeoning Eros. The comic tone remains throughout Act 3 in various ways (most notably in the presence of the Vidūṣaka and the bursting in of Irāvatī, the second Queen), but it does not override the significant treatment of Eros, which carries with it the sacral (but not somber) overtones of fertility ritual.

I have said that Mālavikā's epiphany in Act 3 is not primarily aesthetic, but this is true only in a formal sense, since the *rasika* hero's gaze converts her ceremonial performance and its preparations into a demonstration of her charms. This is also clearly conveyed by the fact that the whole scene has been effectively staged by the Vidūṣaka. It was he who 'accidentally' caused injury to Queen Dhāriṇī's foot, so that she would have to choose another to take her place in the ritual performance. The Vidūṣaka has also informed Mālavikā's closest companion, Bakulāvalikā, who helps her with the ritual preparations, of the King's interest in her friend. The King is therefore in the privileged position of witnessing in action an emissary of his own desires nursing Mālavikā into more open declarations of erotic interest in himself. Thus Bakulāvalikā is an actress in his own private play, whose *mise-en-scène* has been directed by the Vidūṣaka as stage-manager (*sūtradhāra*) or teacher (*nāṭyācārya*). Her role is a supporting one, that of enhancing the *rasa*-appeal of the female lead, to the point where the *rasika* can himself enter into the action as the hero. In view of this metadramatic character of the scene it does not seem far-fetched to understand the word *rasa*, which occurs twice in the verses quoted above (3.11 and 4.1), as a *double*—or shall we say *triple?*—*entendre.* Thus when the King refers to the streak of paint that Bakulāvalikā has applied Mālavikā's foot as *sarasa,* which in an innocent sense means only 'moist', we cannot help thinking that he is also referring to the erotic sentiment (*śṛṅgāra rasa*) being nursed along in him by the scene before him.[23] Likewise, in 4.1, in which he expresses his desire to taste the 'juice' (*rasa*) of love's fruit. This use of the word brings the aesthetic meaning back to its etymological source. King Agnimitra longs to savor the fulfilment of the desire that has been growing in him in conjunction with Mālavikā's artfully constructed epiphanies.[24]

The 3rd Act ends with a disturbance, however. The qualified *rasika,* it turns out, has not been the sole spectator of the performance (*prayoga*) that has just been enacted before him. Midway through it, unknown to the King and his companion, and to the characters 'on stage' (Mālavikā and her friend), the King's current favorite, Irāvatī, has become a spectator along with her maid, Nipuṇikā. She has been searching for the king, ever since he failed to appear at their scheduled rendezvous by the garden swing. She is inebriated in the spirit of vernal amorousness, and because the King's interest is now directed elsewhere her eagerness seems somewhat ridiculous.[25] When she stumbles on to the ritual scene she decides to watch for a while. She already knows that Mālavikā is her potential rival and she suspects that there is more to the ritual performance than meets the eye. Her suspicions are whetted by the insinuations of Bakulāvalikā, who takes every opportunity to bring up the subject of the King's love. And when the King himself enters from his hiding-place to press his own suit in glowing poetic language, Irāvatī leaps out from her own place in the 'audience' to accuse him of faithlessness. She is the spoiler of the aesthetic-erotic mood, an obstacle (*vighna*) to the play-within-the-play's success (*siddhi*).[26] The *nāyikā* (heroine) and her friend exit as quickly as they can, and the King is left to play the unwanted role of appeaser, throwing himself at his wife's feet, declaring Mālavikā a trifling amusement undertaken to pass the time while waiting for Irāvatī to come.

When Act 4 opens the King soliloquizes his frustration in the verse quoted above (4.1: 'Taking root with my desire', etc.). All he has achieved so far—in terms of the conceit—is the arousal of his senses, now including touch, but not the sweet taste of desire's fulfilment. He has made two women angry, three in fact: Irāvatī, whom he has not convinced of his faithfulness; Mālavikā, whom he has disavowed and failed to protect (she is, with Bakulāvalikā, now confined to an underground dungeon); and Dhāriṇī, who having gotten used to Irāvatī as a favorite is not about to accept an impertinent slave as a rival (it is by her authority that Mālavikā has been imprisoned). According to the metadramatic progression, the King has prepared for his own entry into the charmed aesthetic-erotic sphere, the 'poetic universe', only to have the spell broken with a crude reminder of everyday life. He and Mālavikā seem farther apart than ever. But all is not lost. Twice now the Vidūṣaka has staged little dramas to bring her before him (the argument between the *nāṭyācāryas*, the performance around the golden Áśoka), therefore the King has called upon his talents again.

The Vidūṣaka delivers with his finest effort, taking the lead role in the Prologue like the disguised *sūtradhāra* he is. He bursts into the palace courtyard where the King is conversing with Dhāriṇī and swoons with the poison of snakebite. Great commotion: all are aghast. The offstage physician, aptly named Dhruvasiddhi ('Sure-of-success'), suborned to the Vidūṣaka's scheme, calls hurriedly for the queen's serpent ring (the same that symbolized the organic power of art in Act 1) to be used in a homeopathic cure. Once out of Dhāriṇī's sight, however, the Vidūṣaka will present it to Mālavikā's jailer as proof of Dhāriṇī's command to have her and Bakūlāvalikā released. Then the King will be free to court her *ad libitum* in the garden. The plan goes off without a hitch, a comic prelude to what promises to be an undisturbed tryst, in which aesthetic appreciation may indeed serve as an aphrodisiac but no longer as a barrier to savoring the 'juice (*rasa*) of the love-tree's fruit' (*kuryāt klāntaṃ manasijatarur māṃ rasajñaṃ phalasya*, 4.1).[27] Thus again, on the verge of encounter, one finds the structures of aesthetic fixation which seem almost an end in themselves. When the King comes upon Mālavikā she is gazing at a mural in one of the garden pavilions, a mural showing the King at a time when Irāvatī was the apple of his eye; and so he has the delicious experience of watching her become jealous and angry with him, which offers an intoxicating proof of the advance of her erotic interest in him.[28] As he watches he fixes her in a series of what we might call aesthetic snapshots, commenting on the features (*vibhāvas* and *anubhāvas*) that make her disposition so attractive to him. But what a mirror-game this is: he studying her studying him in effigy. What a narcissistic thrill. Then, after savoring the charm of her disposition till it can yield no more, he moves in for the courtly kill, all charm and appealing bashfulness, avowing himself her humble slave, while she expresses amazement to herself that she had come so far under the spell of the art-illusion. Soon the Vidūṣaka and Bakulāvalikā find an excuse to leave them alone, and agree between themselves to stand guard least Irāvatī or another interloper spoil this final drama's success (*siddhi*).

The Vidūṣaka, however, falls promptly asleep, which permits the inevitable to happen. Before the lovers have enjoyed more than a few minutes in private, Irāvatī and her Maid have come upon him muttering Mālavikā's name in his sleep. This prompts Nipuṇikā, the Maid, to drop his curved staff on him, and he awakens thinking he has been attacked by a coiling snake. Out of the pavilion runs the king, Mālavikā following, to his friend's assistance only to be greeted by Irāvatī's sarcastic congratulations. The snakebite stratagem had been the prologue to love, now in another's hands it forces an embarrassed conclusion. Coitus interruptus once again.

But with the same startling suddenness comes now another disturbance, which will succeed in bringing about the consummation of *rasāsvāda* where the Vidūṣaka's efforts have failed. A monkey has bitten the king's young sister, Princess Vasulakṣmī, but this is minor, serving only to get the King immediately off the spot as he runs to her aid. No sooner does he leave the stage than another cry goes up: a great marvel! The golden Aśoka has flowered! Mālavikā's fertility magic, inseparable, as we have found, from her aesthetic-erotic charm, has saved the day. What the King has been unable to achieve by various strategies, employing his 'minister of love' (*kāmatantrasaciva*, 4.17+), Mālavikā has brought to pass by her sexual charisma in her role as the Śrī of the *rasika*'s imagination. In the next Act Dhāriṇī will fulfill her pledge by marrying the King to his dream woman, the Radiant Female who will bring his emotional state to the charismatic condition already symbolized by his prosperous reign. To certify the symbolism, and Mālavikā's Śrī-character, news comes of King Agnimitra's military victory over the unruly King of Vidarbha, achieved by his general (Dhāriṇī's brother Vīrasena) while he 'sported in the gardens on the banks of the Vidiśā like the god of love incarnate'.[29] And to complete the miracle Mālavikā is revealed as a princess, the younger sister, of a certain Mādhavasena of Vidarbha, who had been imprisoned by his cousin (or elder brother?)[30] Yajñasena, the aforementioned unruly King of Vidarbha. The series of aesthetic epiphanies is over. We have gone from art to life, enacting the promise of the burgeoning serpent-ring held out to view in Act 1. Mālavikā is the King's to savor and enjoy; the external world has no further disturbances to send his way, and the public and private meet in the ritualization of love in marriage. It is the perfect wish–fulfilment ending. And the fact that the plot is cast in a series of aesthetic disclosures that move ever closer to life—ending in the marriage ritual that recapitulates the ritual–aesthetic promise of the 3rd Act and Mālavikā's final stepping–forth from artful disguise to her true identity as a princess—only goes to show that we cannot separate wish-fulfilment from the *rasa*–experience. This play is a demonstration piece of the burgeoning aspiration or desire entailed in the classical Indian aesthetic experience.

3. The Arthic Perspective

Yet before we allow ourselves to be carried away by the enthusiasm of the conclusion in all its symbolic aptness, let us look at the metadramatic aspect of the pay briefly from he angle of dramaturgy. Here all is not so sweetly auspicious.

In the symbol of the serpent–ring is combined the perfection of artifice and the organic word of vegetation with its inevitable erotic associations. The ring soon yields to Mālavikā the young actress and desirable woman as the symbol of this duality. We remember the verses the *nāṭyācārya* Gaṇadāsa spoke to celebrate his pupil's transformative artistic powers:

> Whatever I teach her about the realization of emotion (*bhāvikam*) in performance
> the girl seems to reteach me by bringing it to perfection.
> The teacher's art placed in an excellent vessel becomes something more perfect,
> like the raindrop that falls into a shell in the ocean and comes to fruit as a pearl.

This, of course, is precisely the thematic movement we have found in our examination of the play. Mālavikā is the aesthetic object that transforms acting strategies and technical instruction into 'fruitful' aesthetic experience. The Vidūṣaka has taken over from Gaṇadāsa as the play's major acting teacher, staging a number of productions: the quarrel between Gaṇadāsa and Haradatta which led to Mālavikā's dance-performance; Dhāriṇī's hurt foot, which led to Mālavikā's ritual appearance in the garden, and Bakulāvalikā's subornment; and finally the snakebite scenario, serving as introduction to Mālavikā's direct entrance as lover.

The play abounds with technical dramaturgical terms—*prayoga* (performance), *kārya* (the plot's 'aim'), *siddhi* ('success'), *phala* ('fulfilment'), *ārambha* ('undertaking')—all used in *double* or *triple entendre* to link the strategies of dramatic plot-construction and *mise-en-scène* with the Vidūṣaka's prosecution of the love-plot.[31] The overwhelming impression left by these instances is one of concurrence between the Vidūṣaka's 'aim' in bringing King Agnimitra to the savoring (*rasanā*) of his 'fruit' and the play's aim in producing *rasa* for its audience. It has never been sufficiently appreciated how important 'strategy' (*prayoga*) is in drama, but one has only to consider the fact that many of the key dramaturgical terms regarding plot-construction are borrowed from the domain of *arthaśātra* (political science). And further to the point is the fact that both dramaturgy and *arthaśāstra* use the language of organic growth: *bīja* ('seed'), *bindu* ('drop'), *udbheda* ('sprouting'), *garbha* ('womb'), *phala* ('fruit'), etc.[32]

Nevertheless, what we seem to have discovered in the play is an irony. Just as Gaṇadāsa admits that his *upadeśa* or 'instruction' goes only so far, that it is the gifted artist who teaches the teacher and produces the magic of the aesthetic experience, so we have seen that the Vidūṣaka's efforts end in an impasse without the special effect of Mālavikā's fertile beauty. Is this, in some sense, the playwright's confession that *kāvya* cannot achieve its promise for the *rasika* because *rasa* can fulfill itself only in life? Yet the Vidūṣaka is not the playwright, nor does he represent the final dramaturgical intelligence even within the play. That role is reserved for Fate (*daiva*, 5.0, *vidhi* 5.9+), which has mysteriously guided all the elements of the action to their proper conclusion. By its decree—announced by a shadowy, 'infallible' seer (*siddhādeśena sādhunā*, 512+)—Mālavikā was appointed to spend a year disguised as a slave. Fate is the name the unknowing give to the supreme arthic intelligence, whose will is interpreted and carried out in Sanskrit drama mainly by seers and ministers. We can see, then, why the Vidūsaka's plot fails: his embodiment of the arthic force is too servile and benign, domesticated to the *rasika*'s obvious wishes. Whereas the play leaves us with a more severe impression of the dramaturgical genius.

The 5th Act does not simply recapitulate the aesthetic–erotic themes laid out in the 1st Act, but also that Act's political-historical dimension. We have no sense in the intervening Acts that Agnimitra is at war with a recalcitrant vassal, Yajñasena of Vidarbha. Yajñasena has imprisoned his brother/cousin Mādhavasena, because the latter has declared friendship with Agnimitra. In the 5th Act we find out that when Mādhavasena had gone out with a small force to join Agnimitra in Vidiśā he took along his sister, Mālavikā, whom he intended to marry to his overlord. Fate intervened (so to speak), but guided the young woman to Agnimitra's court, where she (and the ascetical Kauśikī, really the sister of Mādhavasena's deceased minister Sumati) saw fit to remain incognito till the yearlong 'curse' had run its course. In the war that goes on behind the scenes, as we have noted, Agnimitra's forces triumph over Yajñasena, with the result that Mādhavasena is freed and set up as equal monarch of a now divided kingdom of Vidarbha. We may therefore see the political plot as serving the love plot, since it plays a part in the recognition of Mālavikā.[33] But I do not think we can so easily overlook the darker side of things.

Mālavikā's fertility magic, reaching through her aesthetic epiphanies to bring the King's hopes and Aśoka tree to blossom, is itself dark and mysterious, but in a non-threatening, organic way. Like the Vidūṣaka's manoeuverings it is clearly subordinate in function to the *rasika*'s fondest hopes and fantasies about art come to life.

The withholding strategy of Fate, however, articulated as it is by a shadowy seer, emanates from a vaguely paternal sphere. It reminds us inevitably of Agnimitra's father, Puṣyamitra, also a shadowy figure in the play, whose letter to his son is read aloud in Act 5. It is a lordly pronouncement, forgiving yet sternly masculine in a way that is wholly foreign to the *rasika* hero. I say 'forgiving' because it contains an unexplained allusion to some anger between them that should now be put aside. The occasion is 'The General's' successful completion of a great military ritual (called the Rājasūya in this text): he has let his horse wander freely for a year, claiming whatever territory it wandered into as his own and defeating all who would oppose him. He has achieved this ascendancy, furthermore, with the military assistance of Agnimitra's son by Dhāriṇī, Vasumitra. Thus Agnimitra, a sportive Krishna figure, the 'love-god incarnate' (5.1-2), is generationally wedged between two more masculine figures, who take action (*pauruṣa*) to implement the will of fate (*daiva*) in sustaining the dynastic family's power and prestige. The world of political action is a threat to the *rasika's* dream of melting desire in palatial pleasure-gardens, as the two Bhāsa plays studied in this book and Viśākhadatta's MR corroborate. It shares the sternness of the paternal No to the pleasure-principle.

With this darker side of things in mind we may return to the symbol of the serpent-ring with renewed appreciation. Not only does it join the organic with the artificial, but averts to the darker force as well. The serpent shows up several times in the course of the play. It is a main feature of the action in Act 4, first as part of the Vidūṣaka's snakebite comedy, then at the end as the metaphorical identity of the staff a that wakes him from his sleep and the lovers from their happy interlude in the Ocean Pavilion. Thus it bites both ways. But two other references are perhaps even more significant. In Act 3 there is a reference (spoken by Bakulāvalikā to the Vidūṣaka) to Mālavikā's being guarded as closely by Dhāriṇī as a jewel by a serpent (*nāgarakṣita iva maṇiḥ*, 3.1+).[34] Then at the beginning of Act 4 the Vidūṣaka tells the King what has happened to Mālavikā as a result of Irāvatī's anger: 'Mālavikā and Bakulāvalikā are now in chains living where they may not see the sun like two serpent-girls in hell' (4.1+).[35] Thus we may see the serpent-ring is a symbol of art that includes a pointed reference to the obstacles that withhold or retard its promise. Like the demonized obstacles (*vighnas*) of the mythopoeic introduction to the *Nāṭyaśāstra* (*NS* 1), the forces impeding the *rasika*'s wish-fulfilment demand recognition and inclusion in his aesthetic representations.

Nor should we fail to take the hint concerning female anger. The final verse of the play is addressed to dhāriṇī as the 'angry one' (*caṇḍī*), and it is hard to avoid the impression of an appeal to the great Goddess of that name, the horrific aspect of Śiva's consort.[36] Female anger is to a large extent trivialized in this play as an element in erotic comedy. As Irāvatī herself confesses, 'Now that my good fortune has passed to another I should only become ridiculous if I still show anger'.[37] Yet it would be wrong to think women posed no threat at court. A disgruntled woman in the harem can be a great source of friction, even a potential conspirator in coup attempts.[38] Dhāriṇī is shown in Act 5 as more interested, finally, in the welfare of her son Vasumitra than in the love-intrigues of her husband. Her own so-called *ārambha* or 'undertaking'—the marriage of Mālavikā with her husband—is not simply an act of generosity or the fulfilment of a promise, but also, and more importantly, a kind of penance undertaken to insure divine favor for her son (5.3+). And it is the news of her son's safety that she first thinks of in her message to Irāvatī at the end of the play (5.17+). Agnimitra is not in so secure a position of power that he can afford to alienate his chief queen. Though in his final prayer her pleads specifically for Mālavikā and all future Mālavikās (dhāriṇī, rivals)—as indeed he should, remembering Mālavikā's underground imprisonment—his plea is really for himself. He, and the *rasika* he represents, is hedged round with menacing powers. Harmony in the harem and a benign fate are necessary for prosperity in the kingdom and his own ability to dream the dreams that are so dear to him.

Notes

1. Two of Harṣa's plays, *Ratnāvalī* and *Priyadarśikā* (7th century AD), seem closely modeled on Kālidāsa here, though it may well be that Kālidāsa himself

was following a paradigm for the *nāṭikā* form set by predecessors whose works are no longer extant. His mention of earlier dramatists in the Prologue might be taken in support of this idea.

2. Some scholars would date Kālidāsa himself to this period (2nd century BC). Most, however, believe he was a Gupta court poet in the 5th century AD. See Upadhyaya, *India in Kalidasa*, and Ingalls, 'Kālidasa and the Attitudes of the Golden Age'.
3. Historically this lends support to the Purāṇic account which says that Puṣyamitra—the general of the last of the Mauryas, named Bṛhadratha—'uprooted' (*uddhṛtya*) his King and inaugurated the Śuṅga dynasty. See Pargiter, *The Purāṇa Text of the Dynasties of the Kali Age*, pp. 31, 70.
4. For the differences between dramatic subgenres see, e.g., the handbooks of Lévi and Keith. G. K. Bhat has excerpted the appropriate passage from the original texts in *Bharata-Nāṭya-Mañjarī* (with English trans.) and *Nāṭya-Mañjarī-Saurabha* (Sanskrit only).
5. Generally the initial stage of love up to physical union—*śṛṅgāra* in the *pūrvānurāga* phase—has a strong admixture of comedy (*hāsya*), while the later *vipralambha* phase is alloyed with pathos (*karuṇa*). This play is comparable, then, to the first of Bhāsa's Udayana plays, the *Pratijñāyaugandharāyaṇa*, or to the first three acts of the *Śakuntalā*, in treating only the *pūrvānurāga* phase of love.
6. M 3.15:
   anāturotkaṇṭhitayoḥ prasidhyatā samāgamenāpi ratir na māṃ prati/
   parasparaprāptinirāśayor varaṃ śarīranāśo'pi samānurāgayoḥ//
   See also 3.3 All translations mine unless otherwise noted.
7. M 1.4:
   devānām idam āmananti munayaḥ kāntaṃ kratuṃ cākṣuṣaṃ
   rudreṇedam umākṛtavyatikare svāṅge vibhaktaṃ dvidhā/
   traiguṇyodbhavam atra lokacaritaṃ nānārasaṃ dṛśyate
   nāṭyaṃ bhinnarucer janasya bahudhāpyekaṃ samārādhanam//
   The 2nd *pāda* alludes, of course, to Śiva's androgynous form, connecting it with the *tāṇḍava* (male) and *lāsya* (female) dance styles. The second half of the *śloka* is a recapitulation of Prajāpati's lesson to the gods and demons in *Nāṭyaśāstra* 1.
8. M 1.1:
   ekaiśvarye sthito'pi praṇatabahuphale yah svayaṃ kṛttivāsāḥ
   kāntasaṃmiśrdeho'pyaviṣaya-manasāṃ yaḥ purastād yatīnām/
   aṣṭābhir yasya kṛtsnaṃ jagad api tanubhir bibhrato nābhimānaḥ
   sanmārgālokanāya vyapanayatu sa vas tāmasīṃ vṛttim īśaḥ//
   I Take *praṇata* as a substantive: 'those who have bowed before him'.
9. I mean 'charismatic' here in the etymological sense of 'radiating (godlike) grace.' I have not been able to find a good English word to express the suggestions of luminosity, fertility, vegetal luxury, auspiciousness, abundance, etc., implicit in the Śrī-idea.
10. Henceforth I shall refer to 'drama' only and to Mālavikā as an 'actress' rather than a 'dancer'. Drama (*nāṭya*) at its core was mimetic dance which had broadened out into stylized acting techniques, dialogue, etc. The performance Mālavikā gives in Act 2, wherein she acts out in dance the stanza she speaks or sings, is part of minimalist drama called a *chalita*, *calita*, or *chalika*, depending on the manuscript. According to Gaṇadāsa's statement just before

the first stanza of Act 2 the original composition seems to have consisted of four stanzas (if the reading *caturthavastukam* is indeed correct; cf. *catuṣpadavastukam* at 2.4+). I have not been able to find any outside reference to the *chalita* form—the commentator Kāṭayavema's remarks are inconsistent and of no help: 1.19+, 2.0, 2.4+. In Daṇḍin *KĀ* 1.39 it is merely a dance-form. For a song-form with love theme known as the *catuṣpada*, however, see M. Ramakrishna Kavi, *Bharatakoṣa*, p. 200. For a technical discussion of Mālavikā's performance see Kapila Vatsyayan, *Classical Indian Dance in Literature and the Arts*, pp. 213-17.

11. 1.3.22-3: *sthāne khalu sajjati dṛṣṭiḥ/ anenāṅgulīyakenodbhinnakiraṇakesareṇa kusumita iva te'grahastaḥ prabhāti/* In all cases I give the Sanskrit *chāyā* of Prakrit passages rather than the Prakrit.

12. 1.5 and 6:

    yadyat prayogaviṣaye bhāvikam upadiśyate mayā tasyai/
    tattad viśeṣakaraṇāt pratyupadiśatīva me bālā//
    pātraviśeṣe nyastaṃ guṇāntaraṃ vrajati śilpam ādhātuḥ/
    jalam iva samudraśuktau muktāphalatāṃ payodasya//

13. See verse 2.3 which appraises her body as an instrument of artistry in a way that it is indistinguishable from erotic appreciation:

    A long-eyed face, lovely as the moon,
    arms curving down from her shoulders,
    narrow torso with plump, swelling breasts,
    sides smooth as polished stone,
    a waist you could put your hands around,
    lovely round buttocks, toes that curl:
    a body put together according to a dance-master's dream.
    dīrghākṣaṃ śaradindukānti vadanaṃ bāhū natāv aṃsayoḥ
    saṃkṣiptaṃ nibiḍonnatastanam uraḥ pārśve pramṛṣṭe iva/
    madhyaḥ pāṇimito nitambi jaghanaṃ pādāv arālāṅgulī
    chando nartayitur yathaiva manasi śliṣṭaṃ tathāsyā vapuḥ//

    Compare 2.6 in which the King studies the heroine's pose after she has finished the performance: formal aesthetic appreciation intensifying erotic interest. The aestheticization of eros is a quintessential ingredient of *kāvya.*

14. For example this delightful poem on Krishna's embarrassment from the *Subhāṣitaratnakoṣa* (number 147, Ingalls' translation):

    Victorious is Hari
    who, thinking it the black of her garment,
    tries to wipe away
    the reflection of his face as dark as raincloud
    from the golden globe of Rādhā's breast,
    whence being laughed at by his mistress,
    he drops his head in shame.
    kanakanikaṣasvacche rādhāpayodharamaṇḍale
    navajaladharaśyāmām ātmadyutīṃ pratibimbitām/
    asitasicayaprāntabhrāntyā muhur muhur utkṣipan
    jayati janitavrīḍānamrapriyāhasito hariḥ//

15. E.g., Hiriyanna, Bishnupada Bhattacharya, S.K. De.

16. 3.4+-5:

    bho vayasya avadhānena dṛṣṭiṃ dehi/ etat khalu bhavantaṃ vilobhayitukāmayā pramadavanalakṣmyā yuvativeṣalajjayitṛkaṃ vasantakusumanepathyaṃ gṛhītam/

nanu vismayād avalokayāmi—
raktāśokarucā viśeśitaguṇo bimbādharālaktakaḥ
pratyākhyātaviśeṣakaṃ kurabakaṃ śyāmāvadātāruṇam/
ākrāntā tilakakriyāpi tilakair lagnadvirephāñjanaiḥ
sāvajñeva mukhaprasādhanavidhau śrīr mādhavī yoṣitām//

17. Edwin Gerow, who translates the play in Barbara Stoler Miller's *Theater of Memory*, regrettably ignores this symbolism in making the tree feminine. He is of course misled by the word *dohada* ('longing'), which usually applies to the unpredictable cravings of pregnant women. This tree's *dohada* is for a kick from the foot of a beautiful woman. As women bear children, trees (always male, as vines are always female) bear flowers and then fruit, and male lovers bear the flower and fruit of their own desire.

18. 3.11:
caraṇāntaniveśitāṃ priyāyāḥ sarasaṃ paśya vayasya rāgarekhām/
prathamam iva pallavaprasūtiṃ haradagdhasya manobhavadrumasya//

19. A mistress's anger due to her lover's peccadilloes was considered an essential part of love-play, giving the male a great thrill. We need not analyse this here, but its reverse logic underlines the male's power in the love relationship.

20. 3.12:
navakisalayarāgeṇāgrapādena bālā sphuritanakharucā dvau hantum arhatyanena/
akusumitam aśokaṃ dohadāpekṣayā vā praṇihitaśirasaṃ vā kāntam ārdrāparādham//
I skip over similar implied comparisons in 3.16-17, which personalize the tree as a lover.

21 3.19:
dhṛtipuṣpam ayam api jano badhnāti na tādṛśaṃ cirātprabhṛti/
sparśāmṛtena pūraya dohadam asyāpyananyaruceḥ//

22. 4.1:
tām āśritya śrutipathagatām āsthāya labdhamūlaḥ
samprāptāyāṃ nayanaviṣayaṃ rūḍharāgapravālaḥ/
hastasparśair mukulita iva vyaktaromodgamatvāt
kuryāt klāntaṃ manasijatarur māṃ rasajñaṃ phalasya//
The touch occurred at 3.17+, when he lifts her up after she has prostrated herself at his sudden (royal) appearance. He is unable to go further because of Irāvatī, who bursts in upon the scene shortly thereafter. The first line evidently refers to his hearing her name when he saw her in the mural (1.3+ in the preparatory scene).

23. Thus the three layers of meaning are the literal ('moist'), the formally aesthetic ('contributing to aesthetic mood'), and erotic ('arousing desire'). *Rasa* is a common word in *kāvya* for 'love' as a delicious feeling or taste. The word has already been used in a clearly aesthetic context at 1.4 (the second verse quoted in this essay) and in Kauśikī's appraisal of her performance at 2.8. I quote the latter here:
Her limbs revealed the matter as if they had their own voice,
her steps were rhythmic, she achieved absorption in the *rasas*,
the gestures of her hands were delicate, and though in the changing sequence
mood nudged mood from view, they were all linked to passion.
aṅgair antarnihitavacanaiḥ sūcitaḥ samyag arthaḥ
pādanyāso layam anugatas tanmayatvaṃ raseṣu/
śākhāyonir mṛdur abhinayas tadvikalpānuvṛttau
bhāvo bhāvaṃ nudati viṣayād rāgabandhaḥ. sa eva//

Of course, this is ironic as well, since her 'absorption in the *rasas*' in fact transcends the fictional situation represented in the performance.

24. *Rasa* is present in 3.10 (*tattvāvabodhaikaraso na tarkaḥ*) in a way that may fit in with its other occurrences. Perhaps even 3.6 (*sārasāt*) could be construed as an echoing of the motif. The word *bhāva* ('mood, emotion, intent') likewise has aesthetic and erotic meanings in this play, though not to the same degree of *double entendre*.. Without going over the passages I simply refer the reader to 1.5 (*yadyad bhāvikam upadiśyate*), 1.10 (*sākṣād bhāvāv iva śarīriṇau*), 2.8 (*bhāvo bhāvaṃ nudati*), 3.3 (*bhāvaśūnyaḥ*), and 3.14 (*bhāvajñānānantaram*).
25. In the typology of heroines she is 'bold' (*pragalbhā*), while Mālavikā is 'naive' (*mugdhā*). The former can never compete with the latter in the 'idealistic' world of Sanskrit drama: virgin territory is always much more promising. It is a matter of the Śrī of a Golden Age springtime as opposed to the Śrī of a familiar summer garden.
26. More on these concepts below; see also Ch. 2.
27. I say 'barrier', because heretofore the King's savoring of Mālavikā has required—against his will—aesthetic distance: he has not been able to get past the introductory 'appreciation' stage with the aesthetic-erotic object.
28. The piquing of a woman's jealousy through infidelities is one of the topoi of *kāvya*. If the woman has already given herself to him, it is a situation that allows him to feel a unique power over her and a narcissistic gratification. He can savor her attachment to him, enjoy other flirtations and conquests, and yet be sure that she cannot reject him. After all where can she go? It is impossible for her to leave him in this cultural context. As Irāvatī will say later in this Act, a woman who remains stand-offish can only appear ridiculous (4.16+).
29. See the uses of *śrī*, *lakṣmī*, and *śobhā* at 5.0)just before the first verse, 5.2, 5.4+, 5.6, 5.8, and 5.8+, and situationally the juxtaposition of flowering tree, marriage, military victory, and the disclosure of Mālavikā's identity.
30. At 5.13 they are called Yajñasena's 'cousin' (*pitṛvyaputraḥ*).
31. It is not within the scope of this essay to examine the numerous usages of these terms. But the reader can easily make the connections between live-plot, ritual, political science, and dramaturgy. Here follows the essential information. *Prayoga*, besides 'performance' or 'application' of theory/instruction (*upadeśa*), means 'stratagem' (borrowed from the domain of political science, *arthaśāstra*) and 'ritual performance' in the context of this play. Thus Mālavikā's ritual performance in Act 3 is simultaneously the result of the Vidūṣaka's strategy and an aesthetic performance. *Prayoga* is used 11 times in the first 4 Acts, and thrice more in verbal cognates: 1.3+, 1.5, 1.8+, 1.12+ (2ce), 1.15+, 1.19+ (2ce), 2.0, 2.9+, 3.0, 4.2+, 4.5, 4.17+. The related *Upadeśa* ('instruction') is used 16 times, thrice more counting cognates: 1.3+ (2ce), 1.5, 1.12+, 1.16+, 1.17+ (2ce), 1.18+, 1.19+ (2ce), 1.20, 2.0, 2.5+, 2.9, 2.9+, 3.0, 3.12+, 3.14+. It is the instruction of the *nāṭyācārya* to his pupil and the Vidūṣaka's—and indirectly the King's—instructions to Bakulāvalikā. *Kārya* ('task, aim') is used 6 times, 3ce in compound with *siddhi* ('success'), which is itself used 11 times, 5 more counting cognates: *kārya* 1.8+, 1.19+, 2.13+, 3.1+, 4.4+, 4.6; *siddhi* 1.8+ (2ce), 1.22, 2.13+, 3.12+ (2ce); 3.15, 4.2+, 4.4+ (4 times), 4.5, 4.5+, 4.6, 5.7+. *Phala* ('fruit, fulfilment') appears 5 times: 1.9+, 3.0, 3.16+, 4.1, 5.3+. *Ārambha* ('undertaking') 5 times: 1.8+, 1.16+, 3.10+, 4.15+, 5.3+. For the technical dramaturgical use of these terms see *NŚ* 21. *Ārambha* and *phala* (or *phalaprāpti*,

phalayoga 'attainment of the fruit') are the first and last 'stages' (*avasthās*) of the dramatic plot. *Kārya* is one of five 'plot constituents' (*arthaprakṛtis*). *Siddhi* is discussed in *NŚ* 27: see 'Aesthetic and Erotic Entrancement' for details.

32. *NŚ* 21.
33. The recognition comes when two captive woman are brought to the court who happen to have been former companions (*sakhyaḥ*) of Princess Mālavikā. They also recognize Kauśikī, who explains the fatal pronouncement, etc.
34. The reading of the phase vary; some MSS have *nidhiḥ* or *nidhī* (both 'treasure') for *maṇiḥ* 'gem'.
35. *mālavikā bakulāvalikā ca nigalavatyāv adṛṣṭasūryapādaṃ pātālavāsaṃ nāgakanyake ivānubhavataḥ/*
36. 5.20:

    Always show me your favor, O angry one:
    this I seek for the sake of your rivals.
    Blessing forfending disaster there will be
    so long as Agnimitra protects his subjects.
    tvaṃ me prasādasumukhī bhava caṇḍi nityam
    etāvad eva mṛgaye pratipakṣahetoḥ/
    āśāsyam ītivigamaprabhṛti prajānāṃ
    sampatsyate na khalu goptari nāgnimitre//
37. *anyasaṃkrānteṣvasmākaṃ bhāgadheyeṣu yadi punaḥ kupyeyaṃ tato'haṃ hāsyā bhaveyam,* 4.16+. Irāvatī, we may confidently predict, is the future of Mālavikā, once her good fortune passes to another, fresher enshrinement of Śrī. Irāvatī too had been an actress—see 1.5+.
38. See the fragment from Viśākhadatta's 3rd play *Abhisārikāvañcitaka,* discussed by V.Raghavan, *Bhoja*'s *Śṛṅgāraprakāśa,* pp. 865-66: King Udayana is alienated from Padmāvatī because he believes she has had his son killed.

CHAPTER 5

The Divided World of the Mudrārākṣasa

What is going here? What purposes does such a text serve? What factors—literary, sociological, psychological, aesthetic, cultural, ideological, linguistic, political, economic—converge here to permit a significant human expression? These are the questions in which any useful methodology of literary criticism must be rooted. A genuine inquiry into the meaning of literature must refuse to accept the ready-made categories that reduce a work to taxonomical status, exemplifying a unitary complex of cultural ideals. On the other hand, the probing of the problematic heart of a work of art requires sympathy and humility in the critic or it becomes self-serving and even nihilistic.[1] What we are after is the understanding of multiple versions of human experience—our own and that of our more or less distant forbears who have left an imaginative record of their sense of things. Literature and all the arts bring us into contact with the human mind operating on the highest level of intuitive awareness. However much language may speak us (a basic tenet of structuralism and its splintered legacy[2]), it is only when we reflect and speak to each other—in the arts and elsewhere—that it can have any meaning. People, not codes or texts, have the interest in 'what is going on' and the hope of using their knowledge 'in the cause of happiness'.[3] It is in this spirit that the present study of Sanskrit drama has been undertaken, a field in which well-intentioned respect for the ideals of classical Indian culture has made it seem either naive or impertinent to ask frankly, 'What is going on here?'

The 'here' in this chapter is a single play, which all critics acknowledge as one of the most important in the corpus, though it has seldom been written on outside of specialist literary histories, handbooks, and editions. It is called the *Mudrākṣasa* in Sanskrit (henceforth *MR*). A literal English translation would be *Rākṣasa of the Signet.*[4] The author is a certain Viśākhadatta or Viśākhadeva about whom we know very little—the usual case for 'early' Sanskrit authors. We have fragments of two other plays and some stray verses that cannot be placed;[5] he lived somewhere in the period AD 400-1000; and the manuscripts call him the son of a *mahārāja*. The last fact is somewhat surprising in view of the *MR*, which depicts a famous historical king—Candragupta Maurya, c. 320-300 BC (Mauryan Empire, c. 320-180 BC) — as passive, subservient, and even fearful with respect to his minister Cāṇakya, whom he regards as his *guru*: royal power and authority pale before the dynamic force of a ruthless and contemptuous Brahmin.[6] On the other hand, the fragments of one of his other plays (*Devīcandragupta* or *Candragupta and the Queen*) show a robust warrior-prince who defeats the enemy with a clever and dangerous deception, saving his elder brother's queen from dishonor and eventually marrying her himself after killing the brother, apparently in self-defence. In both plays we are closer to India's turbulent political history than we are in most of Sanskrit literature, which, if it recalls real events at all, tends to transform them into myth or legend. Modern writers on the *MR* do not have to be embarrassed about an effete and frivolous royal hero (the *dhīralalita* or 'gallant' type found in many dramas), but they are troubled by the lack of a truly moral perspective in the Brahmin Cāṇakya, whose vindictiveness in destroying the previous dynasty (the Nandas) and its hangers-on seems to have little to do with justice. Though we should not minimize their ties to the conventional themes of Sanskrit drama, both plays are unusual in their willingness to take tensions present throughout the literature to a much higher pitch, so that they become as close to problem-plays as one gets in Sanskrit. (Even his third play, of which we have only one fragment, was troubling—King Udayana is alienated from his second wife, Padmāvatī, because he believes she has killed his heir.[7])

My interest in the play has two focuses, one ideological, the other aesthetic, though it is hard to keep the two strictly separate, and indeed I am interested in how they merge. The ideological question centers on the issue of power and authority and features the problematic relationship of emotion and intelligence. But this opposition necessarily entails the aesthetic perspective, for the dominant aesthetic of Sanskrit poetry, and particularly drama, is that of *rasa*, a word meaning literally 'juice' or 'savor' but further designating aesthetically presented 'mood' or 'sentiment'. It is telling too that *rasa*—as well as the related word *bhāva* ('state of being', 'feeling', 'intention')— also typically means 'love' or 'erotic feeling', since the erotic and the aesthetic overlap significantly in classical Indian culture generally. We shall see that Rākṣasa's emotionalism bears both tenors in this play, though the erotic is completely sublimated into personal loyalty to a deceased 'friend', the Nanda king whom he served as chief minister. The goal of Sanskrit drama, according to the earliest manual, is emotional response in the audience, and *rasa* aesthetics concentrates on both the formal means by which this is achieved and its epistemological-ontological status in the qualified hearer-spectator.[8] The qualified recipient is called the *rasika* ('man of taste/feeling') or *sahṛdaya* ('man of heart'), both terms indicating the existence of an aesthetic culture whose professed ideal was a refined sympathetic sensitivity (*hṛdayasaṃvāda*) to whatever held emotional appeal. The poem or play, which typically features love and heroic action and ends on a marvelous note with wish-fulfilling happiness, affords the *rasika* the opportunity to contemplate emotion in what the theorists regarded as an impersonal, universalized form.[9] Some held that the resulting savor—described as a melting, expansive delight—is really a provisional form of unimpeded self-experience, i.e., liberation (*mokṣa*) from all the limiting adjuncts of worldly existence (*saṃsāra*).[10]

The importance of such a claim for us is that it signals the trans-aesthetic, human importance of the catharsis, its vague promise of breakthrough into a realm of emotional freedom. The ideological significance of the *rasa* aesthetic becomes apparent when we understand that the typical protagonist (*nāyaka*) of a Sanskrit play is himself a *rasika*, a model sensibility for the audience, in terms of both sympathetic feeling and erotic sensitivity. The hero's relation to society is a sentimental one, to the extent that it is not simply formulaic. He is the key figure in a utopian vision in which the network of social relations is imagined as an expression of affective bonding. Meanwhile his relation to the heroine (*nāyikā*) is heavily aestheticized in the ways indicated above: he savors her, translating her charms into highly wrought poetic language, and in his longing for her she becomes the symbol of access to a charmed world of emotional freedom. Thus, by thematizing the *rasika* sensibility and confronting it with forces that qualify and diminish it, every play becomes a mythic paradigm of the *rasika*'s fate in the Indian cultural context.

The *MR* takes place in the wake of Alexander the Great's pull-out from the Punjab. Candragupta (called Sandrocottus, or some variation thereof, in the Greek and Latin sources), observing the weakness of the Nanda empire based in the Gangetic valley, overthrew it and expanded his territory by forcing Seleucus I to yield trans-Indus land that had preciously been in Persian control for almost two centuries. The *MR* contains an echo of the Greek-Persian historical presence in making Candragupta's foil, Malayaketu, a *mleccha* (barbarian)[11] and allying him with Greeks, Persians, Scythians, etc. But the *ārya-mleccha* opposition, though significant, is of secondary importance in the play, and virtually non-existent in the rest of the Indian tradition on Candragupta. The real crux for the tradition is an intrafamilial power struggle which highlights the deeper issue of royal *vs.* priestly power.[12] The play extends and modifies this thematic by making the Brahmin Cāṇakya's chief rival another Brahmin, the Rākṣasa of the title, who, however, represents the claims of feeling usually associated with the royal hero. We do not know precisely what tradition the play assumes as the background for its action, since its allusions to past events are sketchy. The best-known account, relayed by the eighteenth-century commentator Ḍhuṇḍhirāja, is as follows. I give it only to provide tentative bearings on the play's themes.

The Nanda king Sarvārthasiddhi had two wives, one a Śūdrā, who gave birth to a splendid son named Maurya.[13] The other woman produced nine sons who are most notable for their antagonism to their half-brother, which increased when the latter miraculously fathered a hundred sons. Since the nine Nandas seem to have had no offspring, the throne was destined to pass to the Mauryas. To prevent this the Nandas had Maurya and all his sons jailed with the intent of starving them. But the prisoners decided to give their meager rations to the eldest son Candragupta, who bore all the bodily marks (*lakṣaṇas*) of a great ruler. One day the king of Laṅkā sent the Nandas a lion in a doorless cage with a challenge: remove the animal without destroying the bars. When all others failed to uphold the kingdom's honor Candragupta was released from prison to try his hand at the puzzle. He immediately deduced that the lion was made of wax and melted it away with a fire set beneath the cage. Thereafter his fame was such that he could not safely be reimprisoned, though his life was constantly in danger.

One day he came upon a Brahmin angrily rooting up and burning a clump of prickly *darbha*-grass which had cut his foot. Such vindictiveness recommended him as a teacher of political science (*arthaśāstra*), so Candragupta explained his situation and secured his assistance. But there is overdetermination of motive on Cāṇakya's side, for just then, feeling hunger, he decided to enter the Nanda eating-hall and sat himself peremptorily in the place of honor. The Nandas had him dragged away, despite the horrified protests of their ministers (any slight to a Brahmin risks the direst of consequences); but before he left the hall, shaking with anger, he dramatically loosened his hair and vowed that he would not bind it again until he had uprooted them. Then he and Candragupta left the capital and formed an alliance with a *mleccha* chief named Parvataka (the aforenamed Malayaketu's father), promising him half the conquered kingdom. In the field the Nanda sons were destroyed, and Candragupta and Parvataka subsequently entered the city in triumph. Then, making his first significant appearance in the story, Rākṣasa, the ultra-loyal minister of Sarvārthasiddhi, led the retired king by a subterranean passage to a hermitage, where nevertheless Cāṇakya later had him assassinated. Meanwhile Rākṣasa remained in the capital, feigning submission, but secretly leading a resistance comprised of noble merchants and other good men. Finally, however, he was forced to set up camp outside the capital and declare open rebellion. Either during this period or while still in the city he sent a poison-girl to assassinate Candragupta, but Cāṇakya shrewdly diverted her to Parvataka, thus eliminating the need to divide the kingdom (this murder of an ally is the first example of Cāṇakya's ruthless absolutism). Numerous other attempts by Rākṣasa's agents similarly fail due to Cāṇakya's ingenuity. The stage is fully set for the play's action when Malayaketu, to whom Cāṇakya has—through agents—told the truth about his father's murder (while leading all others to believe Rākṣasa was to blame) flees to Rākṣasa's camp. A large force is gathered to champion the young *mleccha*'s claim to the throne, Rākṣasa acting as his chief minister and *de facto* general.

The play opens just after Candragupta's coronation. Cāṇakya delivers a long monologue that begins with a ferocious display of wrath as he receives news that Rākṣasa and Malayaketu have joined forces, even though this has been his own plan; for he knows that by attaching Rākṣasa to a headstrong and easily duped young prince he will be able to maneuver him into submission. He then calms himself, gloats over the fulfilment of his vow, and fills us in on the plans he has made to bring Rākṣasa over to Candragupta's side. It is important to understand why this, rather than mere victory, is his ultimate goal. Rākṣasa exemplifies a principle of loyalty that is beyond most men and beneath Cāṇakya himself. The proof of this, in the latter's own words, is that while most men serve a ruler gladly in times of fortune and many will even be found to pin their hopes on his recovery of power when in misfortune, a man like Rākṣasa whose loyalty extends beyond death and the vagaries of fate is extremely rare.[14] For it is clear that for Rākṣasa Malayaketu is nothing but a vehicle of revenge in a lost cause—lost because nothing can ever restore the destroyed Nandas to the throne. He must be made to see that Candragupta is the last legitimate successor and to transfer that unquestioning loyalty to him despite his antagonism to the enemy of his now deceased dearest 'friend'. The securement of Rākṣasa is essential for Candragupta because Rākṣasa represents all that is noble and unselfish in the affective life. His attachment to the deceased Sarvārthasiddhi has all the ideality of love-in-separation, so often celebrated in Sanskrit poetry as the condition in which the lover demonstrates a devotion transcending sensual gratification, which can make love seem only a refined hedonism.

There is no need to go in detail through the plot of the play. Suffice it to say that Cāṇakya cunningly weaves an intricate web of illusion around Rākṣasa to alienate him from Malayaketu and bring his army to ruin. At length, alone and in despair in an abandoned garden, Rākṣasa decides that his final act must be the rescue of a living friend, the merchant Candanadāsa, who has been taken prisoner by Cāṇakya and is about to be executed for having secretly harbored Rākṣasa's wife and child in the city while Rākṣasa was in the field. Realizing the futility of rescue by arms he surrenders to Cāṇakya's men and offers himself as the victim in Candanadāsa's place. Cāṇakya, however, demands a greater sacrifice: that he put aside his earlier, all-consuming loyalty to the Nandas and become the 'servant' (*bhṛtya*) of his enemy. Should he not accept, Candanadāsa will die and not he. This is the major factor in Rākṣasa's accepting ministership under Candragupta, for, despite his formulaic appreciation of the latter's charisma in the last Act,[15] Rākṣasa 'bows to Fate' only when it becomes clear that Cāṇakya will indeed kill the merchant otherwise.[16] The altruistic friendship-bond, a further instance of the ideal emotionality that has linked him to the old order, provides the basis for his functioning in the new order. For his own life he cares nothing: again, this personal disinterestedness with an affective base is precisely what makes him so valuable. By contrast Cāṇakya's disinterestedness is anti-worldly, precluding any affective bond. Therein lies its power.

For Cāṇakya is nothing but a renouncer in disguise.[17] In the Indian context wisdom is worldly only in a secondary, derived sense. All knowledge and authority in the Hindu conception theoretically go back to the Vedas, the sacred texts which are *brahman* in verbal form, or to their source in the wordless absolute. What this means is that the sage who devotes himself to esoteric understanding apart from the world, typically in the forest, is the ultimate power-figure, in psychological and theoretical, if not real, terms.[18] Imagine an ancient Greek world in which priests like Teiresias represented an enormous tradition of sacred texts regarded as the source of *themis* or *dikē*, and were credited with magical powers (omniscience, invisibility, etc.) derived from superhuman ascesis. In classical India virtually every art and science has its ostensible source in the wisdom of shamanlike sage, including, for instance, drama (*nāṭyaśāstra*) and politics (*nīti-* or *arthaśāstra*). Cāṇakya in fact is the attributed author of the primary text of political science, called the *Arthaśāstra.*[19] As Coulson notes in the introduction to his translation of *MR*, we cannot think of Cāṇakya as a character so much as the idealized embodiment of *arthaśāstra* itself. He is a symbol of the omniscience of the esoteric sagely intelligence as applied to practical affairs. His implacable anger is typical of many sages, as one may find by reading the first book of the *Mahābhārata* or looking at present-day 'mythical' films and comicbooks (cf. especially Aurva and Paraśurāma whose wrath was genocidally directed at the entire class of warrior-princes). Its supranormal force, always manifested as a consuming fire (as in Cāṇakya's opening monologue), is due to the energy accrued through ascetical practice: *tapas.*

Cāṇakya in the play has marked figural associations with Yama, the god of Death, with the magical wisdom of the transcendental saint, and with Destiny.[20] His decisions, in other words, carry an indisputable finality that the ordinary person can only take as law of nature or *karma*, or as identical with a suprahuman cosmic intelligence. Ruben seems to me to miss the point in interpreting Cāṇakya as an advocate of an anti-fatalistic world-view in contrast with Rākṣasa who is apt to see the hand of Fate in every failure. The text endorses Rākṣasa's point of view by identifying Cāṇakya's will with Destiny at every juncture. Thus when Cāṇakya in 7.7 ff. seems uncharacteristically humble in attributing his success to Fate (after previously saying that only fools give it credit), he is in fact stating his relationship to the mind-beclouded human world.[21] Especially significant is verse 5.3 which identifies his statecraft with Destiny in terms that are by *double entendre* applicable to dramaturgy.[22] Cāṇakya, in other words, is the author of the play in which the average man may take various roles according to his capacity: sacrificial beast (like the Nandas, 3.27), misguided rebel (Rākṣasa), student and protégé (Candragupta), or willing agents, whether calculating (Bhāgurāyaṇa, 5.4) or sentimental (Siddhārthaka, 5.9).[23] As transcendental saint and healer of delusion (4.17 and 5.2, cited in note 20), however, Cāṇakya delivers from their infatuation those for whom he sees some purpose as servants of Destiny.

A further significant figural identification is with Śiva, whose conflagratory *tapas* is the archetype of Cāṇakya's anger (though he has none of Śiva's playful humor in deception—see the benedictory verse, 1.1). Śiva, the patron-god of drama, is an archetypal fashioner of a deceptive world of appearances that at times ruthlessly bewilders human souls, though his purpose is ultimately salvific. At one critical point in Act 3, in the argument between Cāṇakya and Candragupta feigned to mislead Rākṣasa's spies, the king pretends to find Cāṇakya's policies wanting and attributes his success in destroying the Nandas to Fate. Cāṇakya replies that only fools appeal to Fate (note 20), then flies into rage that makes Candragupta quake with genuine fear as he recalls Śiva's world-destroying Tāṇḍava dance (3.30). [24] Earlier, in the second verse of the play, Śiva had been invoked as the exuberant dancer who must always restrain his gestures lest he destroy the world without intending it. Cāṇakya's *tapas* likewise threatens to breakthrough aesthetic boundaries (see the reference to *rasa*-performance in 3.30: *raudraṃ rasam abhinayatas*) to destroy the very world-order he is engaged in setting aright by staged deceptions. The point here is that his power completely transcends the needs of his protégés and —always threatening to turn to wrath—overrides even his own strategic intentionality.[25] The cosmic perspective here and in the associations given above is not adventitious, since Cāṇakya has the dimensions of an intellect and will so utterly beyond, and contemptuous of, the worldly sphere that his power to fix the course of destiny cannot be questioned.

Critics who see in Candragupta only a passive parody of kingship (showing little resemblance in the play, incidentally, to the quick-witted puzzle-solver who saved the Nanda empire from a reputation for stupidity) have failed to perceive his affinity with the ideal monarch as celebrated throughout *kāvya*. Certainly none of Kālidāsa's plays depicts a king who is other than a child with respect to the real locus of authority. In the *Śakuntalā*, for example, that authority takes form first as the cursing ascetic Durvāsas, then as the benign super-sage Mārīca. Perhaps more interesting are the Bhāsa minister plays (*The Minister's Vows* and *Vision of Vāsavadattā*, probably 4th century. AD).

The hero Udayana is completely enveloped in an affective world of illusion while his Brahmin minister Yaugandharāyaṇa engineers all his affairs from behind the scenes, even directing the course of his love-life. Yaugandharāyaṇa does not have the metaphorical or symbolic status of Cāṇakya, but he has ample association with prophetic destiny-figures and ascetical sages. If we compare the *MR* with these plays, we find the Viśākhadatta has elucidated the paradox of a figure like Yaugandharāyaṇa, who proclaims an affective bond with his sovereign while obviously controlling and condescending to him. For Viśākhadatta has separated out the opposing features, making Rākṣasa the model of the affective servant, while Cāṇakya becomes the transcendent intelligence. A similar division has taken place in the typical hero, who with charismatic pretensions to power (king as visible guardian of the dhārmic order) plays a formulaic or ritualized role in adherence to the prescriptions of the sages, while he inwardly pursues the elation of the paradisal playworld. In the *MR* Candragupta is an emotionalist *manqué*, waiting patiently for the work to be done so that he can devote himself to savoring the delights attendant upon power,[26] while Rākṣasa stumbles through nets of illusion saved only by the ideality of his sentimentalism.

The question inevitably arises, however, concerning Rākṣasa's ability to govern. Throughout the play we have seen him fail to implement any of his designs. He is too humanly involved in the immediate situation to achieve strategic dispassion, too generously disposed to others, as in his unquestioning friendship for Siddhārthaka, who (actually an agent of Cāṇakya) has saved another friend Śakaṭadāsa from execution (2.23 ff.). Yet Cāṇakya praises his intelligence at several points and we are evidently expected to believe that he is the ideal guide for Candragupta. The obvious conclusion is that his intelligence is good enough for everyday purposes and that, even though Cāṇakya retires from the scene at the end of the play, his guiding intelligence is still felt as Destiny itself, to which Rākṣasa pointedly bows (7.17). Ruben is right to see Rākṣasa as a fatalist, but wrong in assuming that this represents defeatism. It is rather, *mutatis mutandis*, an instance of the God-on-our-side idea. The very ruthlessness that frightens the world into submission to Cāṇakya's will—the threat of destructive *tapas* that psychologically enforces allegiance to the dhārmic order—is paradoxically comforting, for it means that no human force can prevail against established values. It can be less troubling to locate all-out destructiveness in the transcendent than in the human sphere. Candragupta is our model: reverence for the *guru* and the transcendental principle that he represents is all that human intelligence need strive to achieve in the practical and ethical spheres. Rākṣasa comes to the same position after resisting, though he himself takes on the role of *guru* in a world now restored to calm. But whenever a real crisis breaks out, one that threatens the principle of established order (*dharma*), Rākṣasa will have to yield to a visitant from the esoteric realm where true intelligence, power, and authority reside.

The ethical thrust of the play then is rigidly conservative, despite or rather because of the fact the Cāṇakya does not act with any moral intention (if he did his power could not suggest the absolute). Though he commends Candragupta as a worthy monarch and decries the Nandas as 'a blight upon the earth' (1.12; see 3.12, 18), their principal sin as far as he is concerned is their affront to himself.[27] The Nandas have failed to treat a Brahmin, symbol of the authority that grounds the dhārmic hierarchy, with unquestioning reverence and humility; but the play itself (and most of the tradition) gives little indication that *dharma* was threatened in any serious way under the Nandas. In other words, it was Cāṇakya who threw everything into confusion, and then rectified the situation by bringing a Śūdra to the throne.[28] Provoked insult to a Brahmin as the source of ruin: this 'ritualistic' concept of sin, coupled with Cāṇakya's near-omniscience-and-omnipotence, is what makes the play seem like Brahmanical propaganda. What defines Candragupta as good king is that he defers to Cāṇakya's authority in every instance (3.6, 32-33). Cāṇakya's concern to stabilize Candragupta's reign by reconciling Rākṣasa to it is gratuitous, an act of largesse. It has a moral dimension—return to a stable order for the functioning of *dharma*—but is not morally grounded in his own intentions, which are dominated by indignation and contempt for the pretensions of the worldly sphere. Cāṇakya is no agent (read 'servant', *bhṛtya*) of *dharma*.

But we can see at a glance that, in terms of a challenge to the transcendent principle of authority that Cāṇakya represents, the real threat lies not with the Nandas, who as typical kings in poetry and legend do not embody any principle of intelligence, but with Rākṣasa, who is himself a Brahmin. Why then is Cāṇakya so lenient with him? Here we get to the essential issue of the play, the proper relationship between emotion and intelligence. The reason Rākṣasa is not convincing as an intelligence figure is because he is really a *rasika* in disguise, having taken over that function from the royal hero. The play envisions a crisis situation in which, unlike Bhāsa's *Svapnavāsavadatta*, the king is not allowed to pursue a private emotional course, merely *representing* authority, while all the engineering goes on in the background. Candragupta is forced to take part in the strategic work of shoring up his own power, contrary to his inclinations which are all for either pleasure or charismatic military action (1.15, 7.11). He longs, like any *rasika*, for the 'taste of pleasure' (*rasaṃ prīteḥ*, 3.4), emblematized by the full-moon festival with its strolling harlots, but he must defer the rewards of the pleasure-principle until the end of the play. Until then he is the humble and fearful Kṣatriya student of the Brahmin guru. Meanwhile the usual emotional center of gravity has been transferred from the erotic to the pathetic (*śṛṅgāra* to *karuṇa rasa*), and Rākṣasa has become the *de facto* protagonist. The cause of his grief, as we know, is the loss of his Master. But what is the significance of this ideologically? We have already said that his loyalty partakes of the ideality of love-in-separation, but we must look deeper than this.

The play is concerned with the solution of a very specific problem, which I would state as the reinvigoration of the symbolism of dhārmic stability with its usual sentimental charge. A good man—Rākṣasa—full of heartfelt feeling for his fellow man has become alienated from the symbols of power and authority appointed by Destiny and has to be brought back into line. The situation is, in fact, not unusual in Sanskrit drama, though never so directly confronted as in this play. Rākṣasa's disaffiliation has links with the attitude of certain kings (Duḥṣanta in *Śakuntalā* or Udayana in *Svapnavāsavadattā*) who give themselves up to the dreamworld of desire, of sentimental effusion, and lose interest in the formulaic performance of their public role. In the case of *Śakuntalā*, it is a curse that forces sentiment to realign itself with the dhārmically sanctioned symbols; in *SV*, it is an elaborate deception engineered by a minister under the direction of Fate. Thus Rākṣasa has to be forced to awaken from the private affective dream and transfer his allegiance to the proper, i.e., fate-sanctioned, representative of authority. That his withdrawal takes the form of nostalgic allegiance to a previous order should not mislead us about its essentially private nature. Cāṇakya's (Destiny's, the Sage's) will is, in a sense, arbitrary, but that is not the point. In the first place it embodies the authority which grounds and establishes the conventional code. In the second it represents the intractability of its—the transcendent authority's—power. In Lacanian terms we could call it the Real, which exists beyond the Imaginary world of the *rasika* sentimentalist and the Symbolic of the cultural code. Even a poetry as indifferent to realism as Sanskrit drama must nevertheless acknowledge a force that undermines which-fulfilment. Rākṣasa must not choose his own symbols, but rather sentimentalize those that Fate or the Śiva-like power of intelligence sets up for him.

One of the things that makes the *MR* unique in its corpus is the clarity with which it reveals that only a transcendent intelligence can effect the desired union of external form and inner feeling. Rākṣasa's purely immanent intelligence—worldly and guided by affective principles—cannot do so without introducing radical problems for the conventional code on both social and aesthetic levels. In Rākṣasa the *rasika* shows a certain desire for self-determination, which he then withdraws in the interest, partly it seems, of comfort or safety and, partly, of delivering himself from a private fantasy-world. The *rasa* aesthetic itself—milking stereotyped or 'idealized' situations for their emotional savor—has no room in it for ideological criticism. It works precisely by investing conventional symbols, including the whole dhārmic structure, with a surfeit of emotion. If a questioning posture were maintained, the rarefied sentimentalism of the *rasa* aesthetic would have to yield to an aesthetic in which thought were as important as, yet concomitant with, feeling. This would further mean that aesthetics even as a formal discipline could not be divorced from intellectual, ethical, and psychological issues. Thus at all costs a firm structure is needed, one that is essentially beyond question. It takes a transcendent intelligence, chastened and empowered by *tapas*, to guarantee certainty where the worldly intelligence can only find confusion.

Thus the *rasika* relegates to an all-powerful cultural Father—the ascetical sage—the resolute capacity for thought and action which he is unable or unwilling to conceive in himself. He endows the sage's will, embodied in tradition, with the ineluctability of Fate in order finally to deliver himself from the confusion resulting from the conflict of emotion and intelligence within his own person, a conflict that threatens the compartmentalization of cultural codes and his own equanimity. What surprise us, however, are the ruthlessness and rage that come to the fore. Can these be as entirely extrinsic to the *rasika* sensibility as they seem to be? If the *rasika* makes use of an anti-sentimental, anti-worldly force to guarantee the preservation of world and sentiment, does this not tell us that the internal conflict has not been resolved? There is one crucially important indication that this must be the case: the fact that Cāṇakya is an authorial figure, in other words that he stands in for the poetic intelligence its strategic capacity. The very terminology of Sanskrit dramaturgy,[29] which casts plot-construction in terms borrowed from the domain of *arthaśāstra*, shows a generic consciousness of the affinity. *MR* 4.3 (see note 22) shows Rākṣasa as the ambitious playwright seeking to write his own story of success, but foundering against the mutually exclusive demands of intelligence and emotion. 5.3, on the other hand, uses the same dramaturgical tropes to show Cāṇakya succeeding where Rākṣasa fails. It does not take much reflection to see that in general the poet is in the same ambiguous position with respect to the *rasika* patron, typically a prince, as the minister: simultaneously servant and master. Is the poet secretly enraged about his position? Most poets were, in fact, Brahmins, though Viśākhadata apparently was not. Nevertheless it is not inconceivable that Viśākhadatta could identify with the idealized Brahmin position to express disgust with what he might have regarded as the stupidity of the conventional mind.

Yet, if this is so, why is Rākṣasa punished in effect for having dared to choose his own symbols? Why must he be reconciled to the hegemony of the prescribed? Could Cāṇakya himself be a figure who represents the failure of a genuinely critical enterprise? Finding no way out of the dilemma the *rasika* slams the door on himself by personifying the creative force as ruthlessly intolerant of experiment. Cāṇakya's rage thus points to the depth of anxiety that the nascent rebellion arouses. As in Freud's description of the genesis of the superego,[30] anger initially directed against proscriptive authority turns against the self and then to outsider scapegoats (cf. the role of Malayaketu, the non-Aryan pretender). The corollary to this is the paradoxical notion that the ostensibly anti-wish-fulfilling figure of the ascetic is in fact the guarantor of the happy ending in which the *rasika* is reassured of his place in the world. The final message is the self-congratulatory one that, though terribly vulnerable, the man of feeling is yet the mainstay of the world, for without his affectivity the world is either the scene of a heartless power-struggle or an empty ritual formalism. The quintessential worldling, he becomes the hero of a world aware of its secondary ontological status, but also aware of its inexplicable necessity. Cāṇakya is the servant of the world and its purposes despite himself. It is as if the *rasika* were saying to the ascetical Father, 'Annihilate me if you wish', knowing that he could afford to call his bluff. But this is a resolution that works only so long as the *rasika* steps out of his self-determining stance and accepts, psychologically, permanent child's status. Intelligence and emotion remain grounded in separate spheres, though each serves the purposes of the other.

The poetic tradition knows of another solution, more overtly benign, but still containing contradictions. I am referring to the archetypal poet-figure Valmīki, the sage-author of the *Rāmāyaṇa*, who, though himself an ascetic, created poetry in sympathy with the affective worlding's plight.[31] We can see variants of this figure in Kāśyapa Mārīca of the *Śakuntalā* (Durvāsas bearing the tenor of ascetical rage) and Yaugandharāyaṇa of the Bhāsa plays. The mythologem alerts us to the significance of the *rasa* aesthetic in justifying the ways of men to gods, so to speak, but it still leaves intelligence and authority transcendent, as in the *MR.* In fact Rākṣasa could be seen as an exposure of the contradiction inherent in the Valmīki synthesis. In a crisis situation, such as Viśākhadatta presents, the sympathetic sage must polarize into his component parts. One cannot be both Rākṣasa and Cāṇakya.

The play leaves us, then, in an unresolved, divided state. We cannot help feeling that the final situation (the ideal world in which worthy king Candragupta is supported by loyal minister Rākṣasa), despite its sentimental charge, is mere posture. Yet the transcendent is itself entirely unappealing. Cāṇakya provides the *rasika* a means of identification with a principle of contemptuous mastery, but this only serves to alienate him from himself. Again, Viśākhadatta has taken a typical situation—the usually benign ironization of the affective hero—and forced it into an all-but-explicit confrontation. We nowhere else get so close to a dismissal of the formulaic sentimentalism on which the whole genre of Sanskrit drama rests and to what seems to me a disclosure of the *rasika*'s self-hatred. One thing is clear: that Cāṇakya's imminent retirement at the end of the play does nothing to banish the specter of disdainful mastery he has raised.

Notes

1. This chapter was originally an essay in *The Scope of Words: In Honor of Albert S. Cook*, ed. by Peter Baker *et al.* The central question 'What is going on here?' is the basis of Cook's protean critical methodology, which could be called a

humanistic 'deconstruction'.

2. See Manfred Frank, *What is Neostructuralism*, Lectures 1-4.
3. A phrase of Louis Armstrong, cited as an inscription to *Good Morning Blues: The Autobiography of Count Basie.*
4. The *MR* has been translated by Michael Coulson in *Three Sanskrit Plays* as *Rākṣasa's Ring*, and more freely by J. A. B. van Buitenen in *Two Plays of Ancient India* under the title *The Minister's Seal.* The Sanskrit editions I have used are those of K. T. Telang; Alfred Hillebrandt; and M. R. Kale. I know of two critical works devoted to the play. The first—G. V. Devasthali, *Introduction to the Study of the Mudrārākṣasa*—is intended for Indian schoolboys, running over the rudiments of plot, character, theme, etc. The second is Walter Ruben, *Der Sinn des Dramas "Das Siegel und Rākṣasa"*, a detailed commentary which offers a *Weltanschauung* interpretation (fatalism vs. human enterprise). All verse-numbering follows that of Coulson's translation.
5. See V. Raghavan, *Bhoja's Śṛṅgāraprakāśa*, pp. 843 ff.
6. Compare also the panegyrical verses honoring Candragupta to the one celebrating Cāṇakya's power, 3.17, 19, 24.
7. Raghavan, *Bhoja's Śṛṅgāraprakāśa*, pp. 865-66.
8. Chapters 6, 7, and 27 of the *Nāṭyaśāstra* (3rd-5th century AD) are the essential ones on emotional response. Ch.1, a mythic origins account, also yields insight into the importance of audience response. The epistemological interest in *rasa* comes later, peaking in the aesthetical works of Abhinavagupta (fl. AD 1000).
9. The main theoretical voices are those of Bhaṭṭa Nāyaka (10th century) and Abhinavagupta, both of whom drew on the work of the more formalistic Ānandavardhana (9th century). All were from Kashmir, which was evidently the early center of theoretical poetics in India. Bhaṭṭa Nāyaka's work is lost, but his was the key concept of universalization (*sādhāraṇīkaraṇa*).
10. Abhinavagupta's thesis.
11. His name, however, would seem to indicate only that he was a non-Aryan from South India (Malaya = Malabar).
12. See V. Raghavan, *The Mudrārākṣasakathā of Mahādeva,* pp. 44-66, for a summary of known literary versions. Both issues—intrafamilial and Brahmin-Kṣatriya conflict—are also at the core of the *Mahābhārata,* perhaps the principal culture-defining Indian text.
13. The four social classes (*varṇas*) in hierarchical order are: Brahmin (priest), Kṣatriya (warrior prince), Vaiśya (farmer, trader, etc.), and Śūdra (servile). In a mythic hymn of the Ṛgveda (1500-1000 BC) the four orders are said to derive respectively from the head, arms, legs, and feet of the primordial sacrificial man. The first three are full ritual members of the Aryan community, though in most of the literature only Brahmins and Kṣatriyas are of any importance. Śūdras are relatively despised, but there are groups even lower who have no place at all in the *varṇa* system.
14. 1.13-14:

    While he has power, people serve their lord for gain,
    And those who follow him into adversity are hoping for his restoration.
    Hard it is to find men with loyalty such as yours,
    Selflessly shouldering the burden of duty even when their master is dead.

    What merit has a timid, stupid man, however loyal?
    What use is a brave and clever man if he lacks loyalty?
    Those who unite brains, courage and devotion, are the servants

That profit a king. In good times or in bad the rest are concubines.
aiśvaryād anapetam īśvaram ayam loko'rthataḥ sevate
taṃ gacchantyanu ye vipattiṣu punas te tat pratiṣṭhāśayā/
bhartur ye pralaye'pi pūrvasukṛtāsaṅgena niḥsaṅgayā
bhaktyā kāryadhuraṃ vahanti kṛtinas te durlabhās tvādṛśāḥ//
aprājñena ca kātareṇa ca guṇaḥ syād bhaktiyuktena kaḥ
prajñāvikramaśālino'pi hi bhavet kiṃ bhaktihīnāt phalam/
prajñāvikramabhaktayaḥ samuditā yeṣāṃ guṇā bhūtaye
te bhṛtyā nṛpateḥ kalatram itare sampatsu cāpatsu ca//

All translations of the text in this essay are by Michael Coulson, unless otherwise noted.

15. 7.12 and 14, both spoken by Rākṣasa:
Here is Candra Gupta, who
Even as a child was known to the world
As one of extraordinary promise,
And by degrees has grown to Emperor
As an elephant grows to be lord of the herd. . . .

This pupil of Kauṭilya [=Cāṇakya] is making me his servant. But no, this is courtesy on Chandra Gupta's part: my jealousy makes me misinterpret it. No wonder Kauṭilya has won such glory:
If he finds a worthy and ambitious man,
The dullest-witted counsellor is sure of renown,
While the cleverest minister, relying on a fool,
Is undermined, like a tree on the bank of a river.

aye candraguptaḥ/ ya eṣa
bāla eva hi loke'smin sambhāvitamahodayaḥ/
krameṇārūḍhavān rājyaṃ yūthaiśvaryam iva dvipaḥ// . . .
spṛśati māṃ bhṛtyabhāvena kauṭilyaśiṣyaḥ/ athavā vinaya evaiṣa candraguptasya matsaras tu me viparītaṃ kalpayati/ sarvathā sthāne yaśasvī cāṇakyaḥ/ kutaḥ/
dravyaṃ jigīṣum adhigamya jaḍātmano'pi netur yaśasvini pade niyatā pratiṣṭhā/
adravyam etya tu viśuddhanayo'pi mantrī śīrṇāśrayaḥ patati kūlajavṛkṣavṛttyā//

16. 7.17:
Love for the Nandas fills my heart, yet I must serve their enemies.
The trees I watered and made tall are all cut down.
To protect a friend I must bear the sword of office.
The things that happen make us all Fate's servants in the end.
nandasnehaguṇāḥ spṛśanti hṛdayaṃ bhṛtyo'smi tadvidviṣāṃ
ye siktāḥ svayam eva vṛddhim agamaṃś chinnās ta eva drumāḥ/
śastraṃ mitraśarīrarakṣaṇakṛte vyāpāraṇīyaṃ mayā
kāryāṇām gatayo vidher api na yantyājñākaratvaṃ cirāt//

I would alter the last line of Coulson's translation:
The course of our duties soon makes us Fate's servants too [i.e., as well as of our human masters].
This renders the force of both *kāryāṇām* and *vidher api.*

17. 'Renouncer' (*saṃyāsin*) signifies one who has ascetically abandoned the world, fixed by dharmic scheme as the fourth stage of life. But asceticism was evidently pre-Aryan in origin and transcended orthoprax Hinduism in any case. In a classic article Louis Dumont has pointed out that the renouncer is the authority figure par excellence in the Indian tradition: 'World Renunciation in Indian Religions'; see also J. C. Heesterman, *The Inner Conflict of Tradition: Essays in*

Indian Ritual, Kingship, and Society, passim, but esp. Chs. 8 and 10, entitled 'The Conundrum of the King's Authority' and 'Power, Priesthood, and Authority'.

18. That is to say, it is the sage, representing the unseen, and not the king, who holds sway over the cultural imagination. Again see Heesterman, *Inner Conflict*, Chs. 8 and 10.

19. Date uncertain, but probably later than the Mauryan period (320-180 BC), to which legend assigns it.

20. I cite a few instances. Death: Cāṇakya's spy in Act 1 is disguised as a street-entertainer who sings in praise of Yama while displaying his image on sheets of cloth (1.16-17); Cāṇakya's sardonic allusion to Citragupta, Yama's accountant (1.19); Candanadāsa interprets his unjust condemnation as proof of Yama's ascendency (7.3). Transcendental sage: Jīvasiddhi, Cāṇakya's spy disguised as a Jain monk, chants with hidden meaning of sages who heal the sickness of illusion with bitter medicine (4.17) and with profound intellect achieve 'success in the world by more-than-worldly means' (5.2)—

    śāsanam arhatāṃ pratipadyadhvaṃ mohavyādhivaidyānām/
    ye muhūrtamātrakaṭukaṃ paścāt pathyam upadiśanti//
    arhataḥ praṇamāmi ye te gambhīratayā buddeḥ/
    lokottarair loke siddhiṃ mārgair gacchanti//

    Destiny: all through Act 2 Rākṣasa and the spy who reports to him attribute the failure of Rākṣasa's covert operations in the capital to the will of Fate; Rākṣasa often repeats this conviction, e.g., 4.2, 5.20, 6.6-8, and 7.17. Meanwhile Bhāgurāyaṇa, Cāṇakya's most cunning spy, makes a direct comparison between his master's plotting and *de facto* destiny (5.3); and in the 3rd Act, when Candragupta, in contentiousness feigned for the benefit of Rākṣasa's spies, attributes Cāṇakya's previous successes to luck or fate, Cāṇakya replies that 'ignoramuses always credit Fate' (*daivam avidvāṃsaḥ pramāṇayanti*, 3.28+). To underscore the impression of omniscient control Cāṇakya declares himself one who even in his dreams is always pursuing his purpose (*na prayojanam antarā cāṇakyaḥ svapne'pi ceṣṭata iti*, 3.19+).

21. Cāṇakya: Tell me, good fellow, tell me—

    Who caught the fire with its leaping flames and put it in his pocket?
    Who roped the restless wind and kept it still?
    Who trapped the lion that reeked of elephant rut and caged him?
    Who swam the ocean, with its sharks and crocodiles?

    Executioner: Why, you, Your Honour, with your strategic brilliance.
    Cāṇakya: No, my man, no! It was Destiny, hating the race of Nanda.
    bhadra kathaya kathaya—

    kenottuṅgaśikhākalāpakapilo baddhaḥ paṭānte śikhī
    pāśaiḥ kena sadāgater agatitā sadyaḥ samāsāditā/
    kenānekapadānavāsitasaṭaḥ siṃho'rpitaḥ pañjare
    bhīmaḥ kena ca naikanakramakaro dorbhyāṃ pratīrṇo'rṇavaḥ//

    nanu nītinipuṇabuddhināryeṇa/
    ma maivam/ nandakulavidveṣiṇā daiveneti brūhi/

    The dramatic entrance that precedes this—Cāṇakya wrapped in the stage curtain with only his face appearing—underlines the symbolic identity.

22. 5.3 (spoken Bhāgurāyaṇa):

    Sometimes revealed, sometimes buried deep out of sight,
    Now complex, now simple, as the task requires,
    Now withering in the seed, now bearing rich fruit—

His statecraft is as manifold as Destiny.
muhur lakṣyodbhedā muhur adhigamābhāvagahanā mu
huḥ sampūrṇāṅgī muhur atikṛśā kāryavaśataḥ/
muhur naśyadbījā muhur api bahuprāpitaphale—
tyaho citrākārā niyatir iva nītir nayavidaḥ//

'Seed' (*bīja*), 'fruit' (*phala*), 'task' (*kārya*) are technical terms of plot-construction (see note 31 of Ch.4 'Kalidāsa's Metadrama'); so too the language of revelation and concealment. This verse should be understood with reference to Rākṣasa's profession of dramaturgy/statecraft in 4.3:

Contriving the first faint outlines of a plot, and then elaborating,
Causing the hidden seeds to germinate unsuspected,
Cleverly managing the crisis, drawing together all the sprawling threads—
In these painful anxieties of creation I am working like a playwright.
kāryopakṣepam ādau tanum api racayaṃs tasya vistāram icchan
bījānāṃ garbhitānāṃ phalam atigahanaṃ gūḍham udbhedayaṃś ca/
kurvan buddhyā vimarśaṃ prasṛtam api punaḥ saṃharan kāryajātaṃ
kartā vā nāṭakānām imam anubhavati kleśam asmadvidho vā//

For the terminology *in proprio situ* see *NŚ* 21.

23. Siddhārthaka's proleptic function is to show that idealistic sentiment can exist within the framework created by Cāṇakya. He prepares the way for Rākṣasa's capitulation.

24. What, can His Honour be genuinely angry?

Though tears of emotion from his quivering eyelids seek to quench it,
The tawny blaze of his eyes bursts into flame beneath his smoking brow.
And as if remembering Śiva in his terror Dance,
The earth trembles violently and scarcely bears the stamping of his foot.

aye kathaṃ satyam evāryaḥ kupitaḥ/ tathāhi/
saṃrambhaspandipakṣmakṣarada-malajalakṣālanakṣāmayāpi
bhrūbhaṅgodbhedadhūmaṃ jvalitam iva puraḥ piṅgayā netrabhāsā/
manye rudrasya raudraṃ rasam abhinayatas tāṇḍaveṣu smarayantyā
saṃjātograprakampaṃ katham api dharayā dhāritaḥ pādaghātaḥ//

25. One might think, in this and other respects of Cāṇakya's character, of parallels to Freud's notion of the death-drive: *Beyond the Pleasure Principle*, sections 5 and 6

26. Cf. 3.4 (my trans.):

Sovereignty affords little scope for pleasure to a king intent on his duties. For—
If intent on his own ends, he ignores the ends of others;
yet to what end a king who ignores his own ends?
Setting others above himself, alas, he becomes a servant,
and how can a servant know the taste (*rasa*) of pleasure?

rājyaṃ hi nāma rājadharmānuvṛttiparasya nṛpater mahad aprītisthānam/
kutaḥ—
parārthānuṣṭhāne rahayati nṛpaṃ svārthaparatā
parityaktasvārtho niyatam ayathārthaḥ kṣitipatiḥ/
parārthaś cet svārthād abhimatataro hanta paravān
parāyattaḥ prīteḥ katham iva rasaṃ vetti puruṣaḥ//

27. Their attempted genocide is never alluded to in the play, nor does it figure in most of the legends (see Raghavan, *Mudrārākṣasakathā*). Alluded to in the play and showing up more often in the tradition is their overtaxation of the populace, but against this as a factor in the play is the fact that Candragupta's

rule was not readily accepted by the people and that the leaders of the resistance—notably rich merchants like Candanadāsa who should have deprecated heavy taxes—were 'the best and brightest' of the citizenry.

28. According to Purāṇic accounts this inaugurated the age of intermittent Śūdra dynasties, one of the chief signs of the degeneration of the present world-age (the *kaliyuga*). Rākṣasa's desperate championing of a *mleccha* has to be seen in context therefore.
29. *NŚ* 21; G.K. Bhat, *Bharata-Nāṭya-Mañjarī*, pp. 160 ff.; or see the appropriate chapters of Lévi, *Le théatre indien*, Keith, *The Sanskrit Drama*, or S. N. Shastri, *The Laws and Practice of Sanskrit Drama*.
30. *Civilization*, section 7; cf. *The Ego and the Id*, section 3.
31. The story is told in *Rāmāyaṇa* 1.2 In sympathetic grief for a curlew deprived of its mate he speaks the first metrical stanza, which then becomes the vehicle for the sorrowful story of Rāma, the Hindu paragon of the choice of duty over desire.

CHAPTER 6

Paradise in a Prison Cell

It takes a determined skeptic to doubt the attribution of the *Svapnavāsavadattā* (*SV*) to Bhāsa, a playwright Kālidāsa himself named as so favored in his time that the younger generation of *nāṭyakāras* had a difficult time getting a hearing.[1] After sifting through the evidence, the most likely conclusion is that the play we have of that name (or a variant), first discovered for Indology by T. Ganapati Sastri in 1909, is a somewhat shorter version of the play known to Śāradatanaya, Rāmacandra and Guṇacandra, Sāgaranandin, Abhinavagupta, Bhoja, and others.[2] And one can scarcely admit the genuineness of SV without accepting the *Pratijñāyaugandharāyaṇa* (*PY*): the two are perfectly complementary in plot, theme, treatment, and style.[3] But even if we could not locate these two plays among the earliest extant of the whole Sanskrit corpus, we would be justified on aesthetic and thematic grounds in including them in any study of the key works of Sanskrit poetry. The plays are simple, yet charming and sophisticated, and more genuinely dramatic—giving us a more complicated sense of conflicting human interests (especially *SV*)—than any play except the *Mudrārākṣasa* (*MR*) of Viśākhadatta, who, however, completely lacks Bhāsa's lightness of touch. The two plays provide a thematic bridge between Kālidāsa and Viśākhadatta, combining the latter's focus on sentiment-negating political demands (*artha, utsāha*) with the former's luxuriating treatment of the inner world of erotic emotion (*kāma, śṛṅgāra*).[4] Bhāsa gives us a perspective on love that is much different from Kālidāsa's : more comic, we would have to say, because it is contrasted not so much with duty (*dharma*) as with a practical sense of reality, yet not so ironic that it alienates our sympathy for the hero. It is that balance of perspectives that I would like to address in this chapter: how it is, for example, that the hero (*nāyaka*), Udayana, can seem to us both foolish and ideally sympathetic. Like all 'steadfast-and-gallant' (*dhīralalita) nāyakas,* as well as some others (e.g., Rākṣasa and Cārudatta of the *MR* and *Mṛcchakaṭika* [*Mṛcch*] respectively), Udayana is a projection of the *rasika* sensibility.[5] What this means for us is that the stakes are higher than they would be if we were dealing with a mere individual hero. The plays allow us to reflect on the *rasika*'s special relation to practical reality, his self–conscious awareness of insulation from it, his apparent powerlessness, the significance of his sentimental values and erotic aspirations, his foolishness in the eyes of the world and perhaps even his own eyes. Once again, the basic question concerns the nature of the playworld of Sanskrit poetry.

The *PY* and *SV* work dialectically together. The former sets up the idea that play (*līlā, krīḍā*) in its most insouciant aspect triumphs over every negative force practical reality and duty can bring to bear, while the latter makes play seem problematic, vulnerable, tinged with sadness, and implicating a certain ethics of sensitivity to others' feelings. In the *PY*, the problems confronting the romantic hero King Udayana are externalized. Despite the fact that it is his incorrigible penchant for recreation and extravagantly impolitic behavior that brings him to a state of imprisonment in his enemy's capital, the very fact of his ironic triumph over good sense makes it seem as if the real barriers to his freedom are creations of the unimaginative, pragmatic, duty-bound world around him. In the *SV*, on the other hand, despite the fact that all Udayana's problems result from specific decisions of his minister Yaugandharāyaṇa in conjunction with the will of Fate, the focus of our attention is always on his—and his wives' —emotional life. In the first play, a prison cell becomes a pleasure garden, and the woman whose beauty performs this magic rides off with the hero to extend the charmed circle of happiness into the broader world beyond. In the second, happiness is so hedged round with ignorance and illusion that it seems only a fragile dream, and pragmatic intelligence (*artha*) reveals its power to cancel pleasure (*kāma*) even as it faithfully delivers it: the pleasure garden becomes again a prison cell. What follows will be in three parts, as we consider each play separately in the light of basic themes and then reflect on our findings in a conclusion.

1. *Pratijñāyaugandharāyaṇa*

a. *The Triumph of Play*

The first Act of *PY* presents us with the basic theme of work vs. play, *artha* (in league with *dharma*) *vs. kāma.* It opens with the bustle in the Vatsa capital, Kauśāmbī. Spies have reported to the minister Yaugandharāyaṇa that the ministers of the Avanti King Pradyota Mahāsena have prepared an ambush for his own King Udayana. He is about to dispatch a messenger to warn his protégé, who is at the moment hunting elephants on the Kingdom's border, when another arrives to tell the minister it is too late. Udayana has walked into the trap in a characteristically grand and thoughtless manner. In the first place the ambush has occurred while the King was engaged in sport instead of attending to state business. Secondly, it is romance that has lured him into the catastrophe. A stranger had approached the hunting party on foot with news of the fabled blue elephant Nīlakuvalaya ('Blue Lotus,' a Moby Dick of elephants) not far away. Unable to resist the appeal of such a prize and ignoring the advice of his attendant minister Rumaṇvān to be cautious, Udayana set out immediately with a small party, determined to capture the beast not with the usual weapons, ropes, and trenches, but by casting a musical spell over him with his marvelous *vīṇā* ('lute') Ghoṣavatī.[6] Thus we have the extravagant image of a charismatic *rasika* walking blindly into a clever trap, armed with mythic illusions and poetic incantations, like the Fool pictured on the Tarot card, stepping off a precipice with his eyes lifted to some enchanting distraction. Once aware of the treachery,[7] however, Udayana suddenly becomes a swashbuckling Kṣatriya hero. He leaps back onto his horse, rouses his men's spirits, calling each by name, then plunges, 'as if playing' (*krīḍann iva,* 1.6+), into the fray, only to be tragically overwhelmed by wounds and lose consciousness just as the sun goes down.[8] And shortly thereafter he is carried off wounded on a litter to Mahāsena's prison in Ujjayinī.

Without discounting the thematic value of the pathos these events arouse in other characters in the play as well as the audience, we can nevertheless look quickly, as the play itself does, to the brighter side of things. Act 2 puts the matter in its proper perspective: there are marriage preparations taking place in Ujjayinī. They are still at an early stage—Mahāsena is receiving ambassadors from neighbouring princes for the hand of his daughter Vāsavadattā—but a contemporary *prekṣaka,* like the modern reader, could have no doubt that Udayana will walk off with the prize. The situational ironies of Act 2 are only too obvious in making the point. So we know already that Udayana's imprisonment will prove to be a blessing in disguise; the only question is how he will pull it off. A little vignette from the same Act provides a hint of what is to come in Acts 3 and 4. Mahāsena is alone with his queen, when she remarks on his uncommon jubilation over the capture of his enemy. She wonders why she has not heard his name among the suitors.

King: My queen, he ignores my very name, not to speak of desiring an alliance by marriage.
Queen: Ignores? Is he a boy (*bāla*) or a fool (*apaṇḍita*)?
King: He may be a boy, he is no fool.
Queen: What makes him so haughty?
King: The Bhārata dynasty, with its long roll of famous Royal Sages and its tradition of deep learning. He is proud of his hereditary knowledge of music. His youthful beauty makes him vain. His people's remarkable attachment (*anurāga*) makes him confident.
Queen: The very qualities one would desire in a son-in-law. By what perversity does one find fault in him?[9]

The Queen sees immediately that his 'childishness',[10] buttressed by good lineage, etc., is an essential part of his charm, which marks him out over the other suitors.[11] Udayana will eventually emerge triumphant because of the very qualities that led to his ostensible downfall in Act 1.[12] Just after this scene, the chamberlain enters with a query about what to do with Udayana's lute. Mahāsena says it should be given to Vāsavadattā, since neither of his sons wants it[13] and Vāsavadattā has already requested instruction on the instrument. We find out in Act 4 that, some time after the events reported in the third Act, Udayana was appointed Vāsavadattā's teacher. Thus the elephant that has proved to be a willow-the-wisp in Act 1 actually points ahead to the lovely princess whom the hero will conquer with the same musical charms. The apparent catastrophe of defeat and imprisonment is revealed as a portal to the garden of delights located at the heart of the courtly playworld.

What Udayana lacks in prudence the play shows him as more than making up for in imagination. Nowhere does this come out more forcefully than in the 3rd Act when we learn that the hero has 'turned his cell into a pleasure garden' (3.5+) by the pure enchantment of his fascination with Vāsavadattā, whom he has seen only once from a distance.[14] This does not, however, come across initially as a positive event. The news comes to Yaugandharāyaṇa on the eve of the implementation of an elaborate covert action to spring Udayana from jail. Panic was to have been created among the palace elephants so that Mahāsena would have had to call upon Udayana to calm them with his lute, after which he would have leapt on the back of the fastest and been back in Kauśāmbī almost before the enemy had time to react. But now the Vidūṣaka informs him and their confederate Rumaṇvān, as all three meet in disguise in a Śiva-temple in Ujjayinī, that the King no longer wishes to go through with the plan. He has fallen in love. Yaugandharāyaṇa's exasperation provokes him to uncharacteristic sarcasm (3.6), but he soon regains his poise with both resignation and resolve. He chides the Vidūṣaka, who has actually gone so far as to suggest that they leave him to his own devices:

> Shall we abandon one who
> is smitten by woe and by love,
> who depends on his friends
> and cannot awake when he should?[15]

We will discuss the loyalty-issue a little later. For the time being, we should simply note that Yaugandharāyaṇa's is the voice of worldly intelligence in a benign, paternal disposition to the hero's childish extravagance. Love, from this vantage, is simply one of life's variables, in this case an affliction ('smitten') or blinding delusion ('cannot awake'). But the political strategist cannot let emotional accident destroy his designs. Yaugandharāyaṇa therefore simply extends his earlier vow to deliver the King to include the young Princess too. And we see in Act 4, in which, off-stage, the King rides away with his Śrī on her elephant, that the plan succeeds.

'Fancying his prison cell a pleasure garden he is set to engage in the royal sport of love.'[16] So the Vidūṣaka sums Udayana's attitude at this critical juncture. A few lines earlier he had characterized his motivation as 'self-interest' (*ātmakāryatā*). This is a loaded word, because *kārya* is a technical dramaturgical term for the motivating goal of all action in the plot. For all other characters in this play, except perhaps the counter-hero (*pratināyaka*) Mahāsena and his ministers,[17] *kārya* falls under the headings of *artha* and *dharma*. Yaugandharāyaṇa is their chief representative: all his efforts (*prayatna*) are directed at furthering the public enterprise (*ārambha*) of restoring the 'master' (*svāmin*) to power. He never thinks of himself, except to take pride in his success or deplore the humiliation of his failure (allowing his protégé to be captured). He explicitly states his willingness to die in the effort so long as the goal is achieved (e.g. 1.14, 4.8). In other words, he and his confederates are motivated by *parakāryatā* 'action for another.' For the King alone the goal of action coincides with private pleasure (*kāma*) rather than work or duty. In his privileged sphere no decision is really painful, basically because he is not called upon to make decisions. As Cāṇakya says in the *MR*:

But then Kingship cannot give pleasure unless it is free from the special vexations that accompany it:
If they must forage for themselves,
Then, however strong they are,
Lords of men and lords of the herds alike
Grow vexed and weary.[18]

It is, therefore, easier for Yaugandharāyaṇa to revise his earlier vow to include the King's new erotic interest than to educate him to the responsibility of his political position.

After all, what is the King's responsibility, when he has ministers who can attend to all the practical aspects of rule much better than he could himself? In a monarchical system there is always the tendency for the kingship to acquire symbolic value at the expense of practical function. The king becomes the public symbol of human aspirations to paradise: he is the focus of government *qua* ritual pageantry, which itself represents the aestheticization, and so transcendence, of the mundane. The Leader is the charismatic personality whom all admire and dote upon: an emotional linkage that allows one a special feeling of participation in the Great One's aura. He is the privileged child the rest of us have had to abandon in the process of growing up; he alone has never left the paradise of infancy; and he thus expresses our own emotional potential.[19] We have ample evidence that in his nobility of character he loves us as we love him.[20] Besides, is it not auspicious to have a leader whose way of life approaches the divine? Are not the women with whom he takes his ease all embodiments of Śrī, the feminine genius of sovereignty who also represents wealth and fertility for the whole Kingdom? Udayana escaping imprisonment and paternal marriage-sanctions[21]: this is Kṛṣṇa himself dancing on the heads of Kāliya, the snake-demon, or prankishly seducing the cowherds' wives. Even Mahāsena gives the ebullient young couple his blessing (4.24+).

So, the play as whole endorses the King's *ātmakāryatā* as a kind of inspiration that complements Yaugandharāyaṇa's *parakāryatā* and brings it to the level of emotional fruition. For all that Udayana's success (*siddhi*, *phalayoga*, etc.) depends on his minister's concerted efforts, the final irony is that his own childish waywardness is the key element in the larger strategy of Fate,[22] viz. the cementing of an alliance between Vatsa and Avantī. Yaugandharāyaṇa rightly interpreted the sage Dvaipāyana's enigmatic actions in Act 1 as 'instruction' (*upadeśá*, 1.,16+) to assume a disguise and work covertly in the enemy's capital, but he did not understand the significance of the Brahmin's laugh as he predicted prosperity (*udaya*) for the house of Udayana. Though he is the principal intelligence figure in the play, Yaugandharāyaṇa fails at first to comprehend the intelligence of Destiny, which awards a privileged place to the romantic imagination. The King is no mere child. he is the supreme Feeler of emotional effects, a true hero of the imaginative life. Despite disaster and humiliation he keeps his sensibility attuned to the regenerative power of Eros. He allows the aura of the Radiant Female of all Sanskrit poetry to pervade, illuminate, and transform his prison cell into a garden. His irrepressible readiness for *līlā* assures us that victory cannot be fully understood in merely political or pragmatic or even moral terms. His championing of the erotic and aesthetic dimension of life tends, at least in its results, to break down the barriers—so prominent in dharmic ideology—between the public and private spheres, for it announces in effect that things have no value if they cannot be savored. Success and rectitude without personal happiness have no meaning for the *rasika*.

b. *Feeling vs. Intelligence*

In order for *līlā* to triumph, as it seems to in this play, intelligence has to be seen as subordinate to feeling, since it is in the affective sphere that sport has its chief value. Yet how can this subordination be made believable, when we see that the chief intelligence figure, Yaugandharāyaṇa, stands in a protective relation to the hero? Part of the answer we have already given, viz., that Yaugandharāyaṇa's intelligence is humanly limited when juxtaposed with the intelligence of Fate. But Fate's concrete spokesman in this play is the ascetic Dvaipāyana, and in fact we could regard the metonymy as an identification. Though Fate as an objective force may be considered either as the net result of myriad *karma* or an independent force limiting human effort (*pauruṣa*), as an intelligent design guiding events to their successful conclusion it is one with the occult Brahmanical intelligence that represents it in the popular imagination. Yaugandharāyaṇa, himself a Brahmin, also has a certain ascetical aspect,[23] though not as much as Cāṇakya in the *MR*. Rather, he is a cross between Cāṇakya and Rākṣasa, representing a successful hybridization of intelligence and emotion. But the two are not of equal weight in his character. In him intelligence clearly holds sway over emotion. In fact, he is emotional only to the extent that it guarantees his *parakāryatā*. For without some basic affective link to the hero and the symbolic order he figureheads what is to keep his intelligence from being indifferent or even subversive? A pure intelligence, as in the case of Dvaipāyana for instance, cannot even be held by ordinary dharmic ties. Strictly speaking, in the Indian world-view a pure intelligence can exist only on the level of renunciation. So the solution of the play, which is the solution of the popular imagination in various legends, is to make the minister an ascetic with regard to sexual feeling but a veritable *rasika* with regard to other kinds of affection.

We can express this relationship in terms borrowed from sixteenth-century *bhakti* aesthetics.[24] Traditional *rasa* theory has one very obvious flaw: it does not recognize the importance of non-erotic human affection, thus excluding friendship, parental feeling, love of child for parent, etc., from the aesthetic domain. This would not be a significant lack if some of these themes were not so important in actual Sanskrit dramas. Thus the Vaiṣṇava aesthetic, despite its lateness and whatever its religious motives, fills a void in Sanskrit critical theory and practice.[25] The system, as articulated by Rūpa Gosvāmin, recognizes five levels of *bhakti* or devotion, which apply to the worship of Kṛṣṇa. The hierarchical structure is a reversal of orthodox notions of salvation based on tranquility and purity, so that the more emotional one's devotion the closer one comes to complete release. Here is the pyramid:

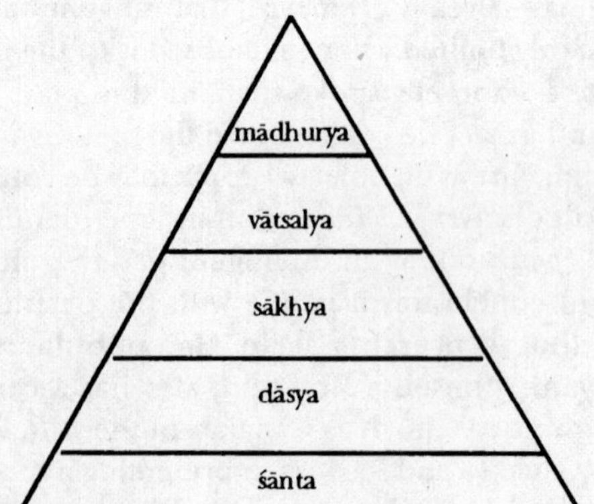

Śānta (the state of transcendental equipoise) is at the bottom with merely a token presence in the system, since it is not really an emotional state at all.[26] Next up is the state of servile devotion (*dāsya*). Still more emotive is the friendship relation (*sākhya*), and more heartfelt than that is parental love (*vātsalya*): but the culmination of emotional intensity is erotic love (*mādhurya*, a synonym for *śṛṅgāra*). If we apply this to the *PY*, what we find is that Yaugandharāyaṇa—let us bracket his confederates—embodies all the lower relations. As a dispassionate intelligence figure he is in the *śānta* stratum, but this is precisely the area where his allegiance to Udayana is least convincing, which accords exactly with the Vaiṣṇava understanding. It requires an emphasis on his intellectual pride (his refusing to accept having been outmaneuvered by the enemy's ministers) to make it at all credible. On the other hand, Act 1 makes repeated allusions to his *dāsya* relation, as for instance in 1.14.[27] The attitude of uncritical devotion to the Charismatic Leader is that in which Yaugandharāyaṇa most represents the naive disposition of the popular audience.[28] But even this is unconvincing, precisely because the minister's uncommon intelligence sets him apart: how could he accept without serious qualification the fiction of Udayana's leadership, charismatic or otherwise?[29] In regard to friendship (*sākhya bhakti*) we are perhaps on firmer ground. The appeal from the Queen Mother in Act 1 and his own statement in Act 3 (that they must help a friend awaken from his affliction) lend support to this idea. But even here we have trouble: how can there be genuine friendship between someone of Yaugandharāyaṇa's intellectual caliber and a naive emotionalist like King Udayana? At best it will involve condescension and pretence. And it is not friendship that explains the affective relationship between the adult and the child. Thus, the most convincing explanation of Yaugandharāyaṇa's emotional ties to Udayana is parental feeling (*vātsalya*), against which the other two seem merely ideological facades. The minister is his 'master's' guardian, a benevolent father, who despite an even mocking exasperation, humors his protégé's incorrigible addiction to fantasy.[30]

Thus, though in Yaugandharāyaṇa taken by himself emotion is subject to intelligence (or else, like Rākṣasa in the *MR*, his plans would result in failure), that same intelligence is subordinate to emotion in the larger sense, since Yaugandharāyaṇa, lacking the sexual dimension, cannot climb to the top of the pyramid. In this purely structural perspective the *dāsya* claims of the text are persuasive after all: in romance terminology Yaugandharāyaṇa is essentially a helper figure. It is the romantic hero who functions as the Indian Everyman.[31] And at the center of the utopian adventure is erotic love with at least the nascent implications of wealth and power: the hero 'getting the girl' and winning or recovering the Kingdom. In Sanskrit court poetry and drama the erotic element of romance undergoes a hypertrophy unparalleled in world literature, since erotic *līlā* offers a psychological experience of freedom unattainable in any other area except extreme ascesis, which is obviously less appealing. In Indian court culture's 'kidnapping' of romance the zenith of attainment is reached in the dalliance of the early stages of the adventure: it is all downhill from there, as the poetry tries to reconcile quasi-mystical heights of pleasure with the social system. Thus, only King Udayana in our play, along with his partner Vāsavadattā, knows what it is to be emotionally free, to savor the juice (*rasa*) of happiness.[32]

Yaugandharāyaṇa is in effect Udayana's ego, in the Freudian sense, whereby the ego mediates pleasure- and reality-principles for the psyche. The King lives by the pleasure-principle alone. We might go even further, still using Freudian terminology, and call his standard the nirvana-principle, since the pleasure he seeks smacks of the transcendent.[33] In this perspective, the outside world is, reductively, only a disturbance, a view shared by Indian metaphysics across the board. Thus, we can see that in a sense Udayana is about that most serious business of finding bliss, while Yaugandharāyaṇa provides the necessary defences against assault from without. Obviously, on a naive psychological level, this is wish-fulfilment. The *rasika* imagines a world in which he has to do nothing but be a 'beautiful soul', sensitive to nuances of feeling, while the Brahmanical or ascetical intelligence, accounting in real life for all those bothersome dharmic regulations which limit one's sense of personal importance, prestidigitates the happy conclusion (wealth, power, universal admiration, and the ease to enjoy erotic *līlā*). There is, of course, a cost, but it is hardly contemplated in this play, which maintains a comic view of the situation. But it is nonetheless clear that the *rasika* in effect renounces all claims to genuine power and authority: he is content to remain emotionally an infant, with ostentatious displays of charisma substituting for even the smallest measure of intellectual and moral self-determination.

Let us recapitulate with another look at the emotional pyramid.

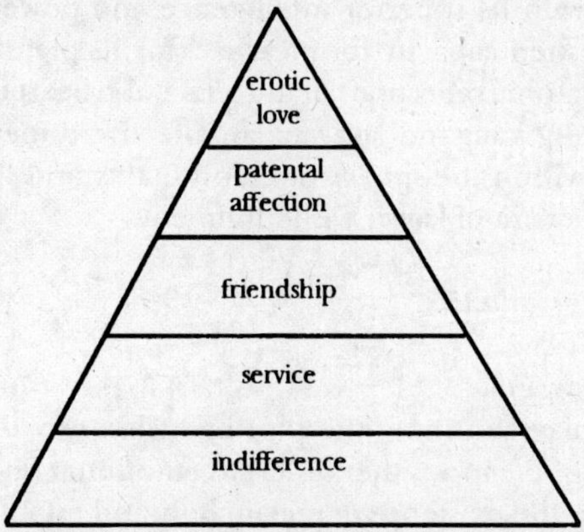

The four lower levels are occupied by Yaugandharāyaṇa and the royal subjects in general, but the radiant peak is occupied only by the *rasika*. There the energy is sexual in that blissfully aesthetic, playful mode celebrated by *kāvya*. We can think of this peak as an area of freedom: the pleasure-garden of the imagination created by the partnership of the *rasika* and his feminine Śrī or Śakti. From the world's point of view it is a prison. But it symbolizes the fantasy potential of the inner life where the laws of romance replace those of nature and society. If we were to look down on the pyramid from directly above the peak it would appear as a ring of concentric circles:

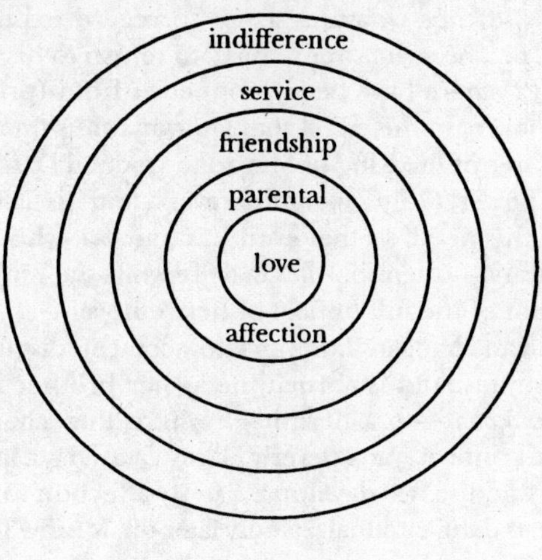

The inmost circle is the prison/pleasure-garden, surrounded by the outer world with its superior intelligence and powers, but also its much diminished capacity for pleasure; for its pleasures are, so to speak, only Platonic reflections of the bliss at the heart of the charmed circle. By giving Yaugandharāyaṇa an affective dimension the play situates him within the sphere of emotionality and thus within the utopian framework of kāvyic wish-fulfilment.

2. *Svapanavāsavadattā*

a. *The Courtly Ethos*

The sequel play continues the plot in such a way that we see the implications of *līlā* in a rather different emotional register, one that acknowledges the existence of melancholy and establishes a certain ethical dimension within the charmed circle itself. I do not know of another Sanskrit play that affords us a deeper appreciation of the human meaning of courtliness (*dākṣiṇya*) in the context of Indian palace culture and the associated *nāgarika* ideal.[34] Let us review the plot very briefly here so that we are spared the trouble of contextualizing the specific incidents discussed below. In the *PY* Udayana triumphs, escaping imprisonment in Ujjayinī, and eloping with 'the boss's daughter' in the process. But the *SV* opens with Udayana and his entourage still in exile, while an usurper (named Āruṇi) sits on the throne in Kauśāmbī. To make matters worse, Yaugandharāyaṇa has engineered a plan to separate the King from Vāsavadattā, for two reasons: (1) with her Udayana seems to regard exile as a sort of honeymoon, i.e., he seems in no hurry to return to his duties in the capital; and (2) there have been prophecies from (probably Brahmin[35]) soothsayers to the effect that Udayana must marry a certain Padmāvatī, sister of the King of Magadha (named Darśaka), before returning to power. Only Yaugandharāyaṇa and his associate ministers know of this need, so that even Vāsavadattā, who—along with Yaugandharāyaṇa—ostensibly dies in a fire while the King is out hunting, is ignorant of the full import of her removal.

Vāsavadattā and Yaugandharāyaṇa now come in disguise—she as a woman whose husband is abroad, he as her brother a wandering ascetic (*parivrājaka*)—to a hermitage where they chance to meet Padmāvatī. Yaugandharāyaṇa cleverly places Vāsavadattā in Padmāvatī's safekeeping, and the two develop a sisterly affection for each other that will serve to defuse mutual jealousy later on. Meanwhile, Udayana, after languishing pathetically for a while, comes by 'accident' (actually steered by his attendant minister Rumaṇvān) to Rājagṛha, the Magadha capital. There he is persuaded to follow the advice of scripture and marry again. Though he is not without erotic feeling for Padmāvatī (4.1), this is really a marriage of convenience—later *ālaṃkārikas* regarded it as an example of *arthaśṛṅgāra* as opposed to *kāmaśṛṅgāra* (political marriage *vs.* love marriage).[36] His heart, as he confesses at a key moment in the play (4.4), is still under the spell of Vāsavadattā's magic. Eventually Udayana recovers his throne, and Vāsavadattā, who has had to witness her husband's marriage to another in silence, is triumphantly revealed to both Udayana and Padmāvatī. As a result, happiness prevails in the harem as it does in the Kingdom.

Thematically, first complication in the relationship between the two heroines comes in the first Act, when a *brahmacārin* enters the hermitage with the news of recent events in the royal camp. Vāsavadattā, ostensibly dead, is nevertheless praised as the happiest of women because of the ardor of the husband's lamentations (1.13). The incident has a revealing metadramatic dimension. Padmāvatī, noticing Vāsavadattā's tears, concludes that they are brought on by her 'tender-heartedness' (*sānukrośa*, 1.12+). She concludes, in other words, that Vāsavadattā is a *sahṛdayā* or *rasikā* listener, responding sympathetically to a tale of tragic romance.[37] The immediate irony is that Vāsavadattā's grief is not at all aesthetically detached, but there are other ironies as well. First, Padmāvatī's own response to the student's tale, apparently only aesthetic, soon reveals its germ of personal interest. At 1.15+ she is asking herself whether or not Udayana will marry again, and finally in Act 2 we learn, with Vāsavadattā, that she has fallen in love with him. And why? Here is the second irony: because of *his* tender-heartedness (*sānukrośa iti*). We need hardly add that it is Pādmavāti's own *sānukrośatva* or *sahṛdayatva* that makes it possible for her to react this way. But can it be merely a quirk of this play that aesthetic capacity is rooted in natural sympathy and what Ānandavardhana calls simply 'passion' (*rāga*)?[38] We are reminded of Bhaṭṭa Tauta's dictum that poet, listener, and protagonist share the same experience.[39] The 'sympathy of hearts' (*hṛdayasaṃvāda*) that qualifies one as a genuine connoisseur of poetry according to Ānandavardhana, Abhinavagupta, and most of their successors is also a bond of sentimental feeling that links the members of the courtly or *nāgarika* community to one another.[40] Udayana, Vāsavadattā, and

Padmāvatī are erotically linked because of their *sahṛdayatva*. Udayana's spotlight self–demonstration of aggrieved love for Vāsavadattā, i.e., of his *sānukrośatva* or *sahṛdayatva*, brings her to tears of relief, but also stirs a sympathetic response in Padmāvatī that inevitably takes on erotic value. *Sahṛdayatva*, as the *Kuṭṭanīmata* says, is sexually appealing.[41]

But this little incident is only a foreshadowing of Act 4, in which Udayana gets to play before the same audience directly, this time with the aid of the Vidūṣaka, whose comic presence adds poignant subtlety to the interpersonal relationships. It is important to understand the implications of what is going on here. The play is basically concerned with a specific problem which is almost precisely the inverse of the problem in the *PY*. There it was a matter of the preposterousnes of the romantic temperament in the context of affairs of state: a way had to be found to integrate Udayana's *sahṛdayatva* into the arthic sphere, and we see in the end that it emerges triumphant. In the *SV* the problem is extricating the *rasika* hero morally from entangled decisions necessitated by practical affairs. In other words, in order for Udayana to remain a *rasika* he must show himself to be innocent of any compromise in his love for Vāsavadattā. The external situation is that King Udayana of Kauśāmabī is required to marry Princess Padmāvatī of Rājagṛha, a matter of political expediency. The first step in the King's exculpation is made in the ascription of the requirement to Fate (1.11). Thus the motivation for the marriage is overdetermined. We would not have blamed Udayana for a calculating decision anyway, because the burden of responsibility has already been assumed by Yaugandharāyaṇa. But the very fact of the overdetermination of Udayana's innocence indicates the seriousness of the issue: Why must he be so decisively distanced from practical responsibility for the marriage? After all, we are in a cultural context where polygyny is the norm, and, as we discover in Act 5, Udayana, despite his enthrallment with Vāsavadattā, has already had a little affair with a maid-servant.

The answer is complex. We are meant to take the enthrallment completely seriously. The affair with Viracikā (5.6+) is regarded as something utterly minor, of no more importance than Purūravas' momentary fascination with the Vidyādharī in *V*4, where the text is very insistent on his innocence. On the other hand, the marriage with Padmāvatī cannot be so treated, because of her social status, and because the text gives us Padmāvatī as a character of *nāyikā* proportions whose sensibility we share. But the principle is plain. Full *sahṛdayatva* requires the hero to be in love, which by the conventions of this poetry means that he must be under the spell of only one woman. Without being in love he is for all practical purposes *vītarāga* and therefore no *rasika* (see note 38). Erotic fascination is the state that fully activates the *rasika*'s capacity for nuanced feeling; without it he is only the promise of himself. But there is also a *de facto* monogyny—or rather 'henogyny'—involved in the kāvyic ideal, at least in its deeper sense, i.e., in passages where the poets are concerned with showing depth of passion whether in *pūrvānurāga* or *viraha* stages. If Udayana, therefore, where simply to give in to the practical demand of taking another wife, it would indicate a concession on his part to a reality which has no importance to the *śṛṅgārin*. The whole point of Ānandavardhana's cited praise of poetry is that its world mirrors the demands of the heart unlike the real one; and the true (which is to say *rasika*) lover is a natural inhabitant of that poetic world. So, if concession to reality must be made, it must be made in ignorance, for in this case ignorance is innocence and ideal. Udayana marries again in complete good faith that Vāsavadattā is dead.

Yet, evidently, this is not good enough. Vāsavadattā, as soon as she hears the news (Act 2), registers disbelief and in this she represents the *rasika* reaction as well. How can one whose melancholy was near-suicidal in the student's account now seem to have become 'indifferent' (*udāsīna*[42]). Do not all the lists of the stages of love indicate that the final stage of love-in-separation is death? (The literary model is Rāma's ancestor King Aja of *Raghuvaṃśa* 8). The text provides Udayana with excuses: the 'hearts of the great are ruled by Scripture' (*āgamapradhānāni . . . . mahāpuruṣahṛdayāni*) and he only passively accepted the proposal made by King Darśaka, Padmāvatī's brother, which was based on that King's admiration of our hero. But the problem is not so easily erased. That is the reason for the careful delineations of Act 4, set in the wistfully erotic garden atmosphere so central to *kāvya*. Engaged in banter with the Vidūṣaka the King is trapped into making the confession of his preference for Vāsavadattā:

> Though I esteem Padmāvatī
> for her beauty, character, and charm
> she does not ravish my heart
> which is still bound to Vāsavadattā.[43]

This settles the issue for Vāsavadattā. She—and the *rasika* spectator—is happy to confirm that there is a gap between public show and private feeling. Whatever the tender-hearted hero is required to do by circumstances does not touch the nuclear purity of his feeling.

But having solved this problem, is the hero not left with another almost as significant? What about Padmāvatī's feeling? Do not the King's overheard remarks indicate a certain lack of feeling for her, an unforgivable *udāsīnatva*? This is precisely what Padmāvatī's maid-servant urges and Padmāvatī herself reflects, but the issue is nonetheless a significant one. Padmāvatī's response implies such an ambiguous definition of 'courtesy' (*dākṣiṇya*) that we are not quite sure whether she is simply being brave and compassionate or elegantly inventing an excuse for her husband.[44] But whatever its exact meaning in context, we can appreciate how necessary it is for the *sahṛdaya* hero not to offend her. This is why the text is careful to establish the fact the the second marriage is not entirely devoid of erotic idealism: Udayana's first words in Act 4 refer to Pādmavatī as the result of the love-god's '6th arrow' (4.1). Thus the situation is a very subtle mix. Udayana, in order to be a convincing sentimental hero, must demonstrate perfect allegiance to Vāsavadattā (thus the pains to show that the marriage is merely an arranged one) as well as genuine sympathy and even erotic appreciation for Padmāvatī. He must navigate between Scylla and Charybdis, showing neither too great nor too little love for either woman. He must tell the truth that erotic idealism demands (monogyny) without offending the second wife who, though required by the circumstances of life, is nevertheless a sharer in the *rasika* sensibility.

But he can only do this by putting the spotlight on himself and acting to arouse a *rasa*-response. Direct appeals would have as little effect as direct statement in poetry. We would have the ornament (*alaṃkāra*) and elegant style (*rīti*) of the *dākṣiṇya* code, but without indirection (*dhvani*) there would be no sharing of an emotional understanding (*rasa*). *Rasa* is the bond uniting the community of the tender-hearted, but it exists primarily on a level that eludes even its own formal causes. Interestingly though—since Eros is at the heart of *rasika* sensitivity—the *rasa* in question here is not *śṛṅgāra*, but *karuṇa*.[45] Ultimately, the hero can only show his innocence by revealing himself as uncomprehending victim of his own destiny. He is the pure soul, the 'beautiful soul,' who lives by the heart's promptings in a dark and confusing world of unfeeling practical and ethical demands.

Thus the climax of Act 4 really comes when, having momentarily succumbed to the banter-induced illusion that Vāsavadattā still lives, he falls back into the real world with a thud. His tears elicit heartfelt sympathy from both wives, and Vāsavadattā urges Padmāvatī to step forward discretely and comfort him in his grief.

It is a poignant moment. Vāsavadattā is now able to rise above her own pain in order to be generous to her co-wife, who must remain, for now, unaware of that generosity. Udayana, for his part, is still further in the dark, being comforted by a woman who he not only thinks knows nothing about his true emotional state, but whom he regards as too weak by nature to be able to bear the truth:

> This newly-married girl
> would tremble if she heard the truth.
> Though she is firm by nature,
> a woman's nature is skittish.[46]

We shall have more to say about the irony of this statement in the Conclusion. Let us content ourselves now with pointing out the distinction between the bearing of the women and that of the hero, which is basically this: they know what they are doing, while he—at least ostensibly—does not. Both Vāsavadattā and Padmāvatī show considerable generosity of spirit and tact in the 4th Act. They are conscious sufferers of moral and emotional ambiguities, who are not allowed to speak what they know and have no power to alter their circumstances. Padmāvatī knows less than Vāsavadattā about the complex situation that unites the three of them, yet her graciousness shows itself most clearly in her ethical demeanor: she refuses to blame her husband or the ghost of the woman who dominates his imagination. She does not pout or play the martyr. By contrast, the hero's moral case is all bound up in his ignorance. He makes no decisions, except to remain silent on the cause of his tears. Since he is the apparent cause of his wives' suffering, his self-display is directed at demonstrating his perfect incomprehension of the moral dimensions of his actions. Powerlessness before destiny and childlike incompetence in the morally ambiguous world of practical reality are the chief ingredients of his self-exonerating pose.

b. *Dream vs. Reality*

The preceding discussion aptly illustrates the fact that as we approach the ethical dimension of the play—and the same is true of other plays—we find ourselves inevitably involved in epistemological questions, such as the extent to which the hero suffers under a delusion and what it means to do so. There is no question that it is precisely here that Udayana emerges as the hero who carries the emotional weight of the play. Vāsavadattā's problem is fundamentally resolved in Act 4: it is now just a matter of waiting for Yaugandharāyaṇa to stage the proper moment for her triumphant self-disclosure. Padmāvatī is still in the dark, but she has learned the essential truth of her situation. Vāsavadattā's appearance will not change that; in fact, due to the 'sisterly' understanding they have already built up,[47] it may help her to be dealing with an affectionate co-wife rather than a haunting erotic ideal. But Udayana still has to be let in on the secret. So in the course of Act 4 the play's center of gravity shifts to him and his unconscious quest for enlightenment. In Act 4 it is banter with the Vidūṣaka that makes Vāsavadattā's presence real, so real that the King falls under the spell of its illusion. The woman whose image was still enshrined in his heart (4.4) seems to step out of the imaginary enclosure—i.e. his heart, a garden world held hostage by Destiny—into the actual garden setting of the Act. But this is only the first of several such evocations, the final one indeed delivering its promise, the Dream-Woman come to life.

The main event occurs in Act 5. Udayana and the Vidūṣaka go to the Ocean Room where they expect to console Padmāvatī in a sudden illness. It turns out she is not there, but the entry into the enclosure anticipates the ambiguity of the vision that will take place there. The Vidūṣaka is startled by what he takes to be a snake writhing at the threshold, but the more preceptive King sees that it is only a fallen festoon stirring in the twilight breeze (5.3)—an apparent advertence to the snake-rope paradigm of Indian epistemology and metaphysics. Once inside and not finding his wife the hero decides to take a nap. The Vidūṣaka's botched bedtime story again evokes the memory of Vāsavadattā, so it is no accident that he begins dreaming of her. The Vidūṣaka departs to get a blanket, but meanwhile Vāsavadattā enters. She too has come to comfort Padmāvatī, and now, in the dark, mistakes the form on the couch for her dear friend. It is important to remember that Udayana has not yet laid eyes on her even in her disguise, since propriety forbids that a married woman be seen publicly without her husband. Vāsavadattā lies down beside him, and then suddenly startles as a voice that is clearly her husband's begins to address her. It is part of the ingenious twilight-ambiguity of this scene that neither Vāsavadattā, nor Udayana himself, nor the reader-spectator is really sure to what extent he is dreaming. Vāsavadattā thinks at first that he is only talking in his sleep. But, uncannily, he sees her in her ornamentless state (Yaugandharāyaṇa's story in Act 1 was that her husband was traveling). Under the spell of the 'illusion' his guilty conscience compels him to interpret her attire as a signal that she is still angry at him for a recent flirtation with the maid-servant Viracikā (see preceding section). The allusion has the interesting effect of drawing her out of the fiction of her decease: she bristles at the memory and scolds him aloud. He reaches for her entreatingly, when suddenly she realizes the danger and flees. Yaugandharāyaṇa's plan and therefore her husband's and her own prosperity depend on her maintaining the fiction. Udayana leaps up to catch her but bumps into a door, the fateful material barrier to the world enshrining the ideal. When the Vidūṣaka returns the King insists that he has really seen Vāsavadattā. The Vidūṣaka objects, voicing the common-sense wisdom of the world, prompting the *rasika*-hero to the following manifesto:

> If this was merely a dream, then how happy never to awaken.
> If this was delusion, let me always be deluded.[48]

As in the Kālidāsa plays, the mirror-play between dream and reality is interesting and significant. Vāsavadattā's pique is, from a certain angle, a momentary surrender to illusion, an entanglement in an emotional complex that draws her out of her appointed role. It has the feel of Udayana's mistake in the preceding Act, when the clever mix of eros, pathos, and humor brought him to the point of telling the Vidūṣaka he would report the latter's words to Vāsavadattā. Or it is not unlike Urvaśī's mistake in confusing her fictive love for Viṣṇu in the play-within-the-play with her actual love for Purūravas: reality breaking in on illusion, but in such a way that reality itself takes the form of an illusion (since Purūravas is not present). Meanwhile Udayana, for his part, is the victim of a fiction who sees through it by means of a dream. But the point of all this ambiguity is contained in Udayana's declaration of allegiance to the ideal over the phenomenal. If he must accept the common–sense judgment of the world, which says that his dream-world is only a fantasy, then the world is not good enough for him. The *rasika-sahṛdaya* chooses to live in a world that mirrors the desires and sentiments of the heart, the world of *kāvya*, which exists, according to Ānandavardhana, Mammaṭa, and other praisers of 'Poetic light' (*pratibhā*), to supplant the real world. But the dichotomy is not just between poetry and fantasy on the one hand and reality and common sense on the other. It is between the private and the public life, between *kāma* and *dharmārthau*. Thus, when we see Udayana at the beginning of Act 6, even though he has risen to the clarion-call of military heroics at the end of Act 5 and recovered his Kingdom, he has withdrawn to a private chamber to brood over the melodies of the lute Ghoṣavatī, so redolent of lost moments with Vāsavadattā. Public success, though graced by Padmāvatī's sweetness and loyalty, cannot overcome a sense of vacuity within. The *rasika* has become, *mutatis mutandis*, a reluctant stoic with respect to duty.

But, with the exception of a few plays like *Urubhaṅga* and *Karṇabhāra*, Sanskrit drama knows no tragedy. We know that there will be a reconciliation between private and public, pleasure (*kāma*) and work-duty (*dharmārthau*), poetic dream and reality. The envoys from Mahāsena's court bring not only the belated blessing of Vāsavadattā's parents on the elopement but celebratory images of the married couple. In a cleverly milked recognition scene, Vāsavadattā emerges finally from the world of poetic image (in the marriage-portrait) into life, becoming once again the inspirational Śrī whose auspiciousness extends from the emotional life to the prosperity of subjects, abundance of crops, resplendence of sovereignty, etc. The *rasika* is not forced to choose between life and art: the latter performs its utopian, wish-fulfilling magic. Harmony reigns in the harem, in the Kingdom, and in Udayana's heart. There is only one discordant note, faintly heard in the jubilance of the resolution, but once heard, altering the major triad to a dominant seventh. It is the matter of Udayana's consciousness of being duped.

The series of 'poetic' intimations of Vasavadatta's presence (banter in Act 4, dream in Act 5, *vīṇā*-melodies and portrait in Act 6),[49] though ultimately productive, depends on a larger fictive framework. Yaugandharāyaṇa has all this time been behind the scenes pulling the appropriate strings to bring the whole puppet-show to its harmonious conclusion. He is the *sūtradhāra* (lit. 'string-holder'[50]) in which the three protagonists have acted with more or less awareness of their role-playing. Or we may think of him as the play's author with his *kārayitrī pratibhā*,[51] artfully constructing a plot which will deliver the fruit of success (*siddhi*, *phalāgama*, etc.) on both political and affective levels.[52] Yaugandharāyaṇa has made it possible for his 'master' to have the best of both worlds: public acclaim and private delight, executing Fate's intentions with what is ultimately only a minor disturbance in the courtly *rasika's* emotional life (which, if anything, he has deepened by arranging a temporary withdrawal of its Śrī).

But is he really the court-poet as servant, delivering the *rasa* bonanza by ever more artful constructions, Kosambi's 'talking house-bird of higher rank'?[53] This can hardly be the case. The first indication comes in a small incident occurring in the context of Vāsavadattā's disclosure. Yaugandharāyaṇa arrives on the scene in the character of the *parivrājaka* claiming his 'sister' of Padmāvatī. Behind a purdah curtain the Nurse has already vouched for Vāsavadattā's identity and the King has, without seeing her yet, directed her to the women's quarters, but Yaugandharāyaṇa keeps up the pretence, accusing him of taking another's wife:

> Born in the Bhārata clan, you are self-controlled, enlightened, and pure. To take her by force were unworthy of you, a model of kingly duty.[54]

Purely in terms of artful dramatic construction this incident serves to force the King to draw the curtain before the eyes of all in a last flutter of doubtful expectation. But it is never enough to explain significant events in formalistic terms. Yaugandharāyaṇa's teasing is a subtle assertion of power over the King's contentment, a reminder that all has depended and will continue to depend on his good will. His subsequent gesture of obeisance (prostration with a humble request for forgiveness)—like his earlier soliloquized foreboding (6.15), which echoes Udayana's own foreboding of Mahāsena's displeasure (6:4)—does little to mitigate our sense of who is really in charge. As in the *PY*, the effort is made to situate Yaugandharāyaṇa within the affective orbit of the King, but this time it does not succeed in establishing the desired hierarchy of emotion over intelligence. This ascetical minister-poet[55] is no mere deliverer of commissioned services.

Thus, the conclusion is less happy than it might be. There is the formulaic *bharatavākya*, in which Yaugandharāyaṇa pronounces blessing over the realm (the fictive one and that in which the play is performed), but just before this comes the King's melancholy awareness of his delusion:

King: Tell me, my dear Yaugandharāyaṇa, what was your object in concealing the queen?
Y: My one idea was to save Kauśāmbī.
King: What was your reason for putting her in the hands of Padmāvatī as a ward?
Y: The soothsayers, Puṣpaka and Bhadraka, had predicted that she was destined to become your queen.
King: Did Rumaṇvān [i.e., the minister who remained in attendance on him throughout] know of this?
Y: Sire, they all knew.
King: Oho! what a rogue he is Rumaṇvān.[56]

The word for 'rogue' is *śaṭha*, a loaded term, since it is used by women who bitterly accuse their husbands of infidelity[57] and is even fixed in the dramaturgical handbooks as the name of the hero who deceives women. In other words, Udayana's discovery puts him in a feminine relation to Yaugandharāyaṇa and his confederates, including even Vāsavadattā. Not even Padmāvatī has been as deluded as he, thanks to her eavesdropping in Act 4.

We can see this better, perhaps, by using an amplified version of the concentric-circle diagram we employed with the *PY*. Udayana, the

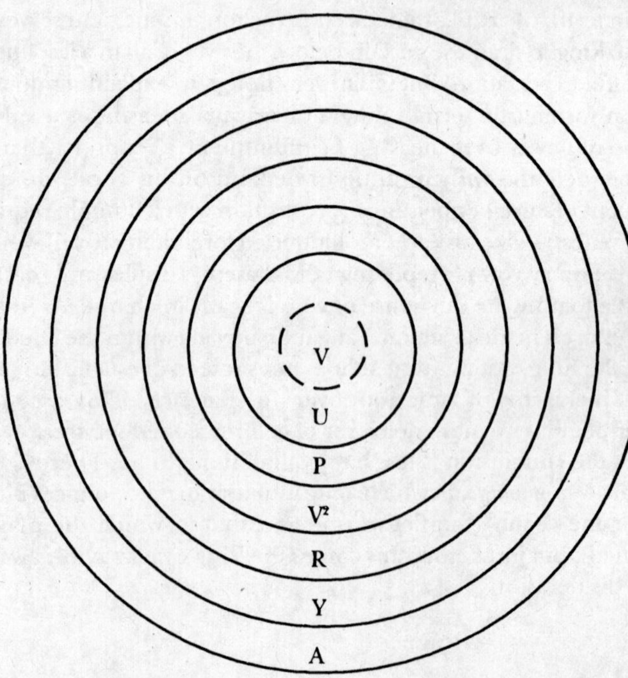

fictive *rasika*, is in the center enshrining the image of Vāsavadattā. This is Vāsavadattā in her capacity as the Radiant Female or Śrī of the imagination, an image or ideal more than a personality or sensibility in he own right (thus the broken line, indicating her dreamlike status). That central locus—including hero and heroine—is either an enchanted garden or a prison cell, according to which criterion is applied, the *rasika*'s or the world's. As we progress through the outer rings we have increased awareness of what is going on. P is Padmāvatī. V^2 is Vāsavadattā *qua* subject. R is Rumaṇvān, who as Yaugandharāyaṇa's agent knows less than he. Beyond Yaugandharāyaṇa are the *ādeśikas* who have a direct insight into the inscrutable intelligence only identified as Fate in these plays. But whereas the *PY* left us with a sense of the *rasa*-vision's triumph, here even Udayana shares the sense of its fragility. He is aware of being in a gilded cage. He is no longer riding charismatically beyond imprisoning barriers on an elephant's back, his Śrī clasping him tightly from behind. He is rather the—literally—disillusioned keeper of the *rasika* faith, now cognizant of the meaning of his own practical impotence (the feminization of his relation to his ministers registers a subtle consciousness of emasculation). The price of *sahṛdayatva* is the sacrifice of claims to charismatic autonomy, even in the private sphere. *Rasāsvāda* itself is seen to depend on outside forces.

Conclusion

We said at the outset that the *PY* and *SV* were complementary plays. The crucial issue is the nature of the poetic playworld: Is this charmed circle more of a pleasure garden than a prison or vice versa? It is hard to avoid the impression that the second play takes a much more profound look at what is involved for the *rasika* hero. It is not simply because it is less comic in tone, or that it deals with love-in-separation (*viraha, vipralambha*) rather than love-before-union (*pūrvānurāga*). It is rather because its perspective is—implicitly, at least—more ethical: how the three protagonists, all *sahṛdayas,* act with respect to each other.

The poignancy of the dream-reality issue is in a certain sense an epistemological red herring. The deeper issue, as in *Śakuntalā* 6, is the hero's good faith. Act 4 centers on a demonstration of the *rasika* hero's good faith that is premised on the formula 'ignorance equals innocence.' But what kind of rationale is this? The *rasika* hero uses his sensibility as a device to silence criticism which centers on the question of callousness (*udāsīnatva, adākṣiṇya*). He says 'Behold my beautiful soul' rather than 'This is what I do and these are my reasons.' We do not want to seem insensitive to the delicacy of courtly evasions. The morality of simplistic frankness at war with all illusion is ultimately a form of brutality, as, for instance, Ibsen shows in his parable *The Wild Duck*. We can, furthermore, see that it is moral sensitivity that informs Act 4; if this were not the case, there would be no reason why Udayana could not openly hurt either Vāsavadattā's or Padmāvatī's feelings. He could simply have married Padmāvatī for reasons of state on Yaugandharāyaṇa's advice. But that was impossible at the outset, because even at that stage (before there was any Padmāvatī in the picture) *sahṛdayatva* implied an intrinsically moral standard: one must not hurt the feelings of another *sahṛdaya*. Nevertheless, the fact remains that the avoidance of the problem leaves us with an impression of weakness in the *rasika* character. The blame is all assigned to the outside world, an inscrutable Fate, Brahmanical cunning.

This is a question of good faith in another sense too, because the *rasika* enjoys the benefits of success in the outside world while refusing to admit complicity with its purposes. We have found Udayana at the end of the second play in a position of feminized impotence with regard to the creative forces that underlie sentimentality. But could this not be a ploy? The *rasika* audience must have found the pathetic self-portrait pleasing (just as the troubador poet and his audience took pleasure in the posture of self-abasement). The question is 'why?' Probably there is no definitive answer, but I would like to suggest two possibilities, which in fact are not mutually exclusive. The first is that the *rasika* was genuinely aware of a fundamental powerlessness vis-a-vis the transcendental authority figurally represented by the ascetic-sage-minister but diffusely present throughout Indian culture in guru-reverence, the *vairāgya* ideal, etc. There is a deep-rooted conviction in the Indian world-view that power and insight come only through self-restraint, i.e., through the denial of the emotional life. Not even the *rasika,* who may have been a person of tremendous wealth and power in actual life, can have escaped the sense that his happiness was not only transient, but deluding and radically disempowering. The metaphysical weight given to *rasa* by poeticians of mystical bent did not succeed in stabilizing it against the ascetical scorn of the cultural superego, except insofar as *rasa* itself is tinged with a solipsistic ascetical detachment (*vairāgya*).[58]

The second explanation is that the *rasika* by portraying himself as impotent avoids bad conscience resulting from his privileged position in society. We should be wary of retrojecting a Marxist sensibility into the past, but let us admit that we are simply being heuristic here. While not every *rasika* was a prince, we can nevertheless say that the cultural center of Sanskrit poetry was the court. Even when it is being experienced imaginatively in the family or monastic library, it is still the courtly atmosphere, its codes and sensibility, that *kāvya* celebrates. Even a bohemian like Bāṇa in his youth must have shared a feeling of privilege simply by belonging to the *rasika* community (not to mention his high birth and good connections). 'Let us grant this,' the skeptic will say, 'but why should any *rasika* have felt the need to exonerate himself for his privilege?' We may, of course, harbor the suspicion that good fortune is never free, never, that is, without that sense of anxiety and guilt that, for instance, underlay tragic consciousness in pre-Marxist Hellas. But let us follow the hints of the text.

There are two areas in which the *rasika* hero shows himself an innocent: with regard to women and with regard to the outside world. As to women we need hardly scratch the surface to see that the relationship between the hero and his beloved(s) is unequal. If she has the magic to transform his world into a pleasure garden, it is basically in her role as Radiant Female. That is to say, she is not a genuine subject in this role, but in fact as much of a ghostly presence as Vāsavadattā becomes in the second play. Though physically present in *pūrvānurāga* and *saṃbhoga* phases, her body enshrines an ideal that will soon depart and take up other residence. It is his—the *rasika*'s—imagination that lends her whatever momentary power she has over him. Vāsavadattā's reign as the Śrī of Udayana's imagination will be short-lived, even if we grant that it has survived intact to the end of Act 6. There is the shadow of the affair with Viracikā, which the text treats as less significant but which, because it suggests a real infatuation, we may see as more significant than the marriage with Padmāvatī. But there is also the legend which the plays draw from, in which—as Harṣa's plays show—Udayana carries on as a playboy. Given the fact that the *SV* records a moral sensitivity to the feelings of women, it is not implausible that polygyny—even on the imaginative level[59]—entailed a certain sense of guilt and required protestations of good faith on the *rasika*'s behalf.

And with regard to the outside world, the texts show the hero benefiting from actions taken by others in his behalf, principally Yaugandharāyaṇa, but Yaugandharāyaṇa himself metonymically suggests the whole range of so-called 'dependents' (*bhṛtya*). We may think back to the *bhakti* pyramid which shows the whole society supporting the privileged sensibility's enjoyment of power, wealth, and happiness. Could it not be that the *rasika* himself is dimly aware of owing a debt to the vast human infrastructure supporting his privilege? This will have meant something different to princes and potentates than it did to bourgeois *rasikas* who might have had a hard time making ends meet (cf. Cārudatta). We have verses in various plays depicting Kings as weary leaders who have earned a moment of respite from their duties, but these of course carry litte dramatic weight. More significant as expiation is the princely *rasika*'s self-depiction as a man of sorrow, with no intrinsic interest in power or wealth, more troubled by the demands of his worldly status than pleased by its rewards. Thus the irony with which the *SV* ends says to all: 'Behold your power over me, despite appearances. If even I am aware of my impotence, how can anyone deny my entitlement to such fragile happiness as comes my way?'

In the section entitled 'The Courtly Ethos' we said that the distinction between the hero and his wives was that 'they are conscious sufferers of moral and emotional ambiguities, who are not allowed to speak what they know and have no power to alter their circumstances,' while his whole concern is to demonstrate ignorance. They are the model, in a sense, of the *rasika* as courtier (or otherwise dependent) rather than as prince, ever mindful of their obligation to forbear and keep silent. What we have tried to show here is that Udayana's behavior is more conscious than it seems. As *rasika* he stands outside his own self–dramatics savoring its effect through all other subjective sensibilities in the play. We called attention to the verse in Act 4 that ironically depicts Padmāvatī as too skittish to bear the truth. Padmāvatī, and by implication Vāsavadattā too, thus emerges as a moral heroine, whose superior vision obliges her to act with restraint. The King in his epistemological prison-house is, paradoxically, not so limited: he is free to fall in and out of love, to exercise his emotional impulses, according to the inspiration of the moment. What seems to be a liability is actually a reinforcement of privilege. But is there any use, on the other hand, in praising the women for a moral sensibility that is forced upon them by circumstances? The fact is that they lack the power or freedom to do as the hero does, so that they have nothing to exonerate: there is nc question of Vāsavadattā 'exploiting' Udayana, i.e., regarding him as the temporary shrine of an exquisite male beauty. It is telling that in the Vaiṣṇava mythology reflecting kāvyic erotics Kṛṣṇa, the love-object *sans pareil*, inspires absolute faithfulness in his female devotees, while he himself is playfully here-and-gone. Indian culture does not seem to support the enshrinement of the female person as permanent erotic object. Rādhā is the woman of privilege, but she has rivals. And the Goddess generally, in her great variety of forms, is more mother than beloved.

I have said that these two takes on the hero's ironization are not mutually exclusive. 'Overdeterminations' of this type are normal in literature as in life, as is acknowledged in the basically formalist New Criticism, not to speak of later 'anticlosural' approaches.[60] It is impossible to exhaust the meaning of a complex work of literature (like *SV*, drawing *PY* into its orbit) because we can only speak of such meaning in relation to an author and an audience. However formulaic the *rasa* aesthetic appears, it does not, in my judgment, mean that emotional symbols (the *vibhāvas*, in a word) were felt without complication. The very existence of the ironies we have discussed (e.g., Udayana's patronizing remarks on Padmāvatī, 4.8) argues against that, as does the practical assumption that the human mind is too complicated for the systems it sets up for itself, especially in the area of the emotions. The interpretations offered here are, as we have indicated, heuristic: the goal is to understand and appreciate what has gone into the making of Sanskrit drama. To deny multivalence, to refuse to allow that beauty may co-exist with all-too-human emotional feints, is to deny the *rasika* his—and her—psychological complexity, and this, I think, is the gravest disservice we can do to Sanksrit literature.

Notes

1. *Mālavaikāgnimitra* 1.2 and preceding.
2. Śāradatanaya's testimony is the most persuasive, since he gives a rudimentary sketch of the plot which includes the lute-verse of Act 6 (6.3). He also cites a portion of a verse we do not have, one which indicates a missing episode: Udayana tentatively concluding from Padmāvatī's artful make-up that Vāsavadattā still lives. Abhinavagupta also cites a verse, not in our play, as do Rāmacandra and Guṇacandra in their *Nāṭyadarpaṇa* (where they name Bhāsa as the author). Rājaśekhara's dictum—that Bhāsa's *SV* survives the fire-ordeal of criticism—is borne out by modern taste as well. See the collected evidence in Ch. 2 of A. D. Pusalker's *Bhāsa: A Study*, which one should also consult for bibliography on the whole attribution debate. The most recent summary known to me is V. Venkatachalam, a Bhāsa advocate.
3. I am agnostic with regard to the claims of other plays in the corpus of thirteen. I see little of Bhāsa's characteristic intelligence and graceful humor in the *Pratimānāṭaka*, for example. On the other hand, I feel certain that the *Avimāraka* and fragmentary *Daridracārudatta* are his. The *PY* is probably also somewhat abbreviated: too much goes on between the extant Acts 3 and 4, and it is after all surprising that we do not even see the conventional hero (see Bharata's definition, *Nāṭyaśāstra* 34.22-23, KSS ed.) on stage. In this essay my citations in both plays are from the Poona edition of C. R. Devadhar, *Bhāsanāṭakacakram: Plays Ascribed to Bhāsa*. I have also used the editions with commentary of T. Ganapati Sastri.
4. Which is not to say that *śṛṅgāra* is not present in the *MR*, as we saw in the last chapter.
5. The distinctions are in a sense arbitrary. Cārudatta, who is regarded as 'steadfast-and-tranquil' (*dhīrapraśānta*), clearly has some of the prominent *dhīralalita* qualities of a romantic hero, but according to *NŚ* 34.17-19, or its interpreters, Brahmins and merchants (and Cārudatta is both) must be *dhīrapraśānta*. Rākṣasa, a Brahmin, strikes us as *dhīrodātta* (steadfast-and-exalted), though, strictly speaking, that slot is reserved for Kings. Conventionally, Rākṣasa escapes such classification altogether. Since the plot can be seen as hinging on the success or failure of Candragupta's bid for power, Rākṣasa becomes a secondary hero (*pratināyaka*). The same is true for Cāṇakya, and for Yaugandharāyaṇa in the *PY*. Thus Ganapati Sastri regards Udayana as the hero of the *PY*, and we shall follow his practice. This makes more sense with regard to *PY*, than *MR* for two reasons. Udayana remains the focus of sentimental interest as the *rasika* figure, while Candragupta is only marginally so. Secondly, while both Yaugandharāyaṇa and Rākṣasa see themselves primarily as loyal aides and dependents of their sovereigns, in Rākṣasa's case this becomes almost a soul-searching issue, since his devotion forces him into rebellion against the status quo. In other words it becomes an ideologically marked locus of feeling that shifts the center of gravity away from the issue of Candragupta's or Cāṇakya's success. But whether one regards Udayana or Yaugandharāyaṇa as the *PY*'s *nāyaka*, the relationship between them is the same, and that is what we are interested in here.
6. Udayana, according to some versions of the legend, was taught this skill by a Nāga. An Indian Orpheus, he charms wild animals, especially elephants, with a stringed instrument. However that may be, the play itself regards the skill as

a family inheritance (2.10+). See, for all variants of the Udayana story, Niti Adaval, *The Story of King Udayana.*

7. A Trojan Horse situation: the blue elephant was artificial, manned by soldiers.
8. The sun-symbolism with its mytho-ritual overtones should not diminish our sense of the Udayana's romantic extravagance. The hero of Sanskrit drama is not an archaic warrior with an exuberant bloodlust. The ethos is courtly, and we are rather to understand such depictions in the spirit of panegyric and aesthetic posture. Ultimately their function is sentimental, adding to his romantic charisma or eliciting pathos for a noble spirit caught in the nets of deception.
9. 2.10+, trans. Woolner and Sarup, except for final sentence.
10. Mahāsena has also already called attention in soliloguy to Udayana's addiction to 'play' (*līlā,* 2.6).
11. She shows herself as susceptible to his appeal as innumerable Indian matrons to that of the child-god Kṛṣṇa; see Kakar, *Inner World,* p. 153.
12. The sage Dvaipāyana Vyāsa at the end of Act 1 has already predicted his resurgence, but left the impression that it would be due solely to Yaugandharāyaṇa's covert activity.
13. One of them is interested only in *arthaśāstra,* the other in warrior's training (*vyāyāma = kṣatradharma*): neither sees the value of music (*gandharvaveda*). Lacking courtly polish, they are philistines who would be incapable of attracting *sahṛdaya* women (cf. the list of desirable qualities in a suitor, 2.4, one of which is *sānukrośatva* [tender-heartedness]), a practical synonym of *hṛdayasaṃvāda*).
14. A modern version of Udayana, with Napoleonic trappings, is Fabrice del Dongo in Stendhal's *Charterhouse of Parma.*
15. 3.7, trans. Woolner and Sarup (I have versified it):
    parityajāma saṃtaptaṃ duḥkhena madanena ca/
    suhṛjjanam upāśritya yaḥ kālaṃ nāvabudhyate//
16. 3.5+: *bandhaṇaṃ dāṇiṃ pamadavaṇaṃ sambhāvia pautto rāaḷiḷaṃ kattuṃ/* [*bandhanam idānīṃ pramadavanaṃ saṃbhāvya pravṛtto rāja-/rāgalīlāṃ kartum*] The *rāaḷiḷaṃ* of the Prakrit yields both *rāja-* and *rāgalīlām* in Sanskrit. Woolner and Sarup have chosen the latter, but it seems to me that the pun is too good to lose.
17. Yet they too serve the purposes of the *nāyaka*'s final 'success' (*siddhi*).
18. *MR* 1.15 (numbering according to Coulson's translation, which is is used here) and preceding: *athavā yat svayamabhiyogaduḥkhair asādhāraṇair apākṛtaṃ tad eva rājyaṃ sukhayati/ kutaḥ—*
    svayam āhṛtya bhuñjānā balino'pi svabhāvataḥ/
    gajendrāś ca narendrāś ca prāyaḥ sīdanti duḥkhitāḥ//
    'Lords of the herds' are elephants.
19. Cf. Freud's essay 'On Narcissism: An Introduction'; also *Group Psychology and the Analysis of the Ego* (1921) on the Subject of identification.
20. E.g., verses like 1.8 which depict him as a generous friend to the good, etc. Or see the panegyric verses at the beginning of *Śakuntalā* 5. The *rasika*-as-King may be impractical and little inclined to duty by temperament but he is depicted as sentimentally bound to his subjects.
21. The elopement is technically either *gāndharva* or *rākṣasa* marriage, depending on one's point of view; cf. *Manusmṛti* 3.32-33.
22. An important motif in this play and the next. A list of allusions to Fate or related Fortune: *PY* 1.3 (*daiva*), 1.5+ (*bhāgya*), 1.6+ (*kṛtānta*), 1.12 (*kāla, bhāgya*), 1.15+ (*vidhāna*), 2.0+ (*daiva*), 2.5 (*bhāgya*), 3.4 (*daiva*); *SV* 1.4 (*bhāgya*), 1.11 (*vidhi*), 3.0+

(*bhāgadheya*), 4.6+ (*vidhi*), 6.4 (*bhāagya*), 6.5 (*daiva*), 6.18+ (*bhāgya*).

23. He has no observable sexual dimension, for example, and acts as an agent of Dvaipāyana's omniscient intelligence. His anger, which comes to the fore in the final Act, has overtones of explosive *tapas*. In the second play he is in fact disguised as a wandering ascetic.
24. The classical work on the subject is S.K. De, 'The *Bhakti-Rasa-Śāstra* of Bengal Vaiṣṇavism.' The latest treatment known to me is Nrisinha P. Bhaduri, '*Bhakti* (Devotion) as an Aesthetic Sentiment.' The essence of the system *qua* aesthetics is the granting of graduated *rasa* status to all positive affective relationships with the charismatic personality.
25. For other systematic attempts to solve the problem see V. Raghavan, *The Number of Rasas*, pp. 119-25, 201-03, and passim.
26. For *śānta rasa* in general the basic source is Raghavan's *Number of Rasas*. See Masson and Patwardhan, *Śāntarasa*, for a speculative treatment of its place in Abhinavagupta.
27. *puruṣāntaritaṃ māṃ drakṣyati svāmī—*

    ripunṛpanagare vā bandhane vā vane vā
    samupagatavināśaḥ pretya vā tulyaniṣṭham/
    jitam iti kṛtabuddhiṃ vañcayitvā nṛpaṃ
    taṃ punar adhigatarājyaḥ pārśvataḥ ślāghanīyam//

    The Master will see me a changed man—

    Sharing his condition in the enemy's city,
    his jail, the forest, or in the next world,
    or, by tricking the King [Mahāsena] who thinks he has won,
    at his side to be praised with his kingship restored.
28. It is clear from *NŚ* 27.40 ff. that the audience of Sanskrit drama did not consist exclusively of *rasikas*. But even the *rasika* shared the naive sentimentality of the popular imagination. *Daivikī siddhi* complements and enhances, rather than excludes, *mānuṣī*, as we have argued in the Introduction.
29. There are two issues here. One is formula, according to which it would be impossible for Yaugandharāyaṇa not to show *dāsya* sentiment. The other is the contradiction between the formula and the idealization of Yaugandharāyaṇa's intelligence which requires that he have a renouncer's independence of mind. See the preceding chapter for a fuller discussion.
30. Can even parental love survive continued exasperation? It would require, at least, a perfect lack of suspicion of bad faith in the indulged child. But this is precisely what Sanskrit drama seeks to demonstrate: that the *rasika*, for all his privileges of power and sexual freedom, is in perfect good faith. One could say that this is the fundamental theme of *SV*.
31. In innumerable stories in world literature, from high romance to fairy- and folk-tale, a disarmingly passive and ignorant, but noble-hearted, hero achieves the pinnacle of success (kingdom, wealth, princess). See Max Luthi, *Once upon a Time*, Ch. 10. *Kāvya* has clothed the romance logic in the courtly and dharmic ideological codes of Indian culture, a phenomenon Northrop Frye refers to as 'kidnapped romance': *The Secular Scripture*, p. 57.
32. A phrase borrowed from *MR* 3.4: *rasaṃ prīteḥ*. See also the image of *Mālavikāgnimitra* 4.1, where *rasa* is the juice of the tree of love.
33. *Beyond the Pleasure Principle*, section 6.
34. The *nāgarika* is the urbane townsman (*nagara* = city) whose culture is a conscious imitation of courtly life. But the relationship was reciprocal:

Purūravas, the royal hero of Kālidāsa's *Vikramorvaśīya* is called a *nāgarika* (3.13+, Velankar ed.). The model lover of the *Kāmasūtra* is called both *nāgarika* and *nāyaka* (protagonist), showing that life imitated art. See the remarks of F.B.J. Kuiper, *Varuṇa and Vidūṣaka: On the Origin of Sanskrit Drama*, pp. 227-28.

35. The occult intelligence need not always be Brahmanical, though it usually is in these plays with their Hindu perspective.
36. Cf. Sarvānanda as cited in Pusalker, *Bhāsa*, pp. 30-31.
37. Cf. *NŚ* 27.55 (KSS):

yas tuṣṭau tuṣṭim āyāti śoke śokam upaiti ca/
dainye dīnatvam abhyeti sa nāṭye prekṣakaḥ smṛtaḥ//

Likewise this is the kind of gentle spectator Kālidāsa calls for in *V* 1.2. *Ś* 3.11+—in which Śakuntalā's friends deduce that she is in love through their familiarity with romances—shows us that the romantic story literature appealed to young girls of court and city (in *Ś*, transposed to the hermitage).

38. Being 'without passion' one cannot be a poet or *rasika*.

apāre kāvyasaṃsāre kavir ekaḥ prajāpatiḥ/
yathāsmai rocate viśvaṃ tathedaṃ parivartate//
śṛṅgāri cet kaviḥ kāvye jātaṃ rasamayaṃ jagat//
sa eva vītarāgaś cen nīrasaṃ sarvam eva tat// DhĀ 3.42+//

Śṛṅgārin is a *de facto* synonym of *sānukrośa*. Cf. the title chapter, section 2.

39. *nāyakasya kaveḥ śrotuḥ samāno' nubhavas tataḥ*, cited by Abhinavagupta, *DhĀL* 1.6+.
40. The community may even include the ascetic, as shown by the example of Valmīki, whose art derives from real-life sympathy for a forlorn *krauñca* bird. See *Dhvanyāloka* 1.5 with Abhinava's commentary. Of greater interest, perhaps, is the passage of the *Abhinavabhāratī* which notes that women are capable of bringing natural sympathy to a state of *rasāsvāda* repose: *tathā hyekaghanaśokasaṃviccarvaṇe'pi loke strīlokasya hṛdayaviśrāntir antarāyaśūny-aviśrāntiśarīratvāt* (Gnoli, *AEAG*, p. 17). But AG need not have singled out women (though his remarks are, incidentally, suggestive of the idea that, as in the West, courtliness indicates a certain feminization of social values). Is not Cārudatta of the *Mṛcchakaṭika* the epitome of the tender-hearted *sahṛdaya*? To insist on a boundary between his aesthetic capacity (*Mṛcch.* 3.3-5) and his whole sentimental bearing in life is to miss the point of the characterization: see the next chapter.
41. Dāmodara, *Kuṭṭanīmata* 548 (Tripathi ed.): see Introduction, note 14. We need hardly mention that such appeal is a cross-cultural phenomenon. Poets and musicians have often found that to move hearts has more than a spiritual value.
42. A key notion, broached at 2.0.72 in Devadhar's edition. Again Vāsavadattā's complaint seems to be made on 'aesthetic' grounds: she complains, in other words, that it is out of character for a *rasika* like Udayana to act with 'indifference' to his deceased wife by marrying again so easily. Cf. a passage in which Abhinavagupta deplores the ascetical-philistine mentality incapable of being affected by beauty: *PTV*, ed. Gnoli, p. 202, translated in Ch. 1, note 37.
43. 4.5, trans. mine.

padmāvatī bahumatā mama yadyapi rūpaśīlamādhuryaiḥ/
vāsavadattābaddhaṃ na tu tāvan me mano harati//

44. Cf. Ch. 3, section entitled 'Courtly Love.' Construed one way what she says is that true *dākṣiṇya* is the avowal of heartfelt sentiment; but also present is the

hint that Udayana's confession is in a sense the polite lie required by the *dākṣiṇya* code when a woman questions her husband about his infidelities. In other words, she may be implying (and this does not negate the first construction) that Udayana is gallantly denying his love for her, Padmāvatī, in the evoked ghostly presence of Vāsavadattā. By offering this fiction she maintains face in a society that appreciates gallant facades.

45. Technical discussion of whether we do not in fact have *vipralambha śṛṅgāra*, since Vāsavadattā is not actually dead, is beside the point. Appeals to pity are an essential part of *rasika* self-display and need to be regarded as such.

46. 4.8, trans. mine.

    iyaṃ bālā navodvādhā satyaṃ śrutvā vyathāṃ vrajet/
    kāmaṃ dhīrasvabhāveyaṃ strīsvabhāvas tu kātaraḥ//

47. A motif sounded several times in the Play, e.g., 1.7+ (twice).

48. 5.9, trans. mine.

    yadi tāvad ayaṃ svapno dhanyam apratibodhanam/
    athāyaṃ vibhramo vā syād vibhramo hyastu me ciram/

    This could be the motto of any *rasika*: the poetic world drenched with sentiment is axiomatically better than the real one.

49. Compare the series of disclosures in *M*: see Ch. 4.

50. I do not accept Pischel's idea that Sanskrit drama originates in puppet-theater and am agnostic as to whether 'string-holder' is to be taken literally with respect to the Stage Manager. The pun is apropos here though.

51. The term is borrowed from Rājaśekhara (*Kāvyamīmāṃsā* 4), who distinguishes between the constructive or strategic (*kārayitrī*) and emotive (*bhāvayitrī*) aspects of the poetic imagination. See J. Nobel, *The Foundations of Indian Poetry*, pp. 64-67, for a short discussion. *Bhāvayitrī pratibhā* belongs to Udayana, the *rasika* capable of realizing the affective meaning of aesthetic fictions, i.e., the series of intimations we have discussed.

52. The Sanskrit terms for the elements of plot-construction are borrowed from the arthic sphere. See Chs. 4 and 5.

53. D.D. Kosambi's characteristically acerbic assessment of the poet's role in Indian aesthetic culture: *The Subhāṣitaratnakoṣa*, 'Introduction,' p. xlvii.

54. 6.16, trans. Woolner and Sarup:

    bhāratānāṃ kule jāto vinīto jñānavāñ chuciḥ/
    tan nārhasi balāddhartuṃ rājadharmasya deśikaḥ//

    Interestingly this harks back to accusation leveled by Mahasena's minister in *PY* 4 regarding the elopement-abduction.

55. His ascetical aspect is suggested in three ways. First, he is asexual (as in the *PY*—see note 23). Second, his decisiveness cuts through the impotence of sentimentality, thus manifesting the Cāṇakya rather than the Rākṣasa side of his character. Third, the metonymy of his disguise aligns him with *saṃnyāsa* and its associated intelligence.

56. 6.18+, trans. Woolner and Sarup.

57. E.g., *M* 4.19+.

58. Discussed in Ch. 1; cf. Ch 2, section 2.

59. Not every *rasika* was polygynous, we can be sure, but the *rasika* ideal itself is. Just as today a male does not have to have enjoyed much 'male privilege' to feel defensive about it.

60. Chari's apt term for various new tendencies in literary criticism: *Sanskrit Criticism*, p. 189.

CHAPTER 7

Cārudatta in Love

The play *Mṛcchakaṭika* or *The Little Clay Cart*, attributed to a certain king Śūdraka, about whom we have no reliable information,[1] has always been praised for its 'realism' in a body of literature—not simply drama (*nāṭya, nāṭaka*) but all of Sanskrit poetry (*kāvya*)—noted rather for its refined, idealizing, courtly sentiment centering in erotic fascination. We welcome *The Little Clay Cart*'s bourgeois setting and picaresque characters, more typical of the less exalted genre of story literature (*kathā*) than of *kāvya*. Critics likewise praise it for the sweetness of its protagonists, the Brahmin merchant Cārudatta and the nobel prostitute Vasantasenā, whose love for each other, in the words of S. K. De, is 'pure, strong and tender' for all the simplicity of its presentation.[2] Yet this blanket praise, which extends to Śūdraka's 'genius' as a constructor of plots and a writer of muscular verse, conceals certain problems. How realistic, for instance, can melodrama be? In what sense can Cārudatta's love be called 'strong', even if we were willing to admit that it is 'pure and tender'? What was the meaning to a contemporary audience of a play which celebrates the ascendancy of an obscure 'man of heart' who never acts in his own behalf, though he spends a remarkable amount of time lamenting his condition? Criticism of the play has to this time hardly scratched the surface.

The principal problem posed by the play is the hero's displacement, and this inevitably involves us in the question of his status as a lover.[3] Like the hero (*nāyaka*) of every play treating love in a serious way, Cārudatta is a *rasika* ('man of feeling') or *sahṛdaya* ('man of heart')—synonymous terms for the idealized representative of India's classical aesthetic culture. But Cārudatta, an impoverished Brahmin merchant, is different from most *sahṛdayas* represented in drama. First of all, most of them are kings, whose charismatic centrality to the socio-political system is taken for granted. Cherished simultaneously as master, friend, childlike protégé, and lover, the royal hero's sensibility represents the privilege of power and sets the standard of taste and feeling for the whole society. The situation is apt enough: few would disagree with the idea that India's aesthetic culture radiated out from the courts. But more important as a marginalizing factor than Cārudatta's hybrid social class as such—a Brahmin functioning as a Vaiśya—is his poverty. There are other non-royal *nāyakas*, such as Mādhava of Bhavabhūti's *Mālatīmādhava* (8th century) who like Cārudatta is a Brahmin, but nevertheless functions as a typical lovestruck hero (*dhīralalita nāyaka*).[4] We should not forget either that when we speak of Indian court culture we are in fact referring a hybrid of the courts and the urban elite.[5] But Cārudatta cannot be a Mādhava primarily because he has the not-so-curious idea that beautiful women belong to the world of wealth and power in which he no longer has a share. Thus, the problem of the hero's displacement hinges on the barrier that lack of means creates between the refined *rasika* sensibility and the *nāgarika* lifestyle that typically goes with it. This in turn implicates love, because erotic feeling (*śṛṅgāra*) is at the very heart of the *rasika* sensibility and indeed of the whole classical Indian aesthetic. What does it mean to be a man of 'heart' or 'feeling' with tastes and inclinations that one cannot afford to indulge? No doubt there were many real-life *sahṛdayas* in Cārudatta's situation, and we would probably not be wrong in seeing this play as speaking directly to their concerns, and incidentally providing them with a wish-fulfilment conclusion.

Let us look first at Cārudatta's credentials as a *sahṛdaya*. We see from his appreciative remarks on music at the beginning of Act 3 (stanzas 3-5) that he has command over the technical vocabulary of connoisseurship, but also, and more importantly, that he has the *sahṛdaya*'s imaginative capacity, as when he praises the lute as 'companion to the longing lover's heart' and 'the delight that increases the passion of the impassioned', and hears in the singer's voice the hidden presence of a beautiful woman. He thus exhibits that subtly erotic sensibility that Ānandavardhana sees as the lifeblood of the 'poetic universe'. Cārudatta also has clear—if erotically muted—links with the *nāgarika* as described in *Kāmasūtra* 1.4: I am thinking especially of the litter of musical instruments in his house, which makes the Brahmin thief Śarvilaka think he has broken into the house of a dance-teacher (3.18+). But more important than these more or less technical recommendations is Cārudatta's tender-heartedness (*sānukrośatva, hṛdayasaṃvāda*). All *sahṛdaya* heroes and heroines have this quality to a marked degree, as when Udayana, the royal protagonist of Bhāsa's *Svapnavāsavadattā* (*Vision of Vāsavadattā*), refuses to disturb a bough on which male and female bees may be enjoying love.

The princess Padmāvatī in the same play falls in love with Udayana simply by hearing an account of his agonies upon the supposed death of his wife Vāsavadattā. Tenderheartedness is thus a sympathy that unites all exemplary 'persons of heart' in a selfconscious community of feeling. Cārudatta has this to an exceptional degree, indeed we know from several passages that he has lost his father's fortune by lavishing wealth on those who have provoked his sympathetic response and we see ample evidence of his generosity even with the little he has throughout the play.

The point of this review is to see that the aesthetic, erotic, social, and ethical features of 'being a person of heart' (*sahṛdayatva*) are all part of one emotional complex. The last item—the ethical perspective—is of special import in *The Little Clay Cart.* Much is made of Cārudatta's 'virtue' or 'merit' (*guṇa*) in this play. But when we examine this concept we see that it is in fact a synonym for sympathetic generosity, i.e., acting on the basis of 'concord of heart' (*hṛdayasaṃvāda*)—what in aesthetic terms is the basis of *rasa*-feeling.[6] In other words, here we have a concept of *dharma* (moral duty) that has little to do with ritualistic obedience to caste norms (*svadharma*), but rather represents an aesthetic-sentimental ideal parleyed into a utopian ethical principle. If everyone were like Cārudatta, if everyone acted upon the impulses of a refined and generous sensibility, then *dharma* would mean the satisfaction of the heart's desire for love, friendship, and an honored place in a world that set the truth of inner goodness over words and appearances. The ending of the play is utopian in just this sense: Cārudatta is made a prince, Vasantasenā is released from prostitution, a fugitive becomes king, a former thief becomes a minister, etc. All men of heart emerge from the obscurity where they had been marginalized by a ruling class that cared only for money, power, and luxury, to inaugurate a new world-order based on respect for the sentimentalized concept of virtue as sympathetic generosity (*guṇa* as *sahṛdayatva*). Cārudatta even extends his generosity to his former tormentor, the Śakāra, the previous king's brother-in-law and a grotesque parody of what it is to be a *nāgarika* without the inner sensibility that makes for true aesthetic taste and courtly erotism.

The mention of the Śakāra brings us back to the question of Cārudatta's character as a lover. Here we encounter a fundamental paradox. The logic of the play demands that we think of Vasantasenā as the ideal beloved (*nāyikā*) of Cārudatta. She is the beautiful woman not of the court who in the corrupt world order can only function as a prostitute, whose *dharma*, we are reminded in the play (1.31-32), is to give herself to whoever can afford her. But beneath the veneer of appearances she is as true a heart as Cārudatta himself, praised by those who know as the virtual goddess of the city (1.27, 1.55+, 5.12, 6.14, 8.39). Thus we would expect Cārudatta, who in fact shares this view, to act upon it or at least to pine for her secretly. And to a limited extent he does. When accident takes her to his house in Act 1 he remarks to himself:

> Ah, it is Vasantasenā—
> The desire inspired by whom
> has, with the end of my wealth,
> subsided within my body
> like the anger of a coward.[7]

Such words would seem to indicate that he has longed for Vasantasenā ever since he met her in the garden of the Love-god's shrine, as she has for him (e.g., 1.32+). But Cārudatta can never make up his mind which Vasantasenā he believes in—the fellow *sahṛdayā* or the venal prostitute who belongs to the power structure from which he is barred. To wit, the 9th verse of the 5th Act:

> The man who has money will be her lover for she can be won with wealth.
> (No, she can be won with virtues!)
> As wealth has abandoned us, so I must abandon her.[8]

Thus Cārudatta as a lover is a great puzzle. Returning to the verse cited above ('Ah, it is Vasantasenā . . . . .'), we can only say that this is a very tepid response for any hero of Sanskrit drama who has been pining for his dream woman. Externally his speech is elegant and deferential: disgusted by the Śakāra's pursuit of her he calls her rather a 'woman fit to be worshipped as a goddess' (*devatopasthānayogyā yuvatir iyam*), and Vasantasenā is sufficiently impressed by signs of his urbanity (*nāgarikatva*) to plan a strategy for seeing him again. But when he walks her home at the end of Act 1 he recites a verse on the moon that seems to raise erotic expectations only to dash them with a comic ineptitude worthy of his rival the Śakāra.

> Behold the rising moon, pale as a lovely woman's cheek,

beacon of the highway, with his retinue of stars,
whose bright rays fall amidst the darkness
like streams of milk in liquid mud.[9]

And this is the way it goes throughout the play, with only one significant exception in Act 5, which I will describe in a moment. Although we have ample evidence of Vasaṇtasenā's pining for Cārudatta (absorption in a love-portrait, inconsequential conversation, virtual death with his name on her lips, etc.), there is not one direct indication in the play of his pining for her. In the scene I mentioned earlier where, walking home at night from a concert, he reveals a sensitivity to music's erotic overtones—one would expect this to lead to some recollection of Vasantasenā's beauty, as it would for any other love-hero in such a situation, but it never comes. He falls into an easy sleep a short time later, having thought of her only in connection with his promise to guard her ornaments. In fact his reference to her in this regard is hardly flattering: he wants the Vidūṣaka to keep the jewels out of the inner quarters since 'they have been worn by a public woman' (*prakāśanārīdhṛta eṣa*, 3.7).[10] In Act 7, though he ostensibly waits for her arrival in an abandoned garden at the edge of town (a situation fraught with potential for poetic expressions of longing), he never spares a thought for her, even before he meets the future king Āryaka who arrives in the coach that was supposed to carry her. In Acts 9 and 10, when he is, respectively, on trial for murdering her and on the way to execution, his thoughts concerning her (with one formulaic exception) have nothing to do with her own plight but rather the ignominy that has fallen on himself in being accused of murder and theft.[11] Cārudatta is an extremely self-absorbed lover—not in the sense that he loses interest in the day-to-day world of work and duty that surrounds him, as other love-heroes do, but in the sense that he can only think of his own misery, society's apparent disregard and contempt of him.

Yet there is the blip in Act 5: Vasantasenā comes to his house as an *abhisārikā*[12] and teases and cajoles him into making love with her. It is hard to avoid the impression of a certain maternal solicitation in this scene: a beautiful woman wise in the ways of the world doting on a bashful quasi-adolescent. But surprisingly enough Cārudatta rises to the challenge with the aplomb of an inveterate 'man of feeling', delivering several *śṛṅgāra* verses on the torture of his lonely vigils, the ecstasy of her touch, the excitatory stimulus of the rains, etc.

We should not downplay this scene, because it does reveal Cārudatta's *rasika* soul in the classical pattern; yet we cannot help seeing it as something of an irregularity in this play. It establishes Cārudatta's credentials as a bona fide *sahṛdaya*, alive to the quasi-mystical satisfactions of erotic thrill, but it does not tip the scales in the direction of erotic love as a rapturous transcendence of mundanity, which is the typical kāvyic treatment. It does not remove the impression that love in this play is the prime example of sentiment as an ethical principle.

To see this in all its clarity we have to move to the climactic moment in Act 10 when Vasantasenā virtually rises from the dead to save him. Just before she arrives, while he is still in the depths of despair, he invokes her in heaven to bear witness to his innocence:

> If *dharma* still prevails for me,
> ruined by Fortune through the lies of the powerful,
> may she herself, in Indra's world or elsewhere,
> remove my crime by her own true being.[13]

The structural opposition expressed here is between true being (*svabhāva*) and virtue (*guṇa*) on the one hand and false speech (*vākya*) and wealth-and-power (*dhana, artha*) on the other. Cārudatta has so little confidence in his own speech as to have allowed himself to subscribe to the confession that his enemy has put in his mouth. But whereas before this he has always tended to include Vasantasenā among those who live in and for the world of appearances, now he explicitly includes her in the circle of mute, inglorious *sahṛdayas* who constitute the inner substance, the *svabhāva,* of society. If *dharma* is a matter of *svabhāva* rather than *vākya,* then somehow a miracle will happen and Vasantasenā will pierce the tissue of corrupt social discourse with the hidden truth. And, of course, this is precisely what happens. She arrives in the nick of time, as he describes her in two apt similes, like 'rain to a withering crop' and 'saving knowledge to a dying man'.[14]

Thus we have to evaluate the significance of love in this play in the socio-ethical context we have described. It is therefore not a matter of momentary transcendence in an aesthetic-erotic bliss and its problematic consequences, as we find in other plays (e.g., Kālidāsa's *Śakuntalā*). Rather here the accent is on love as the most concrete instance of *sahṛdaya* solidarity. Love is the *svabhāva,* the true being, that triumphs over deceptions. As Cārudatta says to his savioress:

> You yourself have redeemed the body
> that was being destroyed because of you.
> How powerful in the lovers' union,
> when even the dead come back to life![15]

For the *sahṛdaya* on the margins of wealth and power, true feeling (*rasa*) is both more and less than a rapturous shiver of delight. It is the ticket to utopia that the proprietors of the beautiful have corrupted by setting a price on it, i.e., by making it a matter of style rather than substance.[16]

Thus it is of critical importance for two reasons that Vasantasenā be the pursuer rather than the pursued in this love affair. Cārudatta is a symbol of the *sahṛdaya*'s essential purity, which in this context means a free-floating emotional sympathy devoid (at least ostensibly) of self-interest. Taking a hint from the vaguely Buddhist atmosphere of the play we might refer to him a secular Bodhisattva, interested in everyone's salvation but his own. Such a function does not sit well with erotic infatuation, which removes lovers emotionally or psychologically from society into a charmed private sphere.[17] Nevertheless, erotic feeling (*śṛṅgāra*) is too important to the *rasika* sensibility for it to be altogether absent. Thus it is given a certain scope to appear in its customary dimensions, but beyond that it is sublimated as a form of devotion to goodness (*guṇa*), not essentially different from—and on the whole inferior to—the all-male friendship-bond.[18]

The second reason is closely related. Vasantasenā is one of several figures in the play who are implicated in the old order but change sides. A good example is the guard Candanaka who lets Cārudatta's coach pass with Āryaka safely inside (Act 6). All of these people choose to follow the dictates of the heart to their own practical disadvantage, and all do so with a direct reference either to Cārudatta or to the affective idea of virtue that he epitomizes.[19] Seen in this light Vasantasenā's choice of Cārudatta despite his poverty and her rejection of wealthy but insensitive clients is an act of self-redemption. Thus her 'death' at the hands of the Śakāra symbolizes her complete severance of ties with the world of venal prostitution,[20] and her recovery—aided by the Buddhist monk whom she had earlier helped in Cārudatta's name—is her decisive rebirth into the value-world of sympathetic generosity (*hṛdayasaṃvāda*). Cārudatta, we remember, was never able to decide who the real Vasantasenā was. This is because the burden of the decision has been entirely upon her shoulders. Cārudatta remains what he is throughout the play, the lodestar of virtue by which others guide their actions. His generosity to Āryaka, his fellow victim, is less a defining moral choice than another instance of his essential character (*svabhāva*).[21] It is for others to make such a choice, and in so doing they choose Cārudatta, the unsung hero of society,[22] or his proxy Āryaka, who regards him as the patron saint of the utopian order ushered in by the successful revolution.[23]

But we cannot end this chapter without reverting to the play's incidental function as wish-fulfilment. For all the ideality of his character we have no trouble seeing that Cārudatta himself is not really free of the idea that wealth and virtue are closely related. He spends an inordinate amount of time brooding on his poverty with its concomitant loss of friends and reputation. Yet why should one who represents true being (*svabhāva*) over appearance (*vākya*) be so concerned with the judgement of superficial people? How, furthermore, can he be so blind to the general esteem in which he is held among all persons of heart? He is never so ashamed as when he cannot display his generosity in material terms. Thus when he has to let the good news whispered into his ear by Vasantasenā's Maid go unrewarded, it launches a series of verses on the theme of impotence:

> Oh misery!
> For a man without money what is the use
> of living in this world at all?
> In his inability to reciprocate
> both his anger and favor are vain.
>
> Furthermore—
>
> A wingless bird, a withered tree, a waterless pond,
> a toothless serpent: a poor man in the human world.
>
> Furthermore—
>
> Poor men are like uninhabited houses,
> waterless wells, withered trees,
> for, forgetting their woes in union with a friend,
> their moments of pleasure thus prove empty.[24]

Again, at that point in Act 3 when his wife provides him with the means of compensating Vasantasenā extravagantly for the loss of her jewels, his first reaction is extreme embarrassment:

What, my wife pities me! Alas! Now I am poor—
My wealth destroyed by a personal fate
and I pitied with a woman's wealth.
Through wealth a man becomes a woman,
and a woman a man through wealth.[25]

If we put all these hints together we emerge with the portrait of a man who sees generosity as a sort of sexual potency and a claim on the general admiration of society. Cārudatta is not vulgar, like the Śakāra and the corrupt ruling class the latter represents. there can be no questioning the sensibility that makes this meek, displaced hero a genuine *sahṛdaya.* But at the same time there is a psychological dimension that we cannot ignore. Cārudatta's version of potency is based on money, not as a means of directly purchasing aesthetic-erotic satisfactions but as a means of inspiring others to love him and act on his behalf. For this reason—and because his very desire for potency is surreptitious—he is essentially passive. It is no accident that when, in the scene mentioned above, Cārudatta reaches for a ring to reward Vasantasenā's maid and then shows embarrassment, Vasantasenā's response is: 'This is why I love you!' (*ata eva kāmyase*), words that almost exactly echo her earlier response when the Vidūṣaka arrived at the brothel with the gift of Cārudatta's wife's heirloom (4.32+). The very manifestion of what he himself feels as impotence wears a charm that borrows power from the admiring beholder. Cārudatta's gestures have, directly or indirectly, the same effect on all noble souls, who rally to his cause, rescue him from his good-hearted passivity, and make him the prince he was always meant to be.[26] Thus the utopian order based on sympathetic generosity corresponds exactly with the acknowledge and empowerment of the *sahṛdaya,* the secular Bodhisattva who, like fairy-tale heroes everywhere, gets the girl and the kingdom too.

Notes

1. He is first mentioned as an author by the poetician Vāmana (fl. AD 800). For further information see such handbooks as M. Krishnamachariar, *History of Classical Sanskrit Literature,* Keith, *The Sanskrit Drama,* and Dasgupta and De, *A History of Sanskrit Literature.*
2. Dasgupta and De, *History,* p. 245.
3. I am bracketing problems of textual accretion, authorship, and where the play stands in relation to the fragment in the Bhāsa corpus called *Daridracārudatta*

or *Cārudatta in Poverty*. Like most scholars I regard Śūdraka's play as an elaboration of Bhāsa's. Śūdraka's dependence on the Bhāsa play was established by Georg Morgenstierne, *Über das Verhältnis zwischen Cārudatta und Mṛcchakaṭika* (1920), though some have contested it, most recently G. H. Schokker, 'Śūdraka, the Author of the Original *Cārudatta*.' See Pusalkar, *Bhāsa*, 2nd ed., for further bibliography.

4. *The Little Clay Cart* and *Mālatīmādhava* are the two prime examples in the extant literature of a type known as the *prakaraṇa*. The requirements of this subgenre are basically that the plot be invented or borrowed from popular stories (*kathā*) as opposed to history and legend (*itihāsapurāṇa*), and that the hero (*nāyaka*) be other than a king, typically a Brahmin, a merchant, or a minister. The heroes of Sanskrit drama are divided into four basic types—exalted (*dhīrodātta*), amorous (*dhīralalita*), serene (*dhīrapraśānta*), and vehement (*dhīroddhata*). According to most sources the hero of a *prakaraṇa* must be serene. Although not entirely artificial, these distinctions (1) are mainly *ex post facto*, (2) cannot be made to fit certain obvious cases, and (3) belie the fact that most *nāyakas* are composite types.
5. Thus the greatest of Sanskrit playwrights, Kālidāsa (probably 5th century AD), can have one of his characters call the royal hero of the *Vikramorvaśīya* a *nāgarika* ('urbane townsman') in order to explain his sophistication (*dākṣiṇya*) as a lover (3.13+). It was the *nāgarika* for whom the *Kāmasūtra*, Vātsyāyana's celebrated treatise on erotics (3rd century?), was written. *Kāmasūtra* 1.4 describes the ideal day of the *nāgarika*, which was devoted entirely to refined amusements and capped by amorous sport. It tells us of *nāgarikas* who joined in *goṣṭhīs* (literary 'clubs'), enjoying cultivated conversation with hetaeras, music, poetry, jaunts to the countryside, etc. Such *goṣṭhīs*, or individual *nāgarikas*, provided important patronage for the arts including troops of actors. In *The Little Clay Cart* Cārudatta's friend Rebhila entertains the members of his *goṣṭhī* with a concert. There is incidentally a whole subgenre of drama devoted to the amorous emploits of the *nāgarika*: the *bhāṇa* or 'monologue play'. Unfortunately it has not received its share of serious study.
6. Cf. the celebrated definition of Abhinavagupta in his commentary on Ānandavardhana's *Dhavanyāloka*:

   Sahṛdayas are those who share in a concordance of heart, i.e., who have an aptitude for identification with what is depicted [by poets] in a mirrorlike mind made clear by familiarity with and practice of poetry. *yeṣāṃ kāvyānuśīlanābhyāsavaśād viśadībhūte manomukure varṇanīyatanmayībhavanayogyatā te hṛdayasaṃvādabhājaḥ sahṛdayāḥ/*

7. 1.55: *aye iyaṃ vasantasenā/*
   yayā me janitaḥ kāmaḥ kṣīṇe vibhavavistare/
   krodhaḥ kupuruṣasyeva svagātreṣveva sīdati//
8. 5.9:
   yasyārthas tasya sā kāntā dhanahāryo hyasau janaḥ/
   (na guṇahāryo hyasau janaḥ)
   vayam arthaiḥ parityaktāḥ nanu tyaktaiva sā maya//
9. 1.57:
   paśya—
   udayati hi śaśāṅkaḥ kāminīgaṇḍapāṇḍur
   grahagaṇaparivāro rājamārgapradīpaḥ/
   timiranikaramadhye raśmayo yasya gaurāḥ

srutajala iva paṅke kṣīradhārāḥ patanti//

Some believe that this is intended to be beautiful and that it only strikes a sour note to our modern sensibility. Parallel examples would have to be adduced to defend this point of view. But even if one could find them, it would still be striking that such a *relatively* unusual simile is the one that occurs to our hero as a romantic gambit, especially in the context of a play which ridicules poetic malapropisms in the Śakāra.

10. It has been suggested that Cārudatta's status as an exemplary householder (*gṛhastha*) explains apparent lack of erotic interest in the heroine: it would not be 'appropriate' for such a hero to pine for a courtesan. Thus, in this instance of the jewels, Cārudatta establishes his credentials as a devout Hindu of his social station, which has the effect of making the love more honorable when it finally gets its due. There is much to this, yet surely the playwright would have been deft enough to infuse his hero with a little more eros (one or two pining soliloquies), if that had been his interest, without damaging our respect for him. After all, if propriety is the deciding factor, why not avoid the love of Brahmin and courtesan altogether? One might indeed point to an underlying ritual pattern, such as the part of the *mahāvrata* rite in which a Brahmin student exchanges smutty invective with a prostitute, which Gonda ('Ascetics and Courtesans') and others have seen as suggestive of an earlier pattern of sexual intercourse (cf. *AV* 11.5). But ritual intrepretations of literature, like psychoanalytic interpretations, interesting and revealing as both are, provide only one set of influencing factors, which do not constitute a sufficient cause. (See Gonda's 'Zur Frage nach dem Ursprung und Wesen des indischen Dramas' for an example of the anthropological-genetic method taken too far.) There is still the question as to why the love of Cārudatta and Vasantasenā was consciously chosen over other literary subjects and why it was treated as it was in this play.

11. The exception is 10.13, repeated after 10.24 and 10.36, according to stage directions:

    O woman with teeth white as pure moonbeams
    and lower lip red as coral,
    after drinking the nectar of your mouth
    must I now drink the poison of infamy?
    śaśivimalamayūkhaśubhradanti suruciravidrumasaṃnibhādharauṣṭhi/
    tava vadanabhavāmṛtaṃ nipīya katham avaśo hyayaśoviṣaṃ pibāmi//

    But even this, though it does raise the specter of her erotic charm, ends in the familiar refrain of self-lamentation.

12. A 'woman who goes (to her lover)', one of eight types of heroine (*nāyikā*) classified according to her disposition to her lover. See Shastri, *Laws and Practice*, pp. 218-20, or any hand-book.

13. 10.34:

    prabhavati yadi dharmo duṣitasyāpi me'dya
    prabalapuruṣavākyair bhāgyadoṣāt kathaṃcit/
    surapatibhavanasthā yatra tatra sthitā vā
    vyapanayatu kalaṅkaṃ svasvabhāvena saiva//

14. 10.39 and 42:

    Who is this who has come to me
    like rain to a withering crop,
    when the sword was poised
    and I was in the jaws of death?

keyam abhyudyate śastre mṛtyuvaktragate mayi/
anāvṛṣṭihate sasye droṇavṛṣṭir ivāgatā//
Whence have you come
with tear-soaked breasts
like saving knowledge
to this dying man?
kuto bāṣpāmbudhārābhiḥ snāpayanti payodharau/
mayi mṛtyuvaśaṃ prāpte vidyeva samupāgatā//

15. 10.43:
tvadartham etad vinipātyamānaṃ dehaṃ tvayaiva pratimocitaṃ me/
aho prabhāvaḥ priyasaṃgamasya mṛto'pi ko nāma punar dhriyeta//

16. By pertinent analogy, one of the main issues of Sanskrit poetics is the distinction made between genuine poetry, which is suggestive and principally concerned with *rasa*, and pseudo-poetry, which does not get beyond rhetorical sport. Ānandavardhana calls all such poetry *citrakāvya* ('picture poetry'), referring to poems whose syllables placed in certain arrangements form a schematic wheel or the like. The only criterion of true poetry is that it please the 'man of heart'. See Ānandavardhana, *Dhavanyāloka* 1.1, 1.13, 3.41-42

17. Cf. Freud, *Civilization and Its Discontents*, section 4.

18. Note the terms in which the Brahmin thief Śarvilaka makes his decision before exiting in Act 4 (4.25):
Two things—friend and woman—
are dear to men in this world,
but now I would chose my friend
over a hundred beautiful women.
dvayam idam atīva loke priyaṃ narāṇāṃ suhṛc ca vanitā ca/
saṃprati tu sundarīṇām śatād api suhṛd viśiṣṭatamaḥ//

He has willingly sacrificed his reputation as a Brahmin out of love for Madanikā, Vasantasenā's servant, yet no sooner does he win her than he gives her up because his friend Āryaka is in trouble. It is no accident, either, that he more than regains his social status as a result.

19. It might be well to refer here to the four 'human goals' (*puruṣārthas*) under which rubric all human behavior can be classified in the Hindu world-view: *dharma* (law, duty), *artha* (profit), *kāma* (desire, pleasure), and *mokṣa* (salvation). Under the old regime *dharma* is confused with *artha*: for example, it is Candanaka's 'duty' to arrest the fugitive Āryaka, just as it is Vasantasenā's duty to surrender to the Śakāra, though both of these actions would really be only self-serving. But in the new order *dharma* will be aligned primarily with *kāma*, with the latter understood altruistically as sympathetic generosity (*hṛdayasaṃvāda*), though eventually *artha* follows suit, i.e., once the revolution succeeds. How different is this notion of *dharma* from the model of *karmayoga* ('the discipline of action') in the *Bhagavad-Gita*, where the ideal is disinterested ritualistic performance of prescribed duty in the spirit of renunciation regardless of the heart's inclinations. Such a notion of *dharma* would offer no hope for Vasantasenā and the other *sahṛdayas* except in the ultimate sense of *mokṣa*. The affective model of *dharma* in this play is distinctly antinomian, since it offered the possibility of a more fluid social structure than the caste system.

20. Lest we dismiss this aspect of Vasantasenā as mere facade we should recall the Vidūṣaka's carnivalesque description of brothel decadence in Act 4. Even if this scene—worthy of a Petronius or a Fellini—is an accretion, it has hermeneutical

value as an indication of the way the indigenous tradition understood the issue at point. Vasantasenā is by implication a queen who presides over a realm of emasculating decadence.

21. Āryaka is Cārudatta's active double, the revolutionary his sympathetic generosity does not allow him to be. By contrast the Śakāra is his 'shadow' or 'evil twin', absorbing all Cārudatta's potential sexual aggressiveness, so that his love can be 'pure' and 'tender' (in S. K. De's terminology). Any anger Cārudatta might feel toward courtesans, who sell their beauty to the highest bidder rather than award it to those with the sensitivity to appreciate it, is transferred to the Śakāra.
22. See the references to his role as 'wishing-tree' (*kalpavṛkṣa*): 1.48, 9.30+, 10.30+ (cf. 2.15+, 4.32, 6.13-14, 10.4).
23. 10.52+ 'Good sir, King Ārayaka proclaims: "I have acquired this kingdom by your goodness. Therefore receive [the principate I confer upon you]." ' *ārya nanvayam āryako rājā vijñāpayati—idaṃ mayā yuṣmadguṇopārjitaṃ rājyam/ tad upayujyatām/*
24. 5.40-42:

bhoḥ kaṣṭam/
dhanair viyuktasya narasya loke kiṃ jīvitenādita eva tāvat/
yasya pratīkāranirarthakatvāt kopaprasādā viphalībavanti//
api ca/
pakṣavikalaś ca pakṣī śuṣkaś ca taruḥ saraś ca jalahīnam/
sarpaś coddhṛtadaṃṣṭras tulyaṃ loke daridraś ca//
api ca/
śūnyair gṛhaiḥ khalu samaḥ puruṣo daridraḥ
kūpaiś ca toyarahitais traubhiś ca śīrṇaiḥ/
yad dṛṣṭapūrvajanasaṃgamavismṛtānām
evam bhavanti viphalāḥ paritoṣakālāḥ//

25. 3.27:

kathaṃ brāhmaṇī mām anukampate/ kaṣṭam/ idānīm asmi daridraḥ/
ātmabhāgyakṣatadravyaḥ strīdravyenānukampitaḥ/
arthataḥ puruṣo nārī yā nārī sārthataḥpumān//

For further expressions of impotence see 1.55 (cited previously) and 5.8.

26. Thus to his composite character of Brahmin and (virtual) Vaiśya he adds the quality of being a (virtual) Kṣatriya: thus emerging as Everyman.

APPENDIX

Rasa Poetics

The system of *rasa* poetics is outlined in detail in chapters 6 and 7 of the *Nāṭyaśāstra.* Despite certain confusions, which I shall mention below, there is a basic theoretical principle, namely that the aesthetic depiction of a group of eight emotional states (the *sthāyibhāvas*) gives rise to a corresponding relishable emotional 'savor' (*rasa*). This emotional savor is regarded as the *sine quạ non* of successful drama: 'without *rasa* nothing useful is achieved' (*na hi rasād ṛte kaścid apyarthaḥ pravartate*).[1]

We can show the relation between *sthāyibhāva* and *rasa* by lining them up in parallel columns:

Principal Emotion	Savor
rati (love)	*śṛṅgāra* (erotic)
hāsa (laughter)	*hāsya* (comic)
śoka (sorrow)	*karuṇa* (pathetic)
utsāha (energy)	*vīra* (manly, heroic)
krodha (anger)	*raudra* (furious)
bhaya (fear)	*bhayānaka* (fearful)
jugupsā (disgust)	*bībhatsa* (grotesque)
vismaya (amazement)	*adbhuta* (wondrous)[2]

The transmutation of *sthāyibhāva* to *rasa* can only occur when there is an aesthetic enhancement of mood through poetic treatment of certain details. In the doctrine laid out in *NŚ* 6.31+ -33+ such treatment entails a careful delineation of the causes (*vibhāva*) and effects (*anubhāva, sāttvika bhāva*) of the emotion as well as a depiction of subsidiary emotions that give the basic mood its color. For example, fear, considered as an abiding feeling (the *sthāyi-* of *sthāyibhāva* means 'abiding') may include momentary feelings (*vyabhicāri-* or *saṃcāribhāvas*) of apprehension, worry, fright, alarm, fatigue, frenzy, and others, in various combinations. Thus the aesthetic enhancement of emotion that produces *rasa* results from a subtle mix of the appropriate 'objective correlatives' of the basic emotion (*sthayibhāva*) and the depiction, again via objective correlatives, of related secondary feelings.[3] The operating metaphor is that of a beverage whose basic substance is enhanced by herbs, spices, sweeteners, etc. (= the *vibhāvas, anubhāvas,* and *vyabhicāribhāvas*), producing a subtle, delicious flavor (the word *rasa* actually means 'flavor').

Given the Indian penchant for theoretical itemization, it was natural that some of these ingredients would become fixed in canonical lists. Thus the *vyabhicāribhāvas* were fixed as a group of 33:

The 33 Transitory States (*vyabhicāribhāvas*)

nirveda (world-weariness)
śaṅkā (apprehension)
mada (intoxication)
ālasya (torpor)
moha (bewilderment)
smṛti (remembrance)
vrīḍā (embarrassment)
capalatā (rashness)
jaḍatā (stupor)
autsukya (longing)
nidrā (sleepiness)
supta (dreaming)
amarṣa (indignation)
avahittah (dissimulation)
vyādhi (sickness)
maraṇa (dying)
vitarka (deliberation)[4]
glāni (weakness)
asūyā (envy)
śama (fatigue)
dainya (misery)
cintā (worry)
dhṛti (contentment)
harṣa (joy)
āvega (alarm)
garva (pride)
viṣāda (dejection)
apasmāra (derangement)
vibodha (wakefulness)
mati (intelligence)
ugratā (cruelty)
unmada (frenzy)
trāsa (fright)

There was also a special group of effects (*anubhāvas*) known as the 'natural states' (*sāttvika bhavas*), which numbered 8:

The 8 Natural States (*sāttvika bhāvas*)

stambha (paralysis)
romāñca (horripilation)
vepathu (trembling)
asra (tears)
sveda (sweat)
svarabhaṅga (faltering voice)
vaivarṇya (loss of color)
pralaya (swoon)

No such attempt was made, however, with respect to the *vibhāvas* or 'causes' of the emotional states in the fictive subjects. Later than the *Nāṭyaśāstra* a distinction was made between two types of *vibhāva*: one called *ālambana* (basic) and the other *uddīpana* (excitatory); but this was already implicit in the *NŚ*. The paradigm case for *kāvya* is a *nāyaka*'s apprehension of a beautiful woman. She is the 'basic cause' (*ālambana vibhāva*) of his erotic feeling, and much care is expended in building up a detailed sense of her physical charm and aura. The 'excitatory causes' are the contextual factors that contribute to the growing erotic mood (*śṛṅgāra rasa*): sweet fragrances, luxuriant vegetation, a full moon, music, ornaments, etc.[5]

The *anubhāvas*, except for the specialized group of *sāttvikabhāvas*, also escaped canonical itemization because of their great variability in context. They are the visible or otherwise concrete signs by which a fictive subject in drama or poetry reveals his emotion: facial expressions, gestures, and words that express delight, sorrow, longing, etc., in relation to his or her basic emotional state.

The system's ambiguities, both semantic and substantial, are also worthy of comment. We detect a certain looseness in the use of the word for 'emotion' or 'state' (*bhāva*). The 'natural states', for instance, are physical conditions which reveal emotion. Even some of the 'transitory states' seem more like physical conditions than feelings: sickness, dying, sleepiness. Others, on the other hand, are mental without appearing to be emotional: intelligence, deliberation, dreaming. *Vibhāva* and *anubhāva* (whatever the value of the etymological explanations at *NŚ* 7.3 + - 5) were obviously chosen because they incorporate the essential term *bhāva*. Thus, though they are categorically referred to as *bhāvas* themselves in certain passages, they are semantically concrete signs relating to 'states' rather than 'states' themselves.

A more substantial problem has to do with the status of *rasa* in relation to *sthāyibhāva*. In *NŚ* 6 it is said that the *rasas* themselves are 'represented' (*prayoktavya*) or 'discerned' (*jñeya, dṛśyate*) through the use of *vibhāvas, anubhāvas*, and *vyabhicāribhāvas*, as if they were themselves emotional states rather than the delicious taste resulting from poetic treatment of the emotional states. The confusion grows when we read *NŚ* 7, where the same exact language is used of the *sthāyi-* and *vyabhicāribhāvas*: they are also 'represented', and by the very same *vibhāvas*, etc. Perhaps we could explain this confusion on the basis of metonymy: the *rasas* are treated like their material causes the *sthāyibhāvas*, even though their existence is outside of the play or text proper in the delectation of the hearer or spectator. We have to make some such assumption to preserve the theory we have outlined above, which is in fact clearly stated in *NŚ* 6.31+ - 33+ (cf. 7.3). But the probability is that this theoretical formulation is later than the elements of the system; *rasa* and *bhāva* probably existed as practical synonyms in early dramatic nomenclature, and only gradually did their semantic connotations, based on their etymological distinction ('flavor, juice' vs. 'state of being, mental state'), harden into a theoretical relationship.[6]

However this may be, the confusion over the status of *rasa* generated a series of positions on the nature of the aesthetic experience. Abhinavagupta (fl. AD 1000) singled out the views of three predecessors, all Kashmiri theoreticians like himself.[7] Bhaṭṭa Lollaṭa and Bhaṭṭa Śaṅkuka (both early to mid-9th century AD) tended to an objectivist interpretation, seeing *rasa* as something to be perceived as immanent in the text or play. AG's criticism of their arguments is often tendentious sophism, but his main point is that they cannot account for the fact that *rasa*-perception is inherently pleasant. On the whole AG subscribes to the view of Bhaṭṭa Nāyaka (fl. AD 900), though only with certain theoretical corrections. But before I can describe BhN's view I have to backtrack a bit and explain how *rasa* crept into poetic theory at large.

Rasa was initially a concept that belonged to the technical and theoretical writing on drama and was not a part of standard poetics, which dealt with verbal poetry (*śravya kāvya*) and focused on the question of what made poetic speech different from ordinary speech. Thus standard poetics revolved around questions of figurality (*vakrokti, alaṃkāra*) and heightened diction (*guṇa, rīti*). It was almost entirely practical and descriptive rather than theoretical. *Rasa* was acknowledged as having a certain value—even the early poeticians Bhāmaha and Daṇḍin (both 8th century AD) say that a major poem (*mahākāvya*) must include all 8 *rasas*—but its place was distinctly secondary. It was accommodated to the *alaṃkāra* system as a vague figure of speech called *rasavat* ('having *rasa*') or in connection with sweetness in diction. The poetician Rudraṭa (fl. 850) was the first to give *rasa* major attention, focusing on *śṛṅgāra*, but he left it unclear how it fit into standard linguistically-oriented poetics. This situation changed with Ānandavardhana (fl. 875), the first to elevate poetics to sophisticated theory.

ĀV shared the linguistic assumptions of his of his predecessors, but he distinguished three levels of linguistic meaning. The first was Denotation (*abhidhā*), in which words mean exactly what they say:

'The village is near the Ganges.' The second is Indication (*lakṣaṇā*), in which the literal meaning has to yield, however slightly, in order to convey the intended meaning: 'The village is on the Ganges', where *on* really means 'near'. This second level of signification is a feature of both ordinary language and poetry, and with regard to poetry it covers all figurality (*alaṃkāra*) as such. But ĀV goes a step further. There is a third level, suggestion (*vyañjanā*), in which language may or may not be figural but the words convey a meaning which goes beyond direct or indirect denotation. The example he gives here is again 'The village is on the Ganges', where the implication is of cool breezes and proximity to the sacred. It is only when language is suggestive, he argues, that we have poetry. He then distinguishes three kinds of suggested meaning: content (*vastu*), figure (*alaṃkāra*), and emotion (*rasa*). Thus if a woman in a poem speaks to a traveler of a lonely spot in the forest where nobody comes, the attentive reader understands that she is suggesting a rendezvous: this is suggestion of content (*vastudhvani*). Or if a poem speaks of the beauty of the moon in a certain way the reader may perceive the intended comparison with a woman's face: suggestion of figure (*alaṃkāradhvani*). But the most significant, most poetic form of suggestion is *rasadhvani*, when the words evoke a delicious emotional response in the sensitive reader (*sahṛdaya*). This is achieved, as we will not be surprised to learn, through the careful depiction of *vibhāvas*, etc., as in dramatics. But whereas in drama these preconditions were conveyed through actions and even costume as well as speech, in verbal poetry language bears the whole burden.[8] Thus it was Ānandavardhana who fully accommodated drama's poetics of *rasa* to verbal poetry and poetics.[9]

Bhaṭṭa Nāyaka, to return to the question of *rasa*'s character, did not accept Ānandavardhana's theory, but he was likewise interested in adapting *rasa* to a general poetic theory. He likewise distinguished three levels of language, beginning with Denotation. Instead of Indication, however, his second level was called Realization (*bhāvakatva*). Here he was speaking only of poetic language. By judicious use of speech (including figures and diction) in describing the objective correlatives of emotion (the *vibhāvas* and *anubhāvas*) the poet released language from its normal referential function so that it generalized what it described as an experience common to every sensitive reader.[10] Beyond this he proposed a third function called *bhojakatva* (the faculty of 'causing delight') which would explain how the generalization of the *vibhāvas*, etc., could lead to the delicious savoring of emotion in the sensitive aesthetic recipient.

Abhinavagupta's principle correction of BhN is the rejection of latter two levels: they are nothing, he ways, but what ĀV means by suggestion (*vyañjanā, dhvani*). But he retains BhN's key concept of generalization (*sādhāraṇīkaraṇa*), now ascribed to suggestion, though ignored by ĀV, as the device by which the magic of *rasa* experience is explained. Thus the question of where *rasa* resides is resolved. It resides in the reader-hearer-spectator of *kāvya* (poetry and drama). So, in fact, does the *sthāyibhāva*. *Kāvya*'s role is to present generalized depictions of the causes and effects of emotion, a virtual reality that touches the chord, so to speak, of the reader's own resident emotional states (*sthāyibhāvas*) but depersonalizes and sublimates them to a condition in which they can be enjoyed as pure savor. Thus poetry becomes a means of savoring the emotional facets of one's own consciousness.

This places the aesthetic subject in the position of a religious adept, who, in AG's brand of Tantra, seeks not to obliterate worldly experience but to experience it as the divine subject who savors the cosmic manifestation as a form of play. For AG perception on the highest level is not distinct from feeling. The *rasa* experience in poetry is a foreshadowing of the permanent transcendence of the personal limitations that occurs only with religious enlightenment. One does not need to believe this, however, to appreciate the high value placed on *rasa* experience by most poeticians from ĀV's time onward. *Kāvya* from Bhāmaha and Daṇḍin had always been idealized. Daṇḍin, for instance, wrote:

> By the favor of words does the course of the world proceed. If the light called 'word' did not shine into this existence, then these three worlds would be in complete darkness. The image of the fame of the earliest kings, reflected in the mirror of speech is rightly called the cow which yields all desires; badly composed, however, it announces the ox-like nature of its user.[11]

This is nothing, however, compared with ĀV's adulation of the 'poetic universe' (*kāvyasaṃsāra*) quoted several times in this book (see Ch. 1, section 2).

Notes

1. The precise translation of *arthaḥ pravartate* in this context is elusive. I myself have translated it somewhat differently in Ch. 3.
2. By the end of the 8th century at latest a 9th *rasa* was accepted: *śānta* (tranquil). Udbhaṭa (fl. 775) was the first poetician to mention it in the extant literature, but it became general. Both Ānandavardhana and Abhinavagupta accepted it for instance. It was, interestingly, never quite clear what its proper *sthāyibhāva* was: see Raghavan, *Number of Rasas*, Ch. 4.
3. The use of Eliot's term seems warranted, as others have noted as well. One wonders if Eliot's poetic theory might not derive from some familiarity, even if slight, with *rasa* poetics. He did study Sanskrit at Harvard for a time before expatriating.
4. The English translations are approximate, since there is no one-for-one fit of English and Sanskrit words. The real meanings of these conditions are elucidated by the particular situations in which they occur.
5. It is especially in the area of the *vibhāvas*, that one comes to appreciate the primary place of *śṛṅgāra* in this poetic system. When we read in the *NŚ* and other manuals and treatises about the *vibhāvas* of other major emotions, the vividness of detail that makes aesthetic depiction successful is either reduced or absent. Here is *NŚ* 6.66+ on the heroic *rasa*:

    > Now the Heroic (*vīra*) sentiment relates to the superior type of persons and has energy [*utsāha*] as its basis [*sthāyibhāva*]. This is created by Determinants [*vibhāvas*] such as presence of mind, perseverance, diplomacy, discipline, military strength, aggressiveness, reputation of might, influence, and the like.

    Presence of mind (*asaṃmoha*) and perseverance (*adhyavasāya*) are qualities in the heroic character, but can hardly be seen as emotional causes. One might see them as a type of *vyabhicāribhāva*, but not a *vibhāva*. Nothing in this whole list has any objective or concrete poetic value. (The above translation is that of Manmohan Ghosh; insertions in square brackets are mine.)
6. Kālidāsa uses *rasa* and *bhāva* together but apparently as synonyms in *M* 2.8.
7. None of their writings are extant except in fragments quoted by other poeticians.
8. In drama one speaks of the four modes of representation (the four *abhinayas*): verbal (*vācika*), bodily (*āṅgika*), 'natural' (*sāttvika*: this refers to the *sāttvika bhāvas* listed above), and costume (*āhārya*) All these together comprise the 'language' of drama as 'spectacle poetry' (*dṛśyakāvya*) as opposed to verbal poetry (*śravyakāvya*).
9. I do not mean to imply that standard linguistic poetics was in fact foreign to dramatics. Under the heading of the verbal mode of representation (*vācika abhinaya*: see preceding note) the *Nāṭyaśāstra* itemizes four figures of speech and ten excellences (*guṇas*) of diction among other things. The *NŚ* is in fact the earliest source of linguistic poetics, though by the time of Ānandavardhana the number of *alaṃkāras* had risen to over 60. However, the *NŚ* did not try to adapt *rasa* to verbal poetry as such.
10. Thus we can see that in doing away with Indication (*lakṣaṇā*) as a separate function of language BhN assigns figurality to the ordinary and poetic realms either as a subsidiary form of Denotation or kind of heightened discourse for the Realization of generalized aesthetic experience.

11. *KĀ* 1.3cd-6:
vācām eva prasādena lokayātrā pravartate//
idam andhaṃ tamaḥ kṛtsnaṃ jāyeta bhuvanatrayam/
yadi śabdāhvayaṃ jyotir āsaṃsāraṃ na dipyate//
ādirājayaśobimbam ādarśaṃ prāpya vāṅmayam/
teṣām asamnidhānẹ'pi na svayam paśya naśyati//
gaur gauḥ kāmadughā samyak prayuktā smaryate budhaiḥ/
duṣprayuktā punar qotvaṃ prayoktuḥ saiva śaṃsati//

Glossary

abhinaya means of histrionic representation; in drama there are four types: *vācika* (verbal), *āṅgika* (bodily: gesture, etc.), *sāttvika* (emotive: tears, etc.), and *ābhārya* (costume)

adākṣiṇya lack of *dākṣiṇya*: gaucheness

ādeśika unspecified type of foreteller of events, such as an astrologer

adbhuta the wondrous or marvelous sentiment (*rasa*)

alaṃkāra 'ornament'; in *kāvya*, any figure of speech

ālaṃkārika used in two senses: (1) a proponent of the point of view that figurality is the most important element in *kāvya*, or a practitioner of this kind of poetics; (2) (by metonymy) a poetician of any sort

alaukika extraordinary, supranormal

anunaya act of conciliation

artha profit, advantage, success, wealth; one of the *puruṣārthas*

ārya honorable person, usually as a title (e.g. by which the Actress addresses the Stage-Manager); also a member of the dhārmic community as opposed to an outsider (see *mleccha*)

āśrama (1) hermitage; (2) stage-of-life, of which there are four, viz. the lives of the student, householder, hermit, and renouncer

ātman soul, self; with a capital *A* it is the self of the universe as described in the Upaniṣads

avatāra 'descent'; the worldly form taken by a major deity, e.g., Viṣṇu as Rāma or Kṛṣṇa

bahumāna respect, esteem

bhakti devotion, loyalty, love; devotional, theistic religion as opposed to austere ritual, meditation, asceticism, etc.

bhāva dominant feeling; used here primarily in the sense of *sthāyibhāva*, the raw material of *rasa*

bhāvaka in Bhaṭṭa Nāyaka's poetics, *kāvya*'s *bhāvaka* capacity makes emotion into an aesthetic universal

bhojaka for Bhaṭṭa Nāyaka, *kāvya*'s *bhojaka* capacity makes the aesthetic universal intrinsically relishable

Brahmā divine personification of *brahman*, the ultimate substance or essence of the universe in the Upaniṣads; synonymous with Prajāpati

Brāhmaṇa a Vedic text concerned principally with ritual

Brahmin see Vaiśya

camatkāra thrill, rapture; a synonym of *rasāsvāda*

caṇḍī angry woman; Caṇḍī is the angry goddess or goddess of destruction

daiva 'divine'; fate

daivikī 'divine' success (*siddhi*); what a drama achieves when it arouses *rasāsvāda*

dākṣiṇya courtesy, urbane or courtly aplomb

dharma law, duty; one of the *puruṣārthas*

dharmārthau *dharma* and *artha* together

dhīralalita 'steadfast and gallant'; the amorous hero of drama and poetry

dhīrodātta 'steadfast and exalted'; the noble hero

dhvani 'sound, overtone'; in poetics, *dhvani* is innuendo or suggestion, and includes the evocation of *rasa*

dṛśyakāvya 'visual poetry,' i.e. drama

gāndharva a form of marriage in which mutually desired sexual intercourse takes the place of familial arrangements and the usual rituals; a *gandharva* is a kind of lesser divinity associated with music and eros

goṣṭhī club of *nāgarikas* dedicated to literary discussion, music, etc.

guṇa virtue; in poetics, a positive feature or 'merit' of diction; the word originally means 'strand' or 'cord'

hṛdaysaṃvāda 'concord of heart'; the sympathetic temperament that qualifies one as *sahṛdaya*

Īśvara Lord: the highest god, personification of the absolute

jīva individual soul/self

kāma desire, pleasure; one of the *puruṣārthas*

karma (n) act, activity; specifically, action or behavior conceived as entailing necessary consequences which have to be lived through; may also refer to the ritual act (whose consequences are always beneficial)

karuṇa, pathos the pathetic sentiment (*rasa*)

kathā tale, story; story literature as distinct from *kāvya*, though often versified *kāvya* poetry: the term includes both prose and verse but only on the sophisticated level; ordinary verse is not included

kāvyasaṃsāra the poetic universe, poetry as an imaginary world

kṛtayuga the Hindu equivalent of the Golden Age, when *dharma* was perfectly observed, there was no disease, and people lived for 400 years; followed by the *tretā, dvāpara,* and *kali yugas,* each worse than the other; we are now—since the end of the Bhārata war—in the *kaliyuga,* characterized by unrighteousness, etc.

Kṣatriya see Vaiśya

līlā play, sport

līlāmokṣa liberation conceived as sport or play

līlāvādin a proponent of play as a metaphysical doctrine

mahākāvya elaborate poetic narrative of major scope, typically in verse; often translated as 'court epic'

mānuṣī 'human' success (*siddhi*); in dramatics this refers to a play's popular success on a level beneath *rasāsvāda;* see *daivikī*

māyā magic, illusion; specifically the world-illusion created by desire and ignorance

mleccha a barbarian or non-Aryan

mokṣa liberation from the cycles of existence (*saṃsāra)*' one of the *puruṣārthas*

nāgarika urbane townsman

nāṭaka drama in general; also a specific dramatic genre with a royal protagonist and a major scope

nāṭikā a *nāṭaka* of smaller scope: *Mālavikāgnimitra* as compared with *Śakuntalā*

nāṭya drama in general; also mimetic dance

nāṭyācārya teacher of dance or drama

nāṭyakāra playwright

nāyaka protagonist, hero, lover

nāyikā female protagonist, beloved

niyati fate, destiny

pāda 'foot'; the fourth part of a stanza considered as a prosodic unit

paṇḍita learned person

pauruṣa 'human'; human effort as opposed to fate (*daiva*)

phalāgama attainment of the fruit of action: the final stage of concerted action in drama

phalayoga synonym of *phalāgama*

Prajāpati 'master of creatures': the creator god or demiurge

pratibhā 'light'; the imaginative capacity: in poetry one of the requirements of a true poet (and *sahṛdaya*); in Śaiva metaphysics the female power by which the universe is manifested (see *śakti*)

prayoga 'application'; in drama this refers to performance or practical application as opposed to learning; also ritual performance and performance of a strategic action

prekṣaka 'beholder'; spectator of drama

puruṣārtha 'human goal'; the four *puruṣārthas* sum up goal-oriented human behavior: duty (*dharma*), profit (*artha*), pleasure (*kāma*), and salvation (*mokṣa*); the first three are subcategorized as the worldly goals

pūrvānurāga the initial stage of love before sexual union, characterized by flirtation and longing

rasa aestheticized sentient; the terms originally means 'juice, liquid' and comes to mean 'flavor'

rasāsvāda *rasa*-savoring, aesthetic rapture

rasika person of feeling, synonym of *sahṛdaya*

rīti 'path'; poetic style catagorized according to certain formal criteria of diction; a synonym is *mārga*

sahṛdaya 'having heart'; person of heart: the ideal recipient of *kāvya*

sahṛdayatva the state of being a *sahṛdaya* (the suffix *-tva* – Eng. *-ness*)

śakti energy; the energetic or immanent power of a transcendent divinity, personified as female and taken as the god's consort; used mostly in Śaivism; also poetic imagination

saṃbhoga 'enjoyment'; love in fulfilment or enjoyment, one of the phases of *śṛṅgāra rasa*

saṃnyāsa renunciation of the world

saṃnyāsin renouncer; one who renounces the world to achieve *mokṣa*

saṃsāra the world, conceived as a realm of ignorance through which one is constantly recycled in changing guises; also, the process of continuous rebirth or reincarnation

saṃskāra 'impression, configuration'; synonym of *vāsanā*
sandhi 'joint'; as used here, one of five possible plot divisions in drama
sandhyaṅga '*sandhi*-part'; one of many incidents which may occur within a *sandhi*; there is a possible total of 64 in a whole play
sānukrośa having a sympathetic temperament
śāstra any body of learning
siddhi success, fulfilment
sneha love, loyalty
Śrī goddess of wealth, fertility, sovereignty
śṛṅgāra the erotic sentiment (*rasa*); divided into *saṃbhoga* (enjoyment) and *vipralambha* (frustration) phases
śṛṅgārin having an urbane erotic sensibility
sthāyibhāva principal emotion such as love, sorrow, fury, regarded as the raw material of *rasa*
Śūdra the lowest of the 4 social orders (see *vaiśya*), the class of menial and servile workers
sūtradhāra stage-manager and leader of an acting troupe
svabhāva 'self-being'; essence
svabhāvokti poetry in the descriptive mode, not utilizing *alaṃkāras*, but still quite elaborate; *svabhāvokti* is sometimes considered a figure in its own right
svayaṃvara 'self-choice'; type of marriage in which the bride chooses her husband among competing suitors
tapas 'heat', especially the heat of asceticism
tejas 'fiery brilliance'; typically associated with royal majesty, but may also be a synonym for *tapas* as well as a word for semen
udāsīnatva indifference
vairāgya dispassion
vaiśya the merchant, farmer, herder, artisan, or otherwise productive class in the dharmic hierarchy, ranked third after Brahmin (priest) and Kṣatriya (warrior, prince)
vākya what is said: appearance as opposed to reality (*svabhāva*)
vāsanā unconscious proclivity resulting from *karma* in a previous existence
vidhi ordained rule in ritual; fate
vidūṣaka the *nāyaka*'s buffoonish companion, the parody of a

food-loving Brahmin who does not even speak Sanskrit

vipralambha — 'disappointment'; love in a state of frustration, either not yet fulfilled (*purvānuraga*) or enduring separation (*viraha*), a phase of *śṛṅgāra rasa* characterized by longing

vīra — the heroic *rasa*

viraha — separation, specifically love-in-separation

viśiṣṭādvaita — 'qualified non-dualism': Rāmānuja's Vedānta, wherein the individual soul (*jīva*) is not wholly identical with the Lord

vītarāga — devoid of passion: what a poet or *sahṛdaya* must not be

Abbreviations

ABh	*Abhinavabhāratī* of Abhinavagupta
AEAG	R. Gnoli, *The Aesthetic Experience According to Abhinavagupta*
AG	Abhinavagupta
AO	*Acta Orientalia* (Hungary)
AOS	American Oriental Series
AS	*Amaruśataka*
AV	*Atharvaveda*
ĀV	Ānandavardhana
BĀU	*Bṛhadāraṇyaka Upaniṣad*
BhN	Bhaṭṭa Nāyaka
BORI	Bhandarkar Oriental Research Institute
BOS	Bhandarkar Oriental Series
BS	*Brahmasūtra* (*Vedāntasūtra*) of Bādarāyaṇa
BSBh	*Brahmasūtrabhāṣya* of Śaṅkara
BSS	Bombay Sanskrit Series
ChU	*Chāndogya Upaniṣad*
CIS	*Contributions to Indian Sociology*
CSS	Chowkhamba Sanskrit Studies
DhĀ	*Dhvanyāloka* of Ānandavardhana
DhĀL	*Dhvanyālokalocana* of Abhinavagupta
DR	*Daśarūpaka* of Dhanañjaya
GOS	Gaekwad Oriental Series
HCIP	History and Culture of the Indian People (series title)
HDS	P.V. Kane, *History of Dharmaśāstra*
HIL	History of Indian Literature (series title)
HOS	Harvard Oriental Series
HSP	S. K. De, *History of Sanskrit Poetics*
IA	K. C. Pandey, *Indian Aesthetics*
IHQ	*Indian Historical Quarterly*
IPVV	*Iśvarapratyabhijñāvivṛtivimarśinī* of Abhinavagupta
JA	*Journal Asiatique* (Paris)
JAOS	*Journal of the American Oriental Society*
JIP	*Journal of Indian Philosophy*
JOI	*Journal of the Oriental Institute* (Baroda)

JRAS	*Journal of the Royal Asiatic Society*
JSAL	*Journal of South Asian Literature*
KĀ	*Kavyādarśa* of Daṇḍin
KM	*Kuṭṭanīmata* of Dāmodaragupta
KP	*Kāvyaprakāśa* of Mammaṭa
KSS	Kashi Sanskrit Series
KSTS	Kashmir Series of Texts and Studies
M	*Mālavikāgnimitra* of Kālidāsa
MBh	*Mahābhārata*
MR	*Mudrārākṣasa* of Viśākhadatta
Mṛcch.	*Mṛcchakaṭika* of Śūdraka
MuU	*Muṇḍaka Upaniṣad*
NŚ	*Nāṭyaśāstra*
PEW	*Philosophy East and West*
PICI	Publications de l'Institut de Civilisation Indienne
PTV	*Parātriṃśikāvivaraṇa* of Abhinavagupta
PY	*Pratijñayaugandharāyaṇa* of Bhāsa
RV	*Ṛgveda*
Ś	*Śakuntalā* of Kālidāsa
SAS	Sanskrit Academy Series
ŚBh	*Śrī-Bhāṣya* of Rāmānuja (comm. on *Brahmasūtra*)
SBE	Sacred Books of the East
SD	*Sāhityadarpaṇa* of Viśvanātha
SOR	Serie Orientale Roma
ŚR	J. L. Masson and M. V. Patwardhan, *Śāntarasa*
SV	*Svapanavāsavadattā* of Bhāsa
SVVSS	Sri Vani Vilas Sanskrit Series
TĀ	*Tantrāloka* of Abhinavagupta
V	*Vikramorvaśīya* of Kālidāsa
VIJ	*Vishveshvaranand Indological Journal*

Bibliography

Note: This list contains some works which, though not cited in the book, have nevertheless had a significant influence on it. The intent is to provide students and others with a basic but also reasonably extensive and up-to-date bibliography on the subject of Sanskrit drama, its background, and the authors treated here.

A. EDITIONS AND TRANSLATIONS

Translations listed after editions despite alphabetical order.

Abhinavagupta.

Abhinavabhāratī

Nāṭyaśāstra of Bharatamuni with the commentary Abhinavabhāratī by Abhinavaguptācārya. Ed. with introduction by R. S. Nagar. 4 vols. 2nd ed. Delhi: Parimal, 1988. See also Gnoli, *Aesthetic Experience.*

Dhvanyālokalocana

Ānandavardhanācāryaviracitaḥ Dhvanyālokaḥ Śrīmadabhinavaguptaviracitalocanavyākhyāsahitaḥ. Ed. with Hindi commentary by Ramsagar Tripathi. 3 vols. 2nd ed. Delhi: Motilal Banarsidass, 1973-81.

The Dhvanyāloka of Ānandavardhana with the Locana of Abhinavagupta. Trans. Daniel H. H. Ingalls, Jeffery Moussaieff Masson, and M. V. Patwardhan. Ed. with an Introduction by Daniel H. H. Ingalls. HOS 49. Cambridge MA: Harvard UP, 1990.

Īśvarapratyabhijñāvivṛtivimarśinī. Ed. M. S. Kaul. 3 vols. KSTS 60, 62, 66. Srinagar, 1938, 1941, 1943.

Parātriṃśikātattvavivaraṇam: Il Commento de Abhinavagupta alle Parātriṃśikā. Ed. with trans. (Italian) by Raniero Gnoli. SOR 58. Rome: Instituto Italiano per il Medio ed Estremo Oriente, 1985

The Tantrāloka of Abhinavagupta with the Commentary of Jayaratha. Ed. R. C. Dwivedi and Navajivan Rastogi. 1st ed. Srinagar (KSTS), 1918-38. Enlarged ed. with introduction. 8 vols. Delhi: Motilal Banarsidass, 1987.

Amaru.

Amaruśatakam: A Centum of Ancient Love Lyrics of Amaruka. Ed. with English trans. by C. R. Devadhar. Rpt. Delhi: Motilal Banarsidass, 1984.

Ānandavardhana.

Dhvanyāloka of Ānandavardhana. Ed. with trans. by K. Krishnamoorthy. 2nd ed. Delhi: Motilal Banarsidass, 1982.

Dhvanyāloka. See Tripathi ed., S. V. Abhinavagupta, *Dhvanyālokalocana*.

The Dhvanyāloka of Ānandavardhana with the Locana of Abhinavagupta. Trans. Daniel H. H. Ingalls, Jeffrey Moussaieff Masson, and M. V. Patwardhan. See s. v. Abhinavagupta, *Dhvanyālokalocana*.

Anon.

Le Vijñāna Bhairava. Ed. with translation (French) and commentary by Lilian Silburn. PICl 15. Paris: E. de Boccard, 1983.

Bharata.

Nāṭyaśāstra of Bharata. Ed. Batuka Natha Sharma and Baladeva Upadhyaya. 2nd ed. Varanasi: Chowkhamba, 1980.

Nāṭyaśāstra of Bharatamuni with the Commentary Abhinavabhāratī by Abhinavagupta. Ed. R. S. Nagar. See s. v. Abhinavagupta, *Abhinavabhāratī*.

The Nāṭyaśāstra (A Treatise on Ancient Indian Dramaturgy and Histrionics), Ascribed to Bharata-muni. Trans. Manomohan Ghosh. Vol. 1 (chs. 1-27). 2nd rev. ed. Calcutta: Manisha Granthalaya, 1967. vol. 2. (chs. 28-36). Calcutta: The Asiatic Society, 1961.

The Nāṭya Śāstra of Bharatamuni. Trans. 'a board of scholars'. Delhi: Sri Satguru, 1981.

Bhāsa.

Bhāsanāṭakacakram: Plays Ascribed to Bhāsa. Ed. C. R. Devadhar. POS 54. Poona: Oriental Book Agency, 1962.

Pratijñāyaugandharāyaṇa. Ed. with Sanskrit Commentary by T. Ganapati Sastri. 3rd ed. Trivandrum, 1920.

Svapnavāsavadattā. Ed. with Sanskrit commentary by T. Ganapati Sastri. Trivandrum, 1924.

Thirteen Trivandum Plays Attributed to Bhāsa. Trans. A. C. Woolner and Lakshman Sarup. 2 vols. London: Oxford UP, 1930.

Dhanañjaya.

The Daśarūpaka of Dhanañjaya. With the commentary of Dhanika and the subcommentary of Bhaṭṭanṛsiṃha. Ed. with introduction and notes by T. Venkatacharya. Madras: Adyar Library, 1969.

The Daśarūpa: A Treatise on Hindu Dramaturgy, by Dhanañjaya. Trans. George C. O. Haas. 1912. Rpt. New York: AMS Press, 1965.

Dāmodaragupta.

Kuṭṭanīmata. Ed. T. M. Tripathi. Bombay: Gujarati Press, 1924.

Inscriptions.

Inscriptions of the Early Gupta Kings and Their Successors. Corpus Inscriptions Indicarum III. Revised by D. R. Bhandarkar. Ed. B. Chhabra and G. S. Gai. New Delhi: Archaeological Survey of India, 1981.

Inscriptions of the Early Gupta Kings and Their Successors. CII 3. Ed. John Faithful Fleet. 1988. Rpt. Varanasi: Indological Bookhouse, 1963.

Kālidāsa.

Mālavikāgnimitra

Mālavikāgnimitra. With the Commentaries of Nīlakaṇṭha and Kāṭayavema. Ed. anon. SVVSS 5. Srirangam: Sri Vani Vilas Press, 1908.

Mālavikāgnikitra: A Sanskrit Play by Kālidāsa. With the commentary of Kāṭayavema. Ed. with English notes by Shankar Pandurang Pandit. BSS 6. 2nd ed. Bombay: Central Book Depot, 1889.

Mālavikāgnimitram of Kālidāsa. Ed. with English notes and translation by C. R. Devadhar. 3rd ed. Rpt. Delhi: Motilal Banarsidass, 1980.

Mālavikā and Agnimitra. Trans. Edwin Gerow. In *Theater of Memory,* ed. Barbara Stoler Miller. New York: Columbia UP, 1984.

Śakuntalā

Abhijñāna-Śākuntalam of Kālidāsa. Ed. with English notes and translation by C. R. Devadhar and N. G. Suru.

Rpt. Delhi: Motilal Banarsidass, 1972.

The Abhijñāna-Śakuntalam of Kālidāsa. With the Sanskrit commentaries of Śaṅkara and Narahari. Ed. Ramanath Jha. Darbhanga: Mithila Institute of Post-Graduate Studies and Research in Sanskrit Literature, 1957.

The Abhijñāna-Śākuntala of Kālidāsa. With the Sanskrit commentary of Rāghavabhaṭṭa. Ed. N. R. Godabole. Revised by Wasudev Laxman Shastri Fanasikar. 5th ed. Bombay: Tukaram Javaji at the Nirnaya Sagara Press, 1909.

Kālidāsa's Śakuntalā. Ed. Richard Pischel. 2nd ed. HOS 16. Cambridge MA: Harvard UP, 1922.

A Reconstruction of the Abhijñānaśākuntalam. Ed. Dileep Kumar Kanjilal. Calcutta: Sanskrit College, 1980.

Śakuntalā by Kālidāsa: The Devanagari Recension of the Text. Ed. with English notes and partial translation by Monier Williams. 2nd ed. Oxford: Clarendon Press, 1876.

Abhijñānaśākuntalam. Trans. Chandra Rajan. In *Kalidāsa: The Loom of Time, a Selection of His Plays and Poems.* Ed. Rajan. Harmondsworth: Penguin. 1990.

Śakuntalā. Trans. Michael Coulson. In *Three Sanskrit Plays.* Ed. Coulson. Harmondsworth: Penguin, 1981. Includes also Viśākhadatta's *Mudrārākṣasa* and Bhavabhūti's *Mālatīmādhava.*

Śakuntalā and the Ring of Recollection. Trans. Barbara Stoler Miller. In *Theater of Memory.* See s.v. *Mālavikāgnimitra.*

Vikramorvaśīya

Vikramorvaśīyam of Kālidāsa. Ed. with English notes and Translation by C. R. Devadhar. 3rd ed. Rpt. Delhi: Motilal Banarsidass, 1979.

Vikramorvaśīyam of Kālidāsa. With the commentaries of Raṅganātha, Koṇeśvara, and Kāṭayavema. Ed. anon. SAS 14. Hyderabad: The Sanskrit Academy of Osmania University, 1966.

The Vikramorvaśīya of Kālidāsa. Ed. with English notes by H. D. Velankar. New Delhi: Sahitya Akademi,

1961.

Urvaśī Won by Valor. Trans. David Gitomer. In *Theater of Memory.* See s.v. *Mālavikāgnimitra.*

Kauṭilya.

The Kauṭilya Arthaśāstra. Ed. and trans. With analytical study by R. P. Kangle. 3 vols. Rpt. Delhi: Motilal Banarsidass, 1986.

Kṣemarāja.

Śivasūtravimarśini. Ed. J. C. Chatterjee. KSTS 1. Srinagar, 1911.

Maheśvarānanda.

La Mahārthamañjarī de Maheśvarānanda. Ed. Lilian Silburn. PICI 29. Paris: E. de Boccard, 1968.

Mammaṭa

The Kāvyaprakāśa of Mammaṭa. Ed. with trans. by Ganganatha Jha. 2 vols. Rpt. Varanasi: Bharatiya Vidya Prakashan, 1967.

Manu.

Manusmṛti. With the commentary of Medhātithi. Ed. anon. 2 vols. Calcutta : Udayacala Press, 1976.

The Laws of Manu. Trans. Georg Buhler. SBE 25. 1886. Rpt. Delhi: Motilal Banarsidass, 1984.

Rājaśekhara.

Kāvyamīmāṃsā of Rajaśekhara. Ed. C. D. Dalal and R. A. Sastry. GOS 1. Baroda: Oriental Institute, 1934.

La Kāvyamīmāṃsā de Rājaśekhara. Trans. Nadine Stchoupak and Louis Renou. Paris: Imprimerie Nationale, 1946.

Rāmānuja.

Bhagavad Bādarāyaṇa's Brahma Sūtra or Śārīraka with Śrī Bhāṣya by Śrī Bhagavad Rāmānuja. With the subcommentary of Abhinavadeśika. Ed. Sri Uttamur T. Viraraghavacharya. 2 vols. Madras: Sreevathsa Press, 1963.

The Vedānta-Sūtras with the Commentary of Rāmānuja. Trans. George Thibaut. SBE 48. 1904. Rpt. Delhi: Motilal Banarsidass, 1976.

Śaṅkara.

Brahmasūtra-Śāṅkarabhāṣyam. With the subcommentaries of Govindānanda. Vācaspatimiśra, and

Ānandagiri. Ed. J. L. Shastri. Delhi: Motilal Banarsidass, 1980.

Vedānta-Sūtras with the Commentary by Śaṅkarācārya. Trans. George Thibaut. 2 vols. SBE 34, 38. 1904. Rpt. Delhi: Motilal Banarsidass, 1980.

Śūdraka.

The Mṛcchakaṭika of Śūdraka. With the commentary of Pṛthvīdhara. Ed. with English notes and translation by M. R. Kale. Rpt. Delhi: Motilal Banarsidass, 1982.

The Mṛcchakaṭika of Śūdraka. With the commentary of Pṛthvīdhara. Ed. with English notes by Hirananda Mularaja Sarma Sastri and Kasinath Pandurang Parab. 2nd ed. Bombay: Nirnaya Sagar, 1910.

The Little Clay Cart. Trans. J. A. B. Van Buitenen. In *Two Plays of Ancient India,* ed. Van Buitenen. New York: Columbia UP, 1968.

Upaniṣads.

Bṛhadāraṇyaka Upaniṣad. In *Ten Principal Upaniṣads with Śāṅkarabhāṣya.* Ed. anon. Delhi: Motilal Banarsidass, 1964.

Chāndogya Upaniṣad. In *Ten Principal Upaniṣads.*

The Thirteen Principal Upanishads. Trans. R. E. Hume. 2nd rev. ed. London: Oxford UP, 1931. Rpt. 1979.

Utpaladeva.

The Śivastotrāvalī of Utpaladevāchārya. With the commentary of Kṣemarāja. Ed. Rajanaka Laksmana. Varanasi: Chowkhamba, 1964.

Vātsyāyana.

The Kāmasūtram of Śrī Vātsyāyana Muni. With the commentary of Yaśodhara. Ed. with Hindi commentary by Sri Devdutta Sastri. KSS 29. 3rd ed. Varanasi: Chaukhambha Sanskrit Sansthan, 1982.

The Kāma Sūtra of Vātsyāyana. Trans. Sir Richard F. Burton. New York: E. P. Dutton, 1962.

Vidyākara.

The Subhāṣitaratnakoṣa Compiled by Vidyākara. Ed. D. D. Kosambi and V. V. Gokhale. HOS 42. Cambridge MA: Harvard UP, 1957.

An Anthology of Sanskrit Court Poetry: Vidyākara's

Subhāṣitaratnakoṣa. Trans. Daniel H. H. Ingalls. HOS 44. Cambridge MA: Harvard UP, 1965.

Viśākhadatta.

Mudrārākṣasa by Viśākhadatta. Ed. Alfred Hillebrandt. Breslau: M. & H. Marcus, 1912.

Mudrārākṣasa by Viśakhadatta. with the commentary of Dhuṇḍhirāja. Ed. with English notes by Kashinath Trimbak Telang. Bombay: Government Central Book Depot, 1884.

Mudrārākshasa of Viśākhadatta. with the commentary of Ḍhuṇḍhirāja. Ed. with English notes and translation by M. R. Kale. 6th ed. Delhi: Motilal Banarsidass, 1976.

The Minister's Seal. Trans. J. A. B. van Buitenen. In *Two Plays of Ancient India.* See s.v. Śūdraka.

Rākshasa's Ring. Trans. Michael Coulson. In *Three Sanskrit Plays.* See s.v. Kālidāsa, *Śakuntalā.*

Viśvanātha.

Sāhityadarpaṇa. Ed. with Hindi commentary by Shalgram Shastri. Delhi: Motilal Banarsidass, 1977.

The Mirror of Composition. Trans. J. R. Ballantyne and Pramadadasa Mitra. 1865. Rpt. Delhi: Motilal Banarsidass, 1956.

B. SECONDARY LITERATURE

Adaval, Niti. *The Story of King Udayana.* Varanasi: Chowkhamba, 1970.

Altekar, A. S. *Catalogue of the Gupta Gold Coins in the Bayana Hoard.* Bombay: Numismatic Society of India, 1954.

Barthes, Ronald. *Mythologies.* Paris: Editions du Seuil, 1957. Trans. Annette Lavers. New York: Hill and Wang, 1975.

Basham, A. L. *The Wonder That Was India.* New York: Grove Press, 1959.

Basie, William ('Count'), and Albert Murray. *Good Morning Blues: The Autobiography of Count Basie as Told to Albert Murray.* New York: Primus, 1985.

Bäumer, Bettina. *Schöpfung als Spiel: Der Begriff līlā im Hinduismus, seine philosophische und theologische Deutung.* Diss. Munchen, 1969.

Baumer, Rachel van M., and James R. Brandon. *Sanskrit Drama in Performance.* Honolulu: University of Hawaii, 1981.

Bhaduri, Nrisinha P. '*Bhakti* (Devotion) as an Aesthetic Sentiment.'

JIP 16.4 (1988): 377-410.

Bhat, G. K. *Appointment with Kālidāsa*. Ahmedabad: L. D. Institute of Indology, 1982.

Bhat. *Bharata-Nāṭya-Mañjarī: Bharata on the Theory and Practice of Drama*. A selection from the *NŚ* in Sanskrit with English translation, notes, and introduction. Poona: BORI, 1975.

Bhat. *Nāṭya-Mañjarī-Saurabha: Sanskrit Dramatic Theory*. Selections in Sanskrit From post-NŚ writers on drama with English notes and introduction. Poona: BORI, 1981.

Bhaṭ *Preface to Mṛcchakaṭika*. Ahmedabad: New Order Book Co., 1953.

Bhat. *The Vidūṣaka*. Ahmedabad: New Order Book Co., 1959.

Bhattacharya, Bisnupada. 'Aesthetic Meaning of Nature—Mode of Reflection: Idealism.' *Our Heritage*, 150th Anniversary Volume (1824-1974): 329-44.

Bloch, Ernst. *Geist der Utopie*. Frankfurt am Main: Suhrkamp, 1964.

Bloch. *Das Prinzip Hoffnung*. Frankfurt am Main: Suhrkamp, 1959.

Bose, Mandakranta. *Supernatural Intervention in The Tempest and Śakuntalā*. Jacobean Drama Studies 99. Salzburg: Institut fur Anglistik and Amerikanistik, 1980.

Brandon, James R. *Asian Theatre: A Study Guide and Annotated Bibliography*. No place given: University and College Theatre Association, 1979.

Brown, W. Norman. 'The Creative role of the Goddess Vāc in the Rig Veda.' In *Pratidānam: Indian, Iranian, and Indo-European Studies presented to F. B. J. Kuiper*, pp. 393-97. The Hague: Mouton, 1968.

Byrski, Maria Christopher. *Concept of an Ancient Indian Theatre*. Delhi: Munshiram Manoharlal, 1974.

Byrski. *Methodology of the Analysis of Sanskrit Drama*. Warsaw: Rozprawy Uniwersitetu Warszawskiego, 1979.

Byrski. 'Sanskrit Drama as an Aggregate of Model situations. In *Sanskrit drama in Performance*, ed. Baumer and Brandon (q. v.), pp. 141-66.

Carstairs, G. Morris. *The Twice-Born: A Study of a Community of High-Caste Hindus*. London: Hogarth Press, 1957.

Chand, Hari. *Kālidāsa et l'art poétique de l'Inde*. Paris: Champion, 1917.

Chari, V. K. *Sanskrit Criticism*. Honolulu: University of Hawaii, 1990.

Christie, Elizabeth. 'Indian Philosophers on Poetic Imagination (*Pratibhā*)., *JIP* 7 (1979): 153-207.

Dasgupta, S. N., and S. K. De. *A History of Sanskrit Literature*. 2nd ed. Calcutta: University of Calcutta, 19745. The body of the text is by De, the introduction and 'Editor's Notes' by Dasgupta.

De, S. K. *Ancient Indian Erotics and Erotic Literature.* Calcutta: Firma K. L. Mukhopadhyay, 1959.

De. ' The *Bhaktirasaśātra* of Bengal Vaiṣṇavism.' *IHQ* 8 (1932): 643-88.

De. *A History of Sanskrit Literature.* See Dasgupta and De.

De. *History of Sanskrit Poetics.* 2nd ed. 1960. Rpt. Calcutta: Firma KLM, 1976.

De. *Sanskrit Poetics as a Study of Aesthetic* (sic). With notes by Edwin Gerow. Berkeley: University of California Press, 1963.

De. *Some Problems of Sanskrit Poetics.* 1959. Rpt. Calcutta: Firma KLM, 1981.

Devasthali, G. V. *Introduction to the Study of the Mṛcchakaṭika.* Poona: Oriental Book House, 1951.

Devasthali. *Introduction to the Study of the Mudrārākṣasa.* Bombay: Keshev Bhikaji Dhavale, 1948.

Dimock, Edward C., Jr., et al. *The Literatures of India.* Chicago: University of Chicago, 1974.

Dumont, Louis. *Homo Hierarchicus.* Trans. Mark Sainsbury. Chicago: University of Chicago, 1970.

Dumont. 'World Renunciation in Indian Religions.' *CIS* 4 (1960): 33-62.

Dyczkowski, Mark S. G. *The Doctrine of Vibration.* Albany: SUNY, 1987.

Frank, Manfred. *What Is Neostructuralism?* Trans. Sabine Wilke and Richard Gray. Minneapolis: University of Minnesota, 1989.

Freud, Sigmund. *Beyond the Pleasure Principle.* 1920. Trans. James Strachey. Standard (English) Edition. *SE.* Vol. 18, pp. 7-64. Rpt. London: Hogarth, 1986.

Freud. *Civilization and Its Discontents.* 1930. Trans. James Strachey. *SE.* Vol. 21. pp. 62-145. Rpt. London: Hogarth, 1986.

Freud. *The Ego and the Id.* 1923. Trans. James Strachey. *SE.* Vol. 19, pp. 12-66. Rpt. London: Hogarth, 1986.

Freud. *Group Psychology and the Analysis of the Ego.* 1921. Trans. James Strachey. *SE.* vol. 18, pp. 69-143. Rpt. London: Hogarth, 1986

Freud. 'On Narcissism: An Introduction.' 1914. Trans. James Strachey. *SE.* vol. 14, pp. 73-102. Rpt. London: Hogarth, 1986.

Freud. *Totem and Taboo.* 1913. Trans. James Strachey. *SE.* Vol. 13, pp. 1-161. Rpt. London: Hogarth, 1986.

Frye, Northrop. *Anatomy of Criticism.* Princeton: Princeton UP, 1957.

Frye. *The Secular Scripture: A Study of the Structure of Romance.* Cambridge MA: Harvard UP, 1976.

Gerow, Edwin. *A Glossary of Indian Figures of Speech.* The Hague: Mouton, 1971.

Gerow. *Indian Poetics.* HIL 5.3 Wiesbaden: Otto Harrassowitz, 1977.

Gerow. 'Plot Structure and the Development of *Rasa* in the Śakuntalā., *JAOS* 99.4 (1979): 559-72; 100.3 (1980): 267-82.

Ghosal, S. N. *The Inception of the Sanskrit Drama.* Calcutta: Calcutta Book House, 1977.

Ghose, Sri Aurobindo. *Kalidasa.* Calcutta: Arya Sahitya, 1929.

Gnoli, Raniero. *The Aesthetic Experience According to Abhinavagupta.* 2nd rev. ed. Varanasi: Chowkhamba, 1968. Text and trans., with introduction and notes, of AG's commentary on the *rasaniṣpattisūtra* of *Nāṭyaśātra* 6.

Goldman, Robert P. 'Fathers, Sons and Gurus: Oedipal Conflict in the Sanskrit Epics.' *JIP* 6 (1978): 325-92.

Goldman. 'Matricide, Renunciation, and Compensation in the legends of Two Warrior-Heroes of the Sanskrit Epics.' *Indologica Taurinensia* 10 (1982): 117-31.

Goldman. 'Mortal Man and Immortal Woman: An Interpretation of Three Ākhyāna Hymns of the Ṛgveda,' *JOI* 18.4 (1969): 273-303.

Gonda, Jan. *Ancient Indian Kingship from the Religious Point of view.* Leiden: E. J. Brill. 1969.

Gonda. 'Ascetics and Courtesans.' *Brahmavidyā* 25 (1961): 78-102.

Gonda. 'Zur Frage nach dem Uraspru͏ng und Wesen des indischen Dramas.' *AO* 19 (1943): 329-453. Rpt. *Selected Studies.* Leiden: E. J. Brill, 1975.

Goodwin, Robert E. 'Aesthetic and Erotic Entrancement in the *Śakuntalā.*' *AO* 43.1 (1989): 99-123.

Goodwin. '*Dākṣiṇya* and *Rasa* in the *Vikramorvaśīya.*' *JRAS* 1988, No. 2, pp. 288-304.

Goodwin. 'The Divided World of Sanskrit Drama: Viśākhadatta's *Mudrārākṣasa.*' In *The Scope of Words: In Honor of Albert S. Cook.* Ed. Peter Baker, Sarah Webster Goodwin, and Gary Handwerk. New York: Peter Lang, 1991.

Goodwin. 'Kālidāsa's Metadrama.' *JSAL* 23.1 (1988): 199-36.

Goodwin. 'Paradise in a Prison Cell: The Yaugandharāyaṇa Plays of Bhāsa.' *JRAS* Series 3, 3.1 (1993): 53-76.

Goodwin. 'The Playworld of Sanskrit Poetry: Model *Śakuntalā.*'In *God's Play: Līlā in South Asia,* edd. William S. Sax and John Carman. New York: Oxford UP, 1994.

Goodwin. Review of *Ratnākara's Haravijaya: An Introduction to the San-*

skrit Court Epic, by David Smith. *JAOS* 110.2 (1990): 374-76.

Goodwin. Review of *Sanskrit Criticism*, by V. K. Chari. *JAOS* 111.3 (1991): 593-96.

Gupta, Chandra Bhan. *The Indian Theatre*. Delhi: Motilal Banarsidass, 1954.

Hart, George L. *The Poems of Ancient Tamil*. Berkeley: University of California, 1975.

Hartmann, Gerda. *Beiträge dur Geschichte der Göttin Lakṣmī*. Diss. Kiel, 1932.

Heesterman, J. C. *The Inner Conflict of Tradition: Essays in Indian Ritual, Kinghsip, and Society*. Delhi: Oxford UP, 1985. (Also published by the University of Chicago.)

Herder, Johann Gottfired. 'Ueber ein morgenländisches Drama.' [*Śakuntalā*] In *Sämtliche Werke*, ed. B. Suphan. Vol. 16, pp. 84-104. Hildesheim: Georg Olms, 1967.

Hillebrandt, Alfred. *Über die Anfänge des indischen Dramas*. Munchen: Königlich-Bayerishe Akademie der Wissenschaften, 1914.

Hiltebeitel, Alf. *The Ritual of Battle*. Ithaca: Cornell UP, 1976.

Hiriyanna, M. *Art Experience*. 1954. Rpt. Mysore: Kavyalaya, 1978.

Ingalls, Daniel H. H. 'Ānandavardhana's *Devīśataka*.' *JAOS* 10.4 (1989): 565-75.

Ingalls. 'General Introduction.' In *An Anthology of Sanskrit Court Poetry: Vidyākara's Subhaṣitaratnakoṣa*. pp. 1-53. See S. V. Vidyākara.

Ingalls. 'Kālidāsa and the Attitudes of the Golden Age.' *JAOS* 96.1 (1976): 15-26.

Ingalls. 'Words for Beauty in Classical Sanskrit Poetry.' In *Indological Studies in Honor of W. Norman Brown*, ed. Ernest Bender, pp. 87-107. AOS 47. New Haven: American Oriental Society, 1962.

Jakobson, Roman. 'Linguistics and Poetics.' 1958. In *Structuralists from Marx to Levi-Strauss*, ed. Richard T. and Fernande M. de George, pp. 85-122. Garden City: Anchor Doubleday, 1972.

Jagirdar, R. V. *Drama in Sanskrit Literature*. 1947. 2nd ed. Bombay: Popular Prakashan, 1967.

Jauss, Hans Robert. *Aesthetic Experience and Literary Hermeneutics*. Trans. Michael Shaw. Minneapolis: University of Minnesota, 1982.

Jhala, G. C. *Kālidāsa: A Study*. Bombay: Padma Publications, 1943.

Kakar, Sudhir. *The Inner World: A Psycho-analytic Study of Childhood and Society in India*. 2nd rev. ed. Delhi: Oxford UP, 1981.

Kane, P. V. *History of Dharmaśāstra*. 5 vols. 2nd rev. ed. Poona: BORI, 1968-77.

Kane. *History of Sanskrit Poetics.* 4th ed. Delhi: Motilal Banarsidass, 1971.

Karmarkar, R. D. *Kālidāsa.* Dharwar: Karnatak University, 1960.

Kavi, M. Ramakrishna. See Ramakrishna.

Kaviraj, Gopinath. 'The Doctrine of *Pratibhā.*' In *Aspects of Indian Thought.* Burdwan, 1966.

Keith, A. The Berriedale. *A History of Sanskrit Literature.* London: Oxford Up, 1920.

Keith. *The Sanskrit Drama.* London: Oxford UP, 1924.

Kinsley, David. *Hindu Goddesses: Visions of the Divine Feminine in the Hindu Religious Tradition.* Berkeley: University of California, 1986.

Konow, Sten. *Das indische Drama.* Berlin: Walter de Gruyter, 1920. *The Indian Drama.* Trans. S. N. Ghosal. Calcutta: General Printers and Publishers, 1969.

Kosambi, D. D. 'Introduction.' In *The Subhāṣitaratnakoṣa Compiled by Vidyākara.* See s.v. Vidyākara.

Krishnamachariar, M. *History of Classical Sanskrit Literature.* 1937. 3rd ed. Delhi: Motilal Banarsidass, 1974.

Krishnamoorthy, K. *Kālidāsa.* New York: Twayne, 1972.

Krishnamoorthy. 'The Sanskrit Conception of a Poet.' In *Essays in Sanskrit Literary Criticism,* pp. 167-86. Dharwar: Karnatak University, 1974.

Kuiper, F. B. J. *Varuṇa and Vidūṣaka: On the Origin of the Sanskrit Drama.* Amsterdam: North Holland Publishing Company, 1979.

Kulshreshtha, R. B. '*Svapnavāsavadatta:* A Study in Mythological Symbolism. *VIJ* 8 (1970): 109-15.

Kulshreshtha. '*Svapnavāsavadatta:* A Study in the Subconscious.' *VIJ* 5 (1967): 63-70.

Kunhan Raja, C. *Kālidāsa. A Cultural Study.* Waltair: Andhra University, 1956.

Kunjunni Raja, K. *Indian Theories of Meaning.* 2nd ed. Madras: Adyar Library, 1969.

Lacombe, Olivier. *L'Absolu selon le Vedānta.* Annales de Musée Guimet 49. Paris, 1937.

Larson, Gerald J. 'The Aesthetic (*rasāsvāda*) and the Religious (*brahmāsvāda*) in Abhinavagupta's Kashmir Śaivism.' *PEW* 26.4 (1976): 371-87.

Lévi, Sylvain. *Le théâtre indien.* 1890. Rpt. Paris: College de France, 1963.

Lienhard, Siegfried. *A History of Classical Poetry: Sanskrit-Pali-Prakrit.*

HIL 3.1. Wiesbaden: Otto Harrassowitz, 1984.

Lingat, Robert. *The Classical Law of India.* 1967. Trans. J. Duncan M. Derrett. Berkeley: University of California Press, 1973.

Lüthi, Max. *Once upon a Time: On the Nature of Fairy Tales.* 1970. Trans. Lee Chadeayne. Bloomington: Indiana UP, 1976.

Manikar, T. G. *Kālidāsa, His Art and Thought.* Poona: Deshmukh Prakashan, 1962.

Mainkar. *The Theory of the Saṃdhis and Saṃdhyaṅgas.* Delhi: Ajanta, 1978.

Madan, T. N. *Non-Renunciation: Themes and Interpretations of Hindu Culture.* Delhi: Oxford UP, 1987.

Madan. *Way of Life: King, Householder, Renouncer.* Essays in honour of Louis Dumont. Ed. T. N. Madan. New Delhi: Vikas Publishing House, 1982.

Majumdar, R. C., A. D. Pusalker, and A. K. Majumdar, edd. *The Age of Imperial Unity.* [HCIP 2.] 5th ed. Bombay: Bharatiya Vidya, 1980.

Majumdar, Pusalker, and Majumdar. *The Classical Age.* HCIP 3. 4th ed. Bombay: Bharatiya Vidya, 1988.

Mankad, D. R. *The Types of Sanskrit Drama.* Karachi: Urmi Prakashan, 1936.

Marcuse, Herbert. *Eros and Civilization.* New York: Random House, 1955.

Masson, J. L. and M. V. Patwardhan. *Aesthetic Rapture: The Rasādhyāya of the Nāṭyaśāstra.* 2 vols. Poona: Deccan College Postgraduate and Research Institute, 1970. Trans. and Commentary of *Nāṭyaśāstra* 6, based on the *Abhinavabhāratī.*

Masson and Patwardhan. *Śāntarasa and Abhinavagupta's Philosophy of Aesthetics.* BOS 9. Poona: BORI, 1969.

Morgenstierne, Georg. *Uber das Verhältnis zwischen Cārudatta und Mṛcchakaṭika.* Halle, 1920.

Miller, Barbara Stoler. 'Kālidāsa's World and His Plays.' In *Theater of Memory,* ed. Miller, pp. 3-41. New York: Columbia UP, 1984.

Narang, Satya Pal. *Kālidāsa Bibliography.* New Delhi: Heritage, 1976.

Nobel, J. *The Foundations of Indian Poetry.* Calcutta: R. N. Seal 1925.

O' Flaherty, Wendy Doniger. *Hindu Myths.* Harmondsworth: Penguin, 1975.

O' Flaherty. *Śiva: The Erotic Ascetic.* New York: Oxford UP, 1981. = *Asceticism and Eroticism in the Mythology of Śiva.* London: Oxford, 1973.

Pandey, Kanti Chandra *Abhinvavgupta: An Historical and Philosophical Study.* 2nd ed. Varanasi: Chowkhamba, 1963.

Pandey. *Indian Aesthetics.* 2nd ed. Varanasi: Chowkhamba, 1959.

Pargiter, F. E. *The Purāṇa Text of the Dynasties of the Kali Age.* London: Oxford UP. 1913.

Parikh, J. T. *The Vidūṣaka: Theory and Practice.* Surat: Shri Chunilal Gandhi, 1953.

Pusalker, A. D. *Bhāsa: A Study.* 1940. 2nd ed. Delhi: Mushiram Manoharlal, 1968.

Raghavan, V. *Bhoja's Śṛṅgāra Prakāśa.* 3rd rev. ed. Madras: Punarvasu, 1978.

Raghavan. *Love in the Poems and Plays of Kālidāsa.* Bangalore: Indian Institute of Culture, 1955.

Raghavan. *The Mudrārākṣasakathā of Mahādeva.* 2nd rev. ed. Rpt. Tanjore: Sarasvati Mahal Library, 1971

Raghavan. *The Number of Rasas.* 3rd rev. ed. Madras: Adyar Library, 1975.

Raghavan. 'Sanskrit Drama in Performance.' In *Sanskrit Drama in Performance,* ed. Baumer and Brandon, pp. 9-44. See s.v. Baumer, Rachel.

Raghavan. *Studies on Some Concepts of the Alaṃkāra Śāstra.* Rev. ed. Madras: Adyar Library, 1973.

Rajan, Chandra. 'Introduction.' In *Kālidāsa: The Loom of Time.* Harmondsworth: Penguin, 1990.

Rakesagupta (sic). *Studies in Nāyaka-Nāykā-Bheda.* Aligarh: Granthayan, 1967.

Ramakrishna Kavi, M. *Bharatakośa: A Dictionary of Technical Terms with Definitions Collected from the Works on Music and Dramaturgy by Bharata and Others.* 2nd ed. New Delhi: Munshiram Manoharlal, 1983. (Sanskrit without trans.)

Ramanujan, A. K. 'The Indian Oedipus.' In *Indian Literature,* ed. Arabinda Poddar, pp. 127-37. Simla: Indian Institute of Advanced Study, 1972.

Rao, K. L. Seshagiri. *The Concept of Śradddhā.* Delhi: Motilal Banarsidass, 1974.

Raychaudhuri, Hemchandra, *Political History of Ancient India.* 6th ed. Calcutta: University of Calcutta, 1953.

Renou, Louis. 'La recherche sur le théâtre indien depuis 1890.' In Sylvain Lévi, *Le théâtre indien,* pp. ix-xxxii. (English trans. 'Research on the Indian theatre since 1890.' *Samskṛta Ranga Journal* 4 [1966]: 1-25.)

Renou. 'Sur la structure du *kāvya.*' *JA* 247 (1959): 1-113.

Rhys Davids, T. W. *Buddhist India.* New York: G. P. Putnam, 1903.

Rosenfield, John M. *The Dynastic Arts of the Kushans.* Berkeley: University of California, 1967.

Ruben, Walter. *Kālidāsa: The Human Meaning of His Works.* Trans. Joan Becker. Berlin: Akademie-Verlag, 1957.

Ruben. 'The *Mṛcchakaṭika,* Its Folkloric and Political Interpretation.' *Oriens* 1 (1948): 74-104.

Ruben. *Der Sinn Des Dramas 'Das Siegel und Rākṣasa'.* Berlin: Akademie-Verlag, 1956.

Sanderson, Alexis. 'Purity and Power among the Brahmans of Kashmir.' In *The Category of the Person,* ed. M. Carrithers et al., pp. 190-216. Cambridge: Cambridge Up, 1985.

Sanderson. 'Trika Śaivism.' In *The Encyclopedia of Religion,* ed. Mircea Eliade et al., vol. 13, pp. 15-16. New York: Macmillan, 1987.

Sankaran, A. *Some Aspects of Literary Criticism in Sanskrit.* Alternate title: *The Theories of Rasa and Dhvani.* 1929. 2nd ed. Madras: University of Madras, 1973.

Sarma, Dimbeswar. *Kālidāsa: An Interpretative Study.* Diss. University of Calcutta. Published by author. Distributed by Chowkhamba. 1968.

Sastri, Gaurinath. *The Philosophy of Word and Meaning: Some Indian Approaches with Special References to the Philosophy of Bhartṛhari.* Calcutta: Sanskrit College, 1959.

Scheftelowitz, Isidor. *Die Apokryphen des Ṛgveda.* 1906. Rpt. Hildesheim: Georg Olms, 1966.

Schiller, Friedrich Von. *Naive and Sentimental Poetry.* 1795-96. Trans. with Introduction and notes by Julius A. Elias. Rpt. New York: Ungar, 1975.

Schokker, G. H. 'Śūdraka, the Author of the Original *Cārudatta.*' In *Pratidānam: Indian, Iranian and Indo-European Studies Presented to F. B. J. Kuiper,* ed. J. C. Heesterman et al., pp. 585-600. The Hague: Mouton, 1968.

Schuyler, Montgomery. *Bibliography of Sanskrit Drama.* 1906. Rpt. New York: AMS Press, 1965.

Sharma, Chandradhar. *Indian Philosophy: A Critical Study.* New York: Barnes and Noble, 1962.

Shastri, Surendra Nath. *Laws and Practice of Sanskrit Drama.* vol. 1. Varanasi: Chowkhamba, 1961.

Shekhar, Indu. *Sanskrit Drama: Its Origin and Decline.* Leiden: E. J. Brill, 1960.

Silburn, Lilian. *Kuṇḍalinī: Energy of the Depths.* Trans. Jacques Gontier. Albany: SUNY, 1988.

Sircar, D. C. 'Date of the *Mahābhāṣya* and *Nāṭyaśāstra.*' In Sircar, *Studies in the Yugapurāṇa and Other Texts*, pp. 17-23. Delhi: Oriental Publishers, 1974.

Smith, David. *Ratnākara's Haravijaya: An Introduction to the Sanskrit Court Epic.* Delhi: Oxford UP, 1985.

Spratt, P. *Hindu Culture and Personality.* Bombay: Manaktalas, 1966.

Tagore, Rabindranath. 'Sakuntala: Its Inner Meaning.' Trans. Jadunath Sarkar. In *Sakuntala*, trans. Laurence Binyon and K. N. Dasgupta. London: Macmillan, 1920.

Thieme, Paul. 'Das indische Theater.' In *Fernöstliches Theater*, ed. H. Kindermann, pp. 26-120. Stuttgart: A. Kröner, 1966.

Upadhyaya, B. S. *India in Kālidāsa.* Allahabad: Kitabistan, 1947.

van Buitenen, J. A. B. 'The Classical Drama.' *In the Literatures of India*, ed. E. C. Dimock, Jr., et al., pp. 81-114. Chicago: University of Chicago Press, 1974.

van Buitenen. 'Dharma and Mokṣa.' *PEW* 7 (1954): 33-40.

Vatsyayan, Kapila. *Classical Indian Dance in Literature and the Arts.* New Delhi: Sangeet Natak Akademi, 1968.

Venkatachalam, V. *Bhāsa.* New Delhi: Sahitya Akademi, 1986.

Warder, A. K. *Indian Kāvya Literature.* 6 vols. to date. Delhi: Motilal Banarsidass, 1972-92.

Wells, Henry W. *The Classical Drama of India.* London: Asia Publishing House, 1963.

Wilson, H. H. *Select Specimens of the Theatre of the Hindus.* 2 vols. Calcutta, 1826-27. 2nd ed. London, 1835.

Zvelebil, Kamil V. *Literary Conventions in Akam Poetry.* Madras: Inst. of Asian Studies, 1986.

Index